Praise For A

"A remarkable, much needed journey through a most potent and potentiating archetypes, a marvelous blend of discursive and exploratory gnosis, and practical and profound methodologies."

-Jean Houston, PhD, Author, Human Potential Leader

"This book offers deep wisdom and guidance for anyone seeking to live in alignment with universal principles. It presents a body of wonderful tools for awakening to our divine nature, showing us how to access the help that is always available to us if we know where to look."

-Susan Campbell, Ph.D. Author, Relationship Expert

"Awaken To Tarot is gift, as it beautifully serves the awakening of the planet. The crystal clear writing is organized, educational, systematic, and very usable. It takes ancient learning and makes it applicable. The reader will find inspiration, timeless guidance, and comprehensive and psychotherapeutic tools to access their own wisdom. The artwork is fabulous! Karen is a much an artist as a writer."

-Donna Hamilton, PhD, MFT. Author

"One of the top ten inspirational books"

-Aspire Magazine, November, 2021

"Awaken to Tarot by Karen La Puma is a superior, practical guide to divination and self-empowerment. What amazes me about Karen's work is the masterful way she weaves together her deep knowledge of Tarot, Astrology, Jungian Archetypes, and Divine Feminine to guide and liberate her readers. Filled with practical, real-life application examples, this book is a treasure that will show you how to tap into inner guidance and awaken your internal allies. That is sorely needed by most people nowadays."

-Darren Starwynn, O.M.D., Author, Seminar Leader

"Karen La Puma has integrated a multiple of modalities in this book. With her unique experience, she combines the classic Tarot, astrology, numerology, the Hero's Journey and the Tree of Life. Take advantage of this author's lifetime of studying to accelerate your learning."

-Kelly de Simone, OD

"This is a beautiful, uplifting and enjoyable book. It is amazing, so poetic and creative with a deep understanding of Life."

-Cathy Coleman, PhD, Astrologer, School Board

"These cards and their symbolism are beautiful and well thought out. As an architect of the spiritual journey, they inspire my own inner counsel to guide me in creative and loving ways."

-Devi Jacobs, CEO Outback/ Temple of Venus Stores

"Wonderful book, great foundation, clear, enjoyable, well-organized and very informative. I know this information, but it would be good for a beginner."

-Susan Stuart, PhD, Intuitive Development Institute

"This lovely and powerful Tarot is original. A guide to a new Life. It is a pioneering adventure of the Now. The River of Life pictograph has an ALIVENESS and PRESENCE. Myriad forms of Life appear. It is invigorating and inspiring to feel the awake possibilities for the human spirit and soul."

-Kathleen Lustman, Acupuncturist and Healer

"As a fellow mystic and priestess, I found Karen La Puma's Awaken to the Tarot a precise and refreshing examination of this ancient system of divination. Her in depth knowledge of astrology, numerology, and the Tree of Life coupled with wisdom and playfulness has produced a Tarot deck that make the teachings of the tarot available to the novice and advanced practitioner alike."

-Shera Renee Sever, MS. ED, Practical Mystic, Soul Coach

"I love this material! It is important, exciting, wonderfully wise, well expressed, organized, and inspiring in its clarity. Karen is perfect as the author of this guide."

-Clive Matson, Poet, Author of Chalcedony

"This book brings a path to face the unknown, like bringing light to the darkness. I went through the pages of this book with such an excitement and joy! The words are energetic and inspirational. Her thoughts energize emotions and provoke a silent tsunami that activated my intellectual spirit and quietly touch my soul. The creative artwork represents a personal history of the unconscious. What was amazing were the words. Like an incredible vision of sunlight on water, they paint universal possibilities from an ancient world into a 'very present space.' Here are transparent canvases for us to start painting our own personal journey."

-Ty Koizumi, Poet, Journalist

"As I reviewed Karen La Puma's tarot book the word that kept coming to mind is encyclopedic, as in comprehensive, inclusive, and a reference work. As a set of supernatural aids one finds on the spiritual path, Karen implicitly encourages readers to take traditional symbols and make them one's own. This is no copy-cat approach to received wisdom. There are endless ways to use Awaken to Tarot."

-Sara R. Diamond, Ph.D., J.D.

"Karen La Puma has gathered our archetypes in a lovely overlapping reference-to-life fabric, in her book Awaken to Tarot. The blending of astrology with tarot creates a brilliant grid that one can attach their own personal knowledge to. It's well organized with highlighting, summary paragraphs and more. Laying out the foundation of psychology, knowledge collected for hundreds of years, even before such a word was invented. Our conscious minds ponder.....certainly 3rd eye opening!"

Andrea La Canela, Flamenco Dancer

An artistic and integrative
digitally created
Tarot Deck in two sizes.

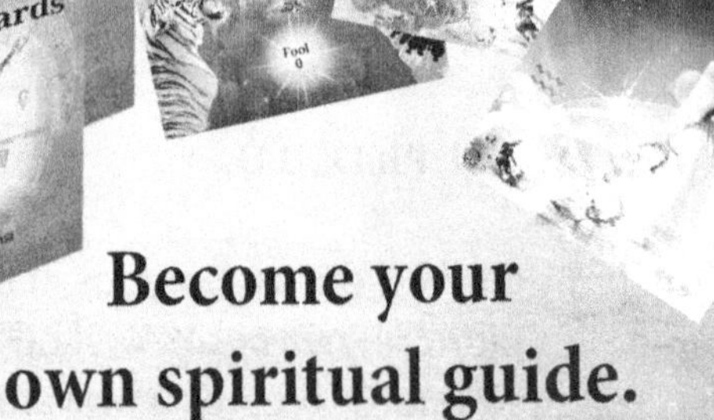

Become your
own spiritual guide.

Learn the magical symbols
that mirrors your soul's journey
and where you are now.

Awaken
To
Tarot

Be Your Own Guide

Using Astrology, Numbers and the Tree of Life

Also By Karen La Puma

Awaken Female Power,

The Way of the Goddess Warrior

Coming Soon

Awaken Magnetic Creation, Manifest Your Dreams

Awaken A New Myth,

Goddess Warrior on the Hero's Journey

Awaken From Ego, Evolve with the Enneagram

Awaken From the Pain Body, Heal Emotionally

Awaken the Inner Archetypes,

Embody the Gods and Goddesses Within

Awaken From Mind, Elevate Consciousness and Communications

Awaken Love, Beyond the Barriers

Awaken the Spiritual Warrior, Empower the Masculine.

Awaken the Sacred, Experience the Ultimate Blessings

Awaken the Hero, The Joys of Giving Back

A Toolkit for Awakening Series

Awaken To Tarot

Be Your Own Guide

Using Astrology, Numbers and the Tree of Life

Karen La Puma

SoulSource

SoulSource Publishing

PO Box 877, Fairfax, CA 94978

Printed in the USA

Cover Art and Interior Layout by
Karen La Puma and Farah Munawar

Spiritual, Psychology, Mythology, Self-Help

Includes Stories, Processes, Photographs, Glossary

ISBN : 978-1-878203-10-6

Edition

10987654321

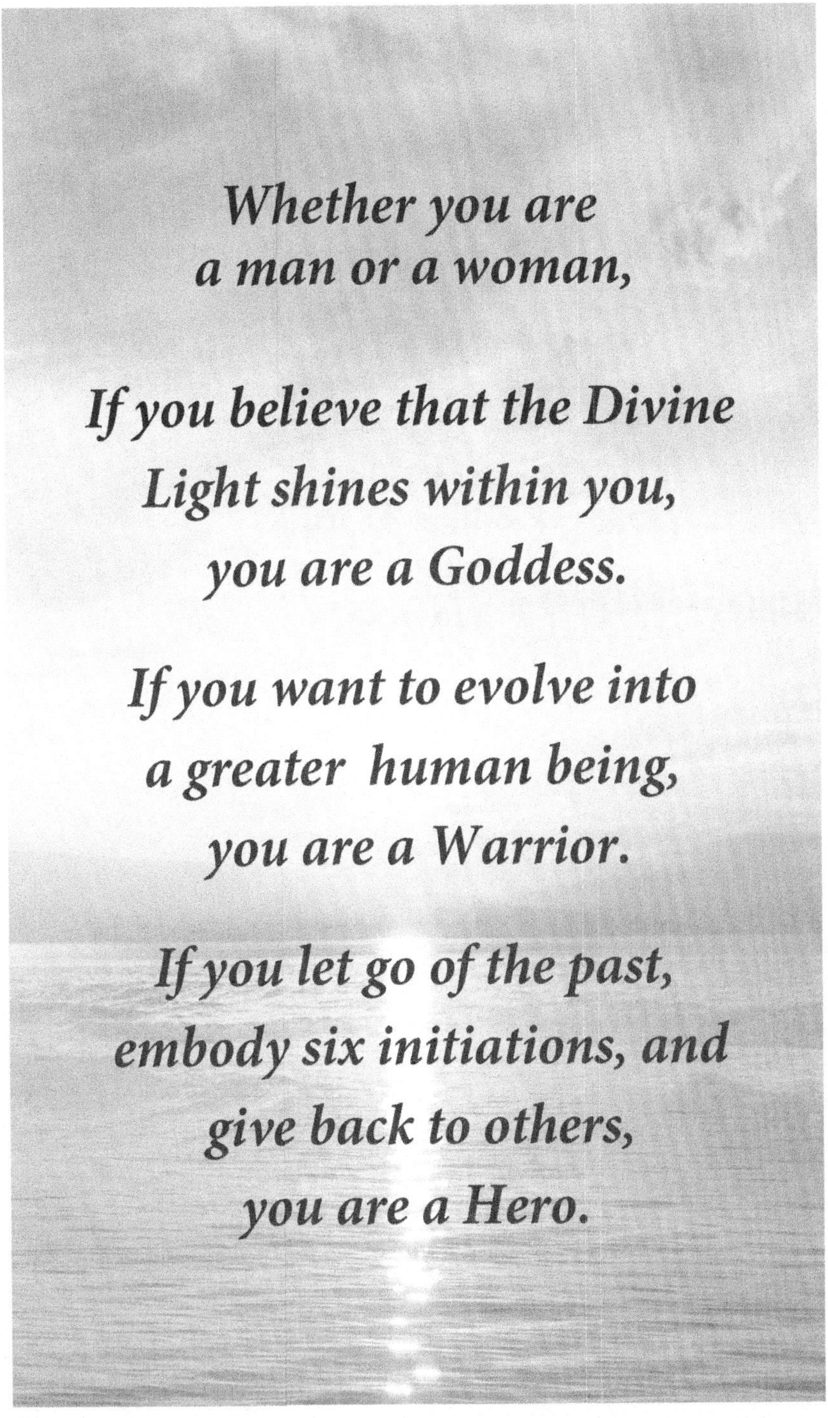

Whether you are
a man or a woman,

If you believe that the Divine
Light shines within you,
you are a Goddess.

If you want to evolve into
a greater human being,
you are a Warrior.

If you let go of the past,
embody six initiations, and
give back to others,
you are a Hero.

To all
Goddess Warriors
on the Hero's
Journey.

"I believe, together, we can inspire,
evolve, awaken, and heal
with the symbolism of
this cosmic model."

-Karen La Puma

Acknowledgements

I was blessed to have studied Tarot with the great, inspirational teacher Angeles Arrien. In 1984, after playing with the Tarot cards about five years, I spent six months researching and writing a book on the Tarot. I realized that as a fairly new practitioner, this massive and deep subject was over my head, so I archived it. After 40 years of reading the Tarot, I have rummaged through those four inches of faded paper files to condense and assemble this version.

My deck of choice has been the genius and innovation of *The Thoth Deck*, which was created by Aleister Crowley and painted by Frieda Harris. I was inspired to create a new deck based on it using digital collage with Internet images. It all started when Shaye McKinney suggested we teach a class together and create our own decks. We had a couple of sessions together and then I took off running. I now can introduce the deck, which I am calling, *Awaken Tarot Cards*.

I greatly appreciate Farah Munawar for her assistance on this series. She helped enhance *Awaken Tarot Cards* and has been my support on all my projects. This new astrological Tarot deck, digitally created into collages was inspiring, fun, and challenging. In spite of not reaching standards of perfection, being an artist immersed in the collective symbolic sea is a wonderful place to play.

Another big thank you goes to Donna Hamilton for always being the first to read my books and offer suggestions.

Editing assistance came from Andrew Ruff, David Cutler and Cathy Coleman.

I have much gratitude to my advocates who have supported me in this long and winding process. I have been bonding with you, my readers, and am thankful for your support.

Contents

Part IV Watery Cups

Part V Fiery Wands

Part VIII Incorporating Tarot

Dear Readers,

Welcome to an offering in the series, A Toolkit for Awakening.

I am pleased to present my new digitally created Tarot deck, called *Awaken Tarot Cards*.

You will see how Tarot symbols bring practical, intuitive, and magical awareness.

You may want to learn this magnificent system or you may desire to use this book as an oracle and open it randomly with a question.

Using the cards and then looking up their meaning is the usual way of divination.

May this book and these cards be a supernatural aid and help make your journey of Awakening a blessed one.

Many Blessings,

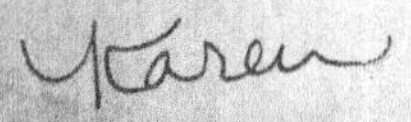

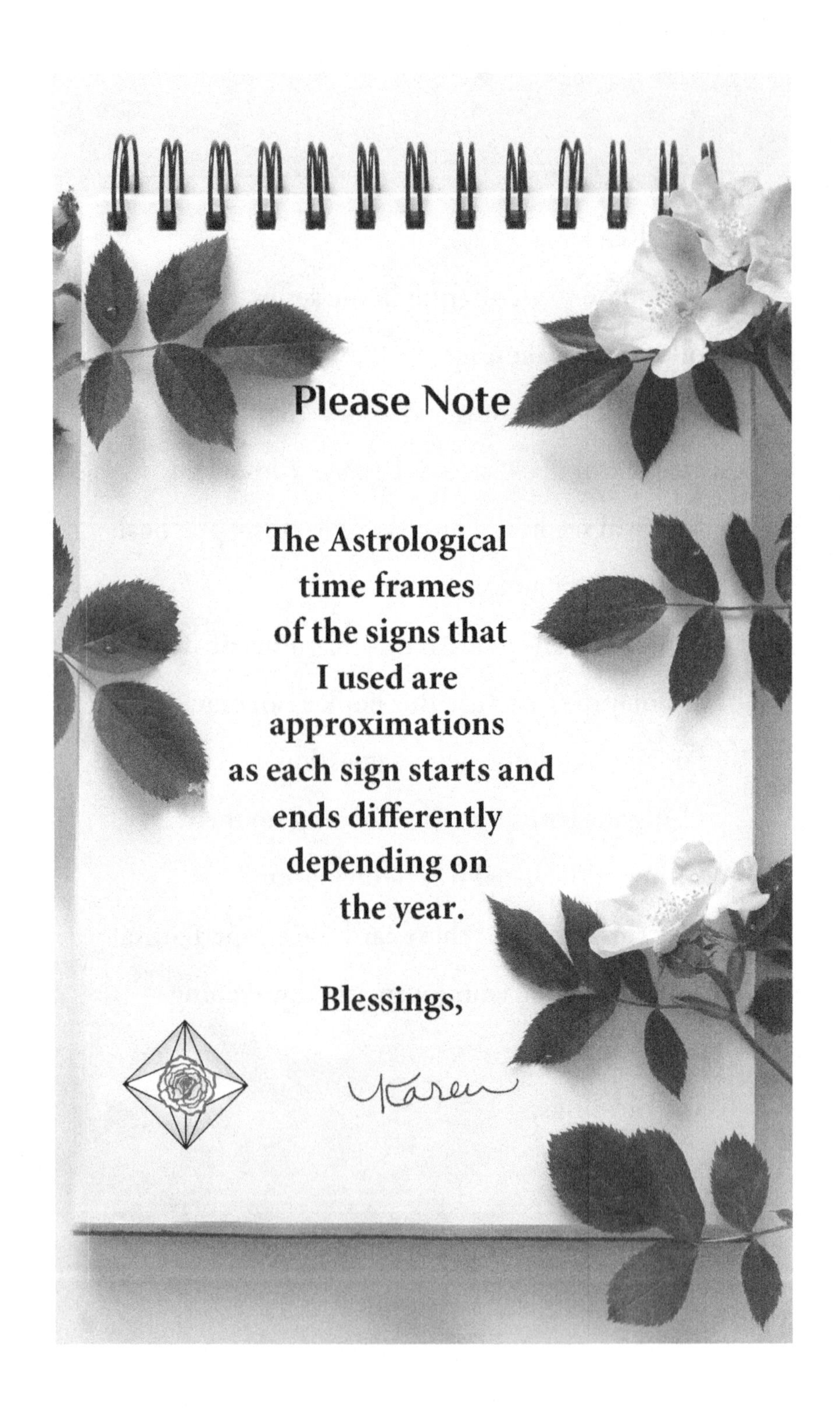

Please Note
The Astrological
time frames
of the signs that
I used are
approximations
as each sign starts and
ends differently
depending on
the year.
Blessings,
Karen

Part I

Opening To Support

I can of mine own self
do nothing.

Jesus Christ

Introducing Supportive Supernatural Symbols

One has only to know and trust
and the ageless guardian will appear.

Joseph Campbell

Throughout history we have wanted to understand the circumstances of our lives and our relationships with others. We have had a profound desire to know ourselves on the deepest levels, to make sound decisions, and to receive guidance from the Divine.

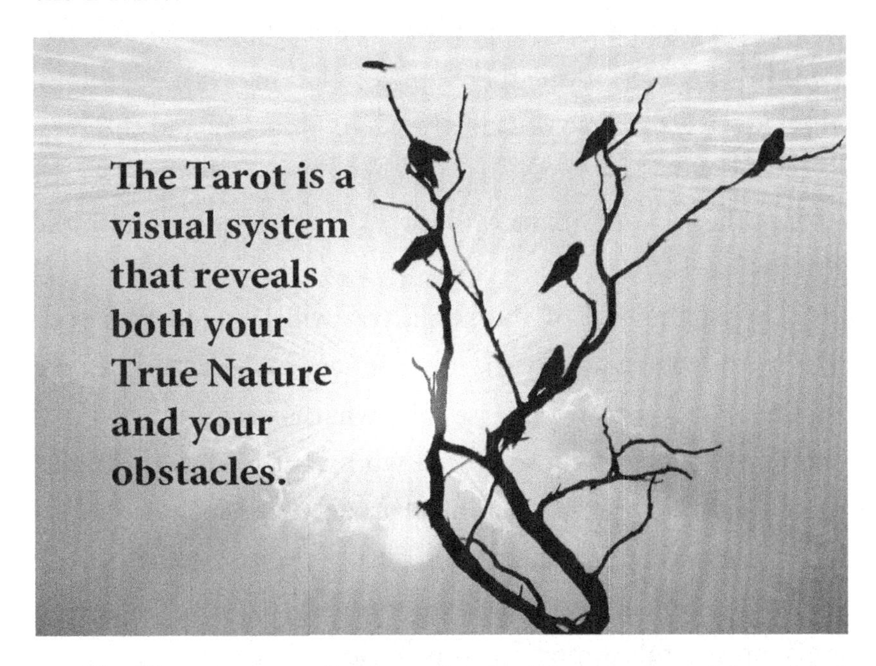

The Tarot is a set of universal principles that provide a visual system which reveals both your True Nature and the obstacles to living from this Unified State of Consciousness. Traditionally and cross-culturally these archetypes communicate all the aspects of existence. Through these rich symbolic mirrors you can receive messages about where you are at present, an external issue, a relationship, your career, and an inner psychological state—in fact all aspects of your evolutionary journey.

In the following pages, you will touch on how to tap into inner guidance and awaken internal allies. This book was written for you to draw assistance from the symbols of your soul's journey as each card is like a magic talisman.

As you explore the visual symbols of each Tarot card, you are given different components that add to your understanding of its meaning. After the visuals there are: a short meaning; descriptions; key words to summarize them; reflective suggestions to go into your process; questions to ponder; and an affirmation. In the descriptions there are correlations with Astrology, Numerology, the Tree of Life, the Hero's Journey, and the general process of evolution. I have included the Hebrew letter for each of the Major Arcana, and the I Ching's association to the Royalty cards.

Toward the end of the book, you will learn to find your life's path, your yearly path, some inner teachers, and sample readings for you to try. Please take what is useful for you and ignore the rest. For those of you who want to dive in deeper, there are several dense teaching chapters that I include in Part VII, "Integrating the Tarot." Altogether these systems can assist your assimilation of each card, as their cosmic voices can exert a powerful support for you. When you use the cards, you not only have a self-reflective tool, a device to awaken intuition, but also a suggestive magnifier of the qualities you want to infuse into your life.

This book is a part of a series called, **A Toolkit for Awakening,** which is based on the eminent mythologist, Joseph Campbell's great blueprint, "The Hero's Journey." It is from his classic book, *A Hero with a Thousand Faces* (1948). This formula for spiritual evolution, presented in Chapter 83 and the conclusion, gives the structure and foundation of this series.

The stage of the Hero's Journey that this book deals with is called "Supernatural Aids." You are encouraged to seek helpers, animate and inanimate, seen and unseen, ancient and modern. You don't have to rely solely upon your own innate powers. Magical helpers appear once you are on the spiritual path as you see abundantly in myths and fairy tales. This book suggests that the Tarot is "a supernatural aid," for these cards are external mirrors from which you can hear your inner guidance.

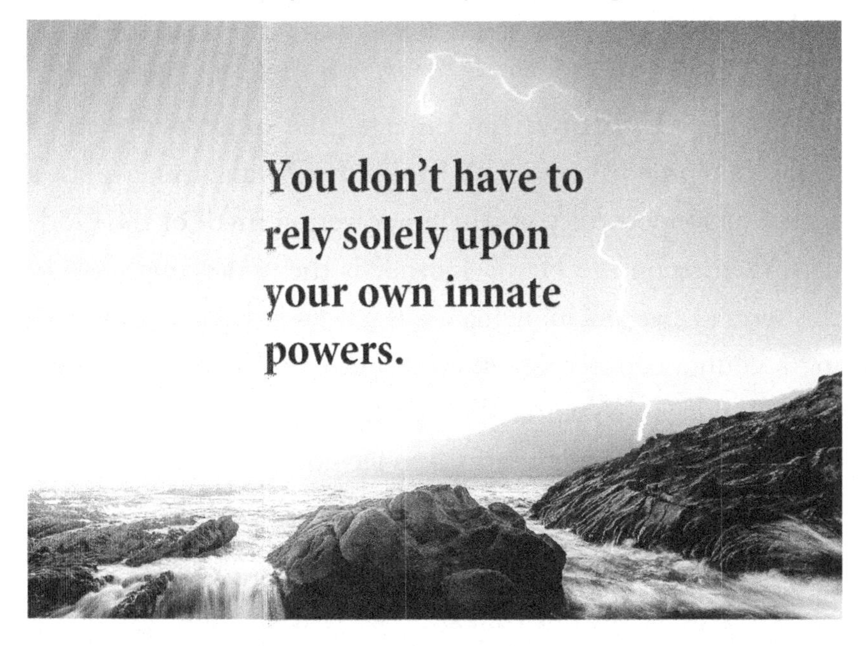

Having support is one of life's most valuable assets. I am thankful for all the support I have received. Yet because I have chosen "a road less traveled," my deepest gratitude has been to those invisible forces—the archetypes (also called universal symbols). Exploring interrelated metaphysical systems, like Tarot, Astrology, and Numerology have given me the keys to the human journey. "Meta" means beyond, for these maps of consciousness go outside the physical to bridge existence with causality. As you play with the archetypes themselves, they become intuitive and active spiritual allies.

There is a vast array of metaphysical oracles to help you gain self-knowledge. You can delve into the many different cosmic looking glasses to muse and reflect. You can pick cards, gaze at charts and maps, throw coins, select stones, add some numbers, dream, visualize, meditate, or open a book randomly for a message, and they will become your guideposts and supportive tools that help you to see another way and wake up to the highest aspects of yourself.

My hope is that the Tarot images, the concepts presented in this book, and the series, **A Toolkit for Awakening**, will be a source of support for you. The empowering myth of the Goddess Warrior on the Hero's Journey is the underlying basis of this series. Love and allowing are the ways of the Goddess. Being accountable for your time, attention and intention is how you embody the Warrior. These archetypes become your helpers and infuse higher vibrations to facilitate new states of consciousness.

My inner and outer helpers guide me and inspire me along my sacred path of expressing Divine Light.

1.

Exploring Tarot

The Tarot is God's Picture Book,
or it could be likened to
a celestial game of chess.

Frieda Harris

The Tarot symbols are amazingly insightful pictorial mythologies that have come down through history as unbound books with seventy-eight cards. With them your inner and outer human experiences operate symbolically, visually, and nonlinearly to reach you in the same states as your dreams and meditations.

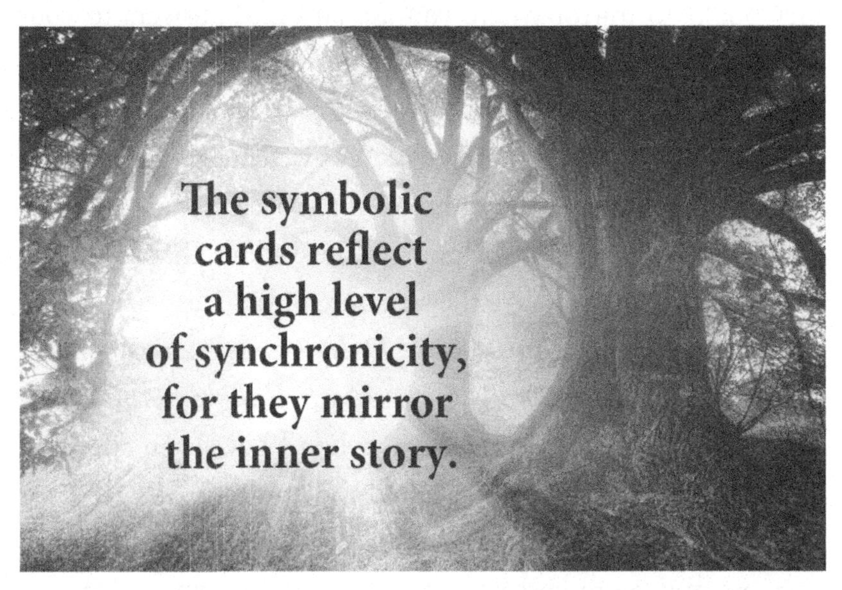

The mystery of how this works is explained by synchronicity, which is a concept that was verbalized by Carl G. Jung in 1960. It is a meaningful coincidence or a psychic orderliness that transcends time and space and activates the archetypes, but that is not determined or caused. The unconscious mind becomes stronger than the conscious mind and reveals the underlying message.

Cosmic symbols are powerful with multiple meanings. They are like throwing a rock into still water. The layers and layers of connotations spread out and draw you into the unconscious realms. Tarot archetypes are steps on the journey and can be seen as *verbs* with actions to take. They are also forces of nature and patterns of being and you can relate to them as *nouns* or a personification of Divinity. They could also be seen as *adjectives*, as they are descriptive paths. The symbols show where you are now and where you are going.

There are many varieties of Tarot decks and complementary books to mirror where you are and find answers to your questions. To name a few: *The Thoth, Waite, Rider, Voyager Tarot, Mythic Tarot, Mother Peace, Jungian Tarot,* and *Goddess Tarot.* With so many decks, you may ask, "Why create another one?" I was called, encouraged, and impelled to co-create its birth.

Some visionary and helpful oracle systems that work the same way, but do not have the structure of the Tarot are: *Medicine Cards, I Ching, Runes, Secret Dakani Oracle, Amulets of the Goddess, Inner Child Cards, Goddess Cards, Enlightenment Cards,* and *Sacred Path Cards.* Sometimes when I have been confused about my writing, I have consulted the quirky *Whack Deck* for fun and direction. There is a wealth of resources on the market as more and more cosmic games are coming out with many spiritual teachers utilizing blessings, teachings, affirmations, and quotes.

The general structure of the Tarot collectively links your being with destiny and time. The universal language is made of twenty-two Trump cards called **Major Arcana**, which represent the universal principles of life. They fit perfectly with Astrology and the ten planets and twelve zodiac signs. Each of the Trump cards has a Hebrew letter with specific attributes.

The Tarot traditionally and creatively connects the ten spheres on the Tree of Life. Each card's placements gives insight into its meaning and a more comprehensive appreciation of the Tarot in general. Robert Wang in his book, *The Qabalistic Tarot* said, "We are to consider the opposite position on the Tree of Life to understand each card." The card opposite on the Tree of Life offers balance and integration to its meaning.

The **Minor Arcana** consist of fifty-six cards. There are four suits with ten cards that signify your opportunities, gifts, and challenges, plus four Royalty Cards, which denote teachers or masters.

The **Swords** cover the element Air and are the mental realm and lessons. They are shown on the card with a sword and the number or designation near it. In regular playing cards, they are the spades. The **Cups** deal with the element Water, which are your emotional trials and gifts; they are the hearts. They are denoted with a cup on the cards. The **Wands** name the Fire element and cover the perceptional and spiritual journey, and alternately are called the clubs, batons, and slaves. They are shown with a fiery wand symbol. The **Disks** signify the Earth element and symbolize the physical and practical concerns. They are the diamonds, and later called coins, rings, and pentacles. They are presented with a golden sphere on the cards.

All these potencies, adepts, and steps can help you discover your own inner knowing, so you can find your own answers. When you allow the Tarot cards to guide your growth, it is like having your own personal psychic on hand. Use their benefits, but do not exploit them. These symbols are sacred. Have fun with them, as they aid in the development and discovery of your full potential. When you open to these universal principles, they become teachers, experiences, initiations, and the path toward greater awareness.

Cosmic archetypes are always available to me for inspiration and inner guidance as I align more and more with the Infinite Intelligence that infuses all symbols and events in my life.

2.

Correlating Astrology and Tarot

Symbols appear as signposts or keys
and function as containers,
revealers, or concealers of meaning.
Our internal and external world intersect
and attempt to dialogue with one another.

Angeles Arrien

Adding Astrology with the Tarot images gives you a gestalt, which is another viewing of the whole that is more powerful than the parts. Let us examine the components of Astrology.

The Planets, including the luminaries, the Sun and the Moon, represent your basic *motivations and human drives.* These are the *actors* and act like *verbs* in your life. Here are their key words and their Tarot designator:

Sun: Conscious will; intention; vitality; ego wrapped in Essence; source of life, creativity and light; **Sun** card.

Moon: Emotions; feelings; instinctual nature; our intuitive response; unconscious self; **High Priestess**.

Mercury: Mind; communications; thinking; writing; making connections; **Magician**.

Venus: Love Goddess; Creator; love, allow, and accept what Is; share; connect, balance and find harmony; **Empress**.

Mars: Initiator; Doer; drive; ambition; instigates, motivates, asserts, and activates; **Tower**.

Jupiter: Benevolent Guru; expansion; abundance; generosity; philosophical faith; **Wheel of Fortune**.

Saturn: Father; Task Master; Cosmic Cop; binds, restricts, limits, controls, brings to form and manifests; **Universe**

Uranus: Rebel Genius; Liberator; Awakener; revolutionizes, synthesizes, changes, and reverses; **Fool**.

Neptune: Mystical Escapist; Dissolver; urge to go higher in consciousness; spiritual, creative and psychic; illusions and delusions; **Moon** card.

Pluto: Rotor Rooter; catalytic reformer; cathartic release; deep; penetrating; transformative; **Aeon/Judgment.**

The **Signs** describe the *mode* and *attitudes* or how the energy manifests. These are your *scripts*. They are like *adjectives* and include all the four elements— Air, Water, Fire, and Earth. Here is a list of the planets; their key words; ruling planet; element; its symbol(s); Tarot designator; and season:

Aries: Initiating; pioneering; self-will for action; dynamic; assertive; independent spirit; Mars; Fire; ram; **Emperor**; March 21 to April 19.

Taurus: Grounded; practical; applied; slow, sure mover toward comfort and security; Venus; Earth; bull; **Hierophant**; April 20 to May 20.

Gemini: Duality; versatility; changeable; exchanging ideas, adaptable, curious, freedom loving; Mercury; Air; twins; **Lovers**; May 21 to June 20.

Cancer: Introspective; reflective; umbilical; family-oriented; setting things in motion; protective; Moon; Water; crab; **Chariot**; June 21 to July 22.

Leo: Dynamic; creative; expressive; playful pleasure; recognition; urge to shine and be your own authority; Fire; Sun; lion; **Lust/Strength**; July 23 to August 22.

Virgo: Practical; service-oriented; detailed; systematizes; organizes; purifying; perfecting; Earth; virgin; **Hermit**; August 23 to September 22.

Libra: Seeks balance and perspective; relationship-orientated; sees possibilities; concern with truth, value, and fairness; Venus; Air; scales; **Adjustment/Justice**; September 23 to October 22.

Scorpio: Intense; probing; psychological power; risk; eliminates; regenerates; Pluto; water; scorpion, serpent, and eagle; **Death/Rebirth**; October 23 to November 21.

Sagittarius: Optimistic; restless aspiration propelling for an ideal; ethics; expansive; philosophical; Jupiter; Fire; archer; **Art/Temperance**; November 22 to December 21.

Capricorn: Prudent; determined; tenacious; patient; ambitious climbing toward a goal or manifestation; Saturn; Earth; goat; **Universe**; December 22 to January 19.

Aquarius: Humanitarian; visionary; reform; altruism; brotherhood; progressive aims of the group; Uranus; Air; water barrier; **Star**; January 20 to February 18.

Pisces: Vacillating; sensitive; imaginative dreamer; mystic visionary; nebulous; sacrificial; surrendering; transcending; savior/victim; Neptune; Water; two fishes; **Moon** card; February 19 to March 20.

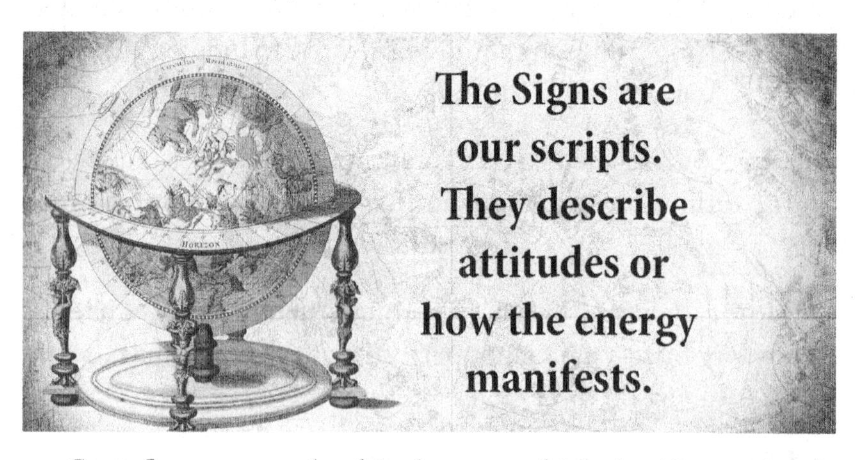

Swords represent the **Air** element, which signify your intellect or mental thought processes and encompasses the self-expressive signs, **Gemini, Libra,** and **Aquarius**. Air signs are observant, conceptual, and communicate ideas, perceptions, and beliefs. There is a quality of versatility, vacillation, cooperation, and detachment. Air signs can be active, masculine, relative, as well as cold, distant, and unemotional.

Cups symbolize the **Water** element, which indicate the emotional realm and comprises the sensitive signs of **Cancer, Scorpio,** and **Pisces**. Water signs equate to feelings and can be receptive and imaginative. The qualities of water are feminine, passive, impressionable, dependent, and submissive to others. Water signs are erotic, indulgent, devotional as well as temperamental, obsessive, and emotional.

Wands encompasses the **Fire** element, and represent the perceptual modes and your inner awareness, and includes the demonstrative signs of **Aries**, **Leo**, and **Sagittarius**. Fire signs are initiating, impulsive, and stimulating. They are expressions of pure energy, such as aspiration, inspiration, will, and daring. Active, masculine, hot, dynamic, and intuitive, Fire signs can be creative, dramatic, intense, and progressive. The feelings of joy, enthusiasm, and anger are associated with Fire signs.

Disks denote the **Earth** element, which deal with practical, physical, financial, and material manifestations and includes the signs, **Taurus**, **Virgo**, and **Capricorn**. The Earth signs create, build, sustain, and possess. Slow sure movers, they are solid, stable, passive, feminine, industrious, and conservative. There is reliability, common sense, as well as stubbornness, distance, and a resistance to change in the Earth element.

Each of the elements falls into one of the three modalities—Cardinal, Fixed, and Mutable. The **Cardinal** signs are the **Movers—Aries**, **Cancer**, **Libra**, and **Capricorn**. They are goal-directed and dynamically move out of the self to set up a situation. Cardinal signs initiate each season. Determined, they strive and engage in activities that explore and nurture their aptitudes and skills.

The **Fixed** signs are the **Sustainers—Taurus**, **Leo**, **Scorpio**, and **Aquarius**. They dig in and are able to hold steady in their goals to achieve something solid. They are resistant to change and can be stubborn. Respected for their self-containment and sense of purpose, Fixed signs are good at centering, meditating, and manifesting.

The **Mutable** signs are **Changers—Gemini, Virgo, Sagittarius**, and **Pisces**. They are flexible, adaptable, and restless for movement. Being versatile enables them to see life from many perspectives, to be great communicators, and adept with people, selling and promoting. Seasonally it is a breakdown or transition time, which is demonstrated in their dualistic natures.

The twelve signs also have a life view that is Personal, Social, or Universal. The **Personal** signs are concerned with an individual self and its outlook and include the first four signs of **Aries, Taurus, Gemini,** and **Cancer**. The **Social s**igns are more communal and concerned about being with others and inclu**de Leo, Virgo, Libra**, and **Scorpio.** The **Universal** signs are interested in the collective and the group and encompass **Sagittarius, Capricorn, Aquarius,** and **Pisces**.

The astrological formula for the numbered cards within the Minor Arcana deal with the division of the zodiac signs. The ten cards in each suit show a sequence of development. Aces are always the most abstract and highest of the element. The **Twos, Threes, and Fours** deal with the **Cardinal** and are more action-oriented and follow the three decanates of the sign. The **Fives, Sixes, and Sevens** are the **Fixed** signs and stabilize and sustain the process. The Fives represent the first 10 degrees. The Sixes are from 10 to 20 degrees and the Sevens, from 20 to 30 degrees. The **Eights, Nines, and Tens** connect with the **Mutable** signs, which are more adaptable and lead to change. These numbers continue to follow the three decanates of the signs.

The astrological formula is not so clear for the **Royalty** cards, except for the Princes. Royalty cards are the masters, the teachers who mediate and reconcile the lessons of the elements.

The **Knights** are the Awarded Chiefs and all have the added qualities of **Fire** with its elements. The Knight of Swords is a passionate, determined Thinker and associated with all the air signs. The Knight of Cups is the Loyalist and master of emotional rewards and is designated to the sign Cancer. The Knight of Wands is the Visionary and associated with all the fire signs. The Knight of Disks, the Healer and the Harvester, represents all the earth signs and the fiery Leo through its shield.

The **Queens** are the feminine leaders. All have a receptive element of **Water** within them. They also have a strong Cardinal influence that provokes dynamic action. The Queen of Swords, the Mask Cutter, is connected to all the Air signs, especially Libra. All the Water signs, but especially Cancer and Pisces, represent the Intuitive Mother, Queen of Cups as she holds the symbol's Neptune. The Queen of Wands, the Seeker, covers all the Fire signs, especially Aries with the added perception of Pisces. The Queen of Disks, the Nutritionist, has mastery of building new worlds, especially related to diet, and signifies grounded Capricorn plus qualities of dynamic Aries.

The **Princes** have an element of **Air** added to their element. They traditionally ride chariots and show a need for movement, but relate to the Fixed Signs, which sustain, manifest, and hold fast to their element. The Prince of Swords, the Paradox Cutter, is progressive Aquarius. The Prince of Cups, the Lover-Boy, is deep Scorpio. The Prince of Wands, the Creator, is Leo. The Prince of Disks, the Builder, is practical Taurus. All the fixed signs are shown in the Hierophant, Chariot, and Universe card, which represent how the laws of the Universe are fixed.

Princesses have an abundance of initiative energy. All have an added quality of **Earth**, which grounds the mastery in their element. The Princess of Swords, the Mood Fighter, goes beyond moodiness to alignment and is represented by all the air signs. The Princess of Cups, the Detacher, has overcome possessiveness, manipulation, seduction, and jealousy and astrologically represents all the Water signs. The Princess of Wands, the Liberator, overcomes internal blocks and has the attributes of Aries. The pregnant Princess of Disks, the Earth Mother, denotes creative power and astrologically there is a quality of Aries and Scorpio to this earthy disk.

You can blend this rich reservoir of symbolic meaning with the visual representations to your intuitions, experiences, and intentions and when you do, you have a great mirror to reflect your life.

I integrate the Astrological components with the Tarot, which add rich meanings to the archetypal symbols.

3.
Reading the Cards

Synchronistic phenomena are similar
if not identical to phenomena studied in
parapsychological experiments.

Carl G. Jung

It is important to have a quiet, respectful objective when you consult this magical oracle. The process of shuffling the cards is a ritual in which you are invoking a communication with your own inner guidance. It is like a prayer as you are setting a sacred intention. You may even want to say:

> ***"Dear Divine, guide me with your wisdom through these cards so that I may hear what I need for my understanding and growth at this time."***

Because the symbolic cards reflect a high level of synchronicity, they mirror the inner story. When a card comes up in reverse, it indicates change, for the energy of the archetype is either coming in or leaving.

It is also important how you word your questions. I try and avoid yes and no answers. My favorite is: What is the energy around this situation? If you are deciding between two issues, pick cards for each consideration. When you get a negative card, read it constructively with positive commands. For example, if you choose The Nine of Swords, self-cruelty, say "Love yourself more. Be gentle with yourself. Can you name some things you appreciate about yourself."

When you pick a card, notice which symbols catch your eyes, as that is an intuitive message and start the reading from there.

Notice if it is a Major Arcana, a Royalty card, and/or which suit or area of life it is, and which number.

When you look at the cards spread out, take note of the colors and if there are any that are prominent.

Record all your readings in a journal, as this would be helpful to see reoccurring energies.

I have a personal visual system of designating the cards and suits: I put a box around the Major Arcana; a check mark for Swords; a small circle for Cups; an underline for wands; and an x for Disks. I also notice if the card is reversed and if it is, I mark it with Rx. Then I note the number of each area, that gives insight to the emphasis of elements for which I receive guidance. This tells me which areas of my life are more prominent. I have a category for the challenges; one for the Royalty cards; and one for which numbers are repeated. I also translate the cards to their astrological significators to see repetitive patterns.

I started to compare what spheres in the Tree of Life are activated and which planets and words are being emphasized. All this analysis gives a gestalt to help me with the unfoldment of the meanings of what is occurring in my life.

You may want to develop your own system. The symbols are there as pebbles being thrown into a pond; let your mind lead you through the ripples and layers of meanings to see what your particular message is for this moment.

Seeing the timing for events is a tricky proposition in the Tarot. For this purpose I generally use Astrology because it has more parameters. Angeles Arrien always related to the numbers on the cards and included weeks and months. You could always look at the seasonal time of the signs of the Zodiac, if that is applicable. (For example, Leo's (11) Lust card, could be 11 days, weeks, or months or its season of July 23 to August 22.) A general guideline, but not a sure way, is: Swords represent days, Cups symbolize weeks, Wands reveal months, and Disks denote years.

The way I started to truly develop my intuition was to learn to read these Tarot cards. Before I took an intensive Tarot course with my beloved teacher, Angeles Arrien, I let the cards reveal their magic by picking cards each morning. If you are a beginner, start with just one card. My "Daily Reading," was one card was for the body, one for the mind, and one for the emotions. At the end of the day, I would read the interpretation of the symbols in a corresponding book plus my day would reveal the cards' meanings. Later I began adding three more cards to reflect my unconscious body, mind, and feelings and a seventh card for my soul. Using different oracles and decks, I did a variety of readings and wrote their messages out in my journal as if I were getting counsel from a great guru.

Sometimes sharing the wisdom of reflections with friends can be fun. Once before a friend and I had a visit, we randomly picked three cards and then just went on talking together. After we were finished, we checked the cards and were amazed. They reflected our exact conversation.

Sometimes in our groups we have cards available, each individual will pick one as their cosmic expression in the moment and the feedback is often a feeling of delight and amazement.

One afternoon in the mid 1970's, I was a flight attendant on a trip to a resort inland in the Pacific. I was reading the cards of a co-worker in our hotel cafe. I had been studying and playing with the Tarot for a couple years by then. While we were playing with the cards, this curious native woman watched us for a while and then came up to me and asked if I would read her. She randomly picked three cards, the pregnant and autonomous Princess of Disks and the sorrowful Three of Swords were two of them. I innocently asked her if she was pregnant, unmarried, and sad about it. She was in shock, for I had hit her dilemma on the head. The next day she had told about thirty-five people in her village how incredible my prediction was. They lined up for me to read them. That was a memorable afternoon. Since the locals only spoke English as their second language, I had to read the cards in the simplest terms as if I was speaking to a child. I felt challenged as well as privileged for that experience. My reward was that everyone was so very appreciative. Many asked if I would do it again the next day, as they wanted to share the experience with their friends.

Another unique incident happened to me while on a layover in Singapore. It was a Full Moon at the same time as my Moon astrologically. As I went out to dinner with several of my fellow coworkers, I told them, "This is an auspicious night. Let's be open to having fun." As soon as we sat down in the restaurant, a group of six sailors noticed us and asked if we would join them. We were delighted and didn't hesitate. After treating us to dinner, they invited us to a party. A Navy ship was at port with many more sailors on board. Somehow our dinner companions learned I could read Tarot cards. When I got to the party, the word had spread. Sailors were lined up for me to read their cards. Although most of these Navy guys regarded the opportunity as just fun, I was told that the experience stimulated awe, deep thinking, and psychological probing. The general buzz was how amazingly revealing the cards were.

Somehow the Moon's energy helped opened my psychic channel that night. In general whenever someone reads the cards, the value and quality of their answers is dependent upon their level of consciousness. When you do a reading with an open heart, the insights you receive can be a great teacher and helper, and provide synchronistic revelations of your inner process.

Use some cosmic play as a guiding force to mirror your life. Explore a metaphysical bookstore or an App. store and discover the numerous tools and divination devices available and see what calls to you.

Draw on the *Awaken Tarot Cards* or, if this deck does not call you, be open to purchasing something that attracts you with a book to explain the symbols.

In the morning choose something to reflect what you need for your day and let it sit on your table or dresser. Then, in the evening, reflect on your symbols for insight into how they mirror the issues of your day.

Whenever you have a question, sit quietly and reflect, then ask the symbol what you should do.

Meditate on a card if you want to invoke more of the qualities represented by the symbol.

As a deeper meditation, draw and color a card or symbol with your own rendition of the quality.

Whenever you use your hands to creatively express, you have an opportunity to bring what is inside out. As you play with these sacred symbols, you can find a direct channel to your soul's journey.

As I place my sacred intentions on the Tarot their meanings are revealed to me, and add insight, clarity, and inspiration to my life.

Part II

Major Arcana

The psychological mechanism for transforming is the symbol.

Carl Jung

Fool: Take a risk and dare to be who you really are. Trust yourself to embark on a new path from a place of courage. Revolutionary change and electrical energy are available now to awaken and transform your life.

4.

Beginning and Ending with the Mystical (0) Fool

True liberation involves coming to the point where
all structure is taken by choice
and life is self-created.

Robert Hand

The **Fool** is the most well known of all the Tarot cards. Having the number 0, the Fool is not foolish, but is the **Adventurer** who is ready, willing and able to embark on new territory—his own path. Stepping on the spiritual adventure, he represents the state of mystical, ecstatic wonder that is inherent within us. This **Cosmic Being** is the **Wanderer** for he begins the transformative spiral journey and ends it.

Here you have the **Universal Person** who is taking a quantum leap into an expanded state of consciousness, shown through emanation of rays coming from the Fool. Crossing the crevasse from the past to the future, this **Humanitarian** is outlined in the celestial Universe. An androgynous being that has both male and female characteristics within, the figure is illustrated with the body of man and the face of woman.

The planetary ruler of the Fool is **Uranus**, which is electrically charged and links the Fool to those intuitive channels where powerful forces flow into awareness with electrical rapidity. S/he deals with what ought to be, where rules don't apply. His realities are your ideals. The Fool is capable of finding new ways of achieving, for s/he sparks the mind into new creativity, beyond reason and the established view of things. Sometimes the feeling of uprootedness and unsettledness can occur, because Uranus symbolizes reversals and surprises.

The Fool is leaping away from the tiger, which symbolizes past fears and conditioning, into a new world of humanitarian community. His greatest assets are courage and freedom from fear and limitation.

The symbolism of the cosmic hand shows that s/he has the new world and the potential for new growth. The timing of this archetype is now, as there is a readiness and willingness to take action.

The snake and the butterfly represent regeneration and transformation. The dove denotes a sensitive, compassionate, peaceful nature. The crystal reveals clarity of perception. The rising sun shows the potential and pervading life force of this archetype.

The Hebrew letter for the Fool is its first letter, *aleph,* which means "**ox**" and is associated with power at work, strength, and the all-pervading creative energy or breath that animates all life. The Fool is full of this life-breath manifesting as a primal aspect of universal consciousness.

On the Tree of Life, the Fool travels (the upper masculine Pillar of Expansion) between **Crown** (*Kether*) and **Wisdom** (*Chokmah*). The universal Fool is the **Divine** spark that resides within the entire dynamic Zodiac. The Magus, in the opposite position on the Tree of Life, brings an understanding of spiritual Love that balances the Fool's spiritual and inspirational doing.

Let the Fool inspire you to get ready for the unexpected, open new doors, and create opportunities and changes in your life's patterns as well as your consciousness.

Fool Key words: *Uranus; Awakener; Cosmic Adventurer; Wanderer; Revolutionary; courage; absence of fear; liberation; openness; freedom; ecstasy; peak experience.*

Meditate on courage and taking risks.

Contemplate on ecstasy and wonder in your life.

Imagine you are filled with electrical energy to revolutionize your life.

Where is there fear in my life?

Who am I without my fears, pains, and the limiting labels?

What adventure is calling me?

How can I bring anticipation, awe, and curiosity into my life?

I am ready, willing, open, and able to follow the path of my heart and higher mind with courage and radiance.

Magician: You have all you would ever need to communicate brilliantly, with humor and an artful sense of timing. Trust your mind to be proactive and to speak from knowledge.

5.

Communicating with the (1)Magician

All magic and miracles have an
attitude of hopeful expectancy.

Carl Jung

The **Magician** or the **Magus** represents the principle of communication. Often called the **Juggler**, this **Expert Communicator** speaks with inspiration, resilience, and a sense of humor. A **Master of Symbols,** the Magus manipulates words, concepts, images, and psychological realties. As you open to the Magician, you tap into your ability to observe, converse, discriminate, analyze, and adapt.

Having the number one, the right use of mind is the first step to becoming a conscious person. **Mercury** (Hermes to the Greeks), the winged Messenger of the gods is the Magus. The rendition in *Awaken Tarot Cards* is feminine since Mercury represents an androgynous being. The smiling golden figure represents flexibility. S/he holds within all the symbols and is gifted with timing. In her right hand is a sword for air signifying intellect and logic. On top of it is the caduceus, which denotes healing and regeneration. In the left hand is a fire wand, symbolizing inspiration and the spiritual and inner world. Within the wand is an arrow that denotes directness, honesty, and purpose. Around the body are several floating symbols. A cup with a snake denotes regenerating and transforming emotions. A coin or disk symbolizes the physical, financial world. A winged egg reveals extra-sensory perception. A key signifies the tools to awakening; and a book shows bringing the information to the world. In addition to the gifts and talents, all the symbols show the power of choice.

The Hebrew letter for the Magician is *beth,* which means "**house**" and translates as "that which goes on within us." Eliphas Levi said, "All magic is in the will." So this symbol represents the self-conscious phase of mental activity.

The Magus or Magician deals with magic and the Hermetic philosophy, "As above, so below." This Principle of Correspondence also says, "As Within, So Without," which basically means that everything—all of the planes of existence—are connected and in correspondence. These influencing ideas open your mind to look to the enchantment of metaphysics.

On the Tree of Life, the Magician traverses (from the upper feminine Pillar of Form) between **Crown** (*Kether*) and **Understanding** (*Binah*). It blends our spiritual nature with **Saturn's** comprehensiveness and willingness to manifest into form. Creative energies take form through the wonders of this archetype. There is an activating power that changes one thing into another. The Magician understands that spiritually we are One with the **Divine**. The Fool with its inspiration and dynamic wisdom balances the Magus by his position on the Tree of Life.

With the Magician, you get in touch with the spark of Divine Will that is a part of all of us, where all truth lies. Yet throughout history the Magician reveals the dynamic connection with the world of spirit and matter. Mercury is said to rule thieves. There is a duality to the mind: it stands for both truth and falsehood.

Let the Magician help you see beyond projection to the real truth, so you can bridge the inner and outer. The Magician tells you to correctly apply your mind, and be responsible for the thoughts you think. The subconscious acts according to the instructions of your thoughts. Being proactive and focusing on what you want to become, rather than what you want to overcome, is the power of mind to change your life.

Magician Key words: Mercury; communication; flexibility; intelligence; timing; humor; intuitive knowing; mental connections; skillful use of symbols.

Realize your mind as your tool and not your master by watching its workings during the day without judgment.

What do I need to do to become mindful of my thoughts?

Be watchful of your thoughts and then notice, are they are positive or negative?

Do I want to create more of that in my life?

I am a master communicator and I use my mind skillfully and magically.

High Priestess: Whenever you pull this card, you know the answer. Go inside, pay attention, and ask your inner self. Trust your intuition and feelings. Give in a balanced, independent way.

6.

Intuiting with the (2) High Priestess

Why are you afraid of the silence,
silence is the root of everything.
If you spiral into its void,
a hundred voices
will thunder messages
you long to hear.

Rumi

The **High Priestess** is that step on the path when you withdraw from outer involvement and turn inward to listen to the silence. The Priestess observes and absorbs the quiet so that the inner voice can speak and be heard. She is the **Psychic** of the deck. As the **Intuitive Knower**, her perceptions dissolve the separateness in the mind, for she has a direct link with universal knowledge. Her receptivity embraces the sensitivity of her ruler, the **Moon**. Her power, contained and hidden, has the ability to awaken the unconscious and how we telepathically communicate with each other, whether we are aware of it or not.

The High Priestess sits facing her left, for her intuitive wisdom is not expressed in rational terms. The infinity symbol in front of her eyes, shows her extra-sensory awareness and extended vision. At the bottom of the card are crystals, which signify perception and clarity of vision. Her acute sensitivity perceives visual and mental images. Her special gift is memory, the principle of recollecting knowledge already possessed within.

Clothed in luminous light, she goes beyond the conscious mind to a deep inner wisdom. She sits in swirls of light that represent implosive feminine energy, yet within the curves are straight lines and squares, which denote dynamic, direct, and purposeful masculine energy. The symbol of the Sun and Moon together represent balance and new beginnings. The number two reinforces the feminine, balancing, and harmonizing aspect of the High Priestess.

In myth, the **Moon Goddess** was the Egyptian **Isis**, or the Greek and Roman, **Artemis/Diana**, which reveals a self-contained ingenuity and power. She sits on her throne as the symbol of female power, showing how the High Priestess is her own person. Near her is a bow and arrow, which represents her need for independence. She will give love in a balanced way but will not be restricted. The secret of this path is equilibrium or balancing the male and female and expressing independence.

The Hebrew letter for the High Priestess is *gimel,* which means "**camel**" and gives the idea of transition and movement. Like the camel that can travel long distances without water, the Priestess possesses both self-sufficiency and resourcefulness.

Astrologically the Moon reflects your deepest needs, your self-image, and how you perceive and feel. The Moon influences our tides, as water is her element and her domain is emotions. When the High Priestess comes up in a reading, she may be telling you to listen to the depths of your feelings to know what choices to make.

The pomegranate was considered a special fruit to the Egyptians, which they served to their dignitaries. The High Priestess has rare and fruitful gifts. The sunflower follows the sun and as you learn to track your inner light, you engage in an expanded consciousness.

On the Tree of Life the High Priestess dwells (in the upper, central vertical path on the Pillar of Integration) between **Divine Crown** (*Kether*) and **Sun's Beauty** (*Tiphareth*). This is the longest and most important path on the Tree of Life, as you infuse and radiate your spiritual nature with your personal self. You intuitively know that you are Whole and connected to the Source. The Infinite activates the Higher Self, and you have excellence and elegance.

By withdrawing from outer involvement, you allow the High Priestess to open you to the wisdom of the personal unconscious and the collective unconscious. As you quiet your mental chatter, you can listen within to hear your inner, visionary psychic speak to you. Then you can truly know yourself.

High Priestess Key words: Moon; balance; receptivity; intuition; psychic ability; independence; emotions; sensitivity.

Contemplate on pulling inward for self-care, meditation, and quiet time each day.

Am I listening to my intuition? What is it telling me?

How can I express my independence more?

What do I need to do to have more balance in my life?

I listen and trust my inner knowing.

Empress: You are magnetically creative and beautifully fertile with new life. Love, allow others, and accept whatever is. Open to receive and give generously.

7.

Creating with the (3) Empress

Being deeply loved by someone gives you strength,
while loving someone deeply gives you courage.

Loa Tzu

The **Empress**, the second feminine archetype is the third path of the Tarot Journey, which represents love with wisdom. Ruled by **Venus**, the **Goddess of Love** and **Beauty**, the Empress implies that the fundamental law of the Universe is love. Love is a compelling force that binds us together. With Venus you look for what is similar, and connect, unify, cooperate, and harmonize. You come from your heart, allow others to be as they are, and accept what Is.

Her power of imagination is the beginning of all creative processes. She is the great **Earth Mother** as shown with the swan and her duckling.

The Empress' world is a **Fertile Garden**, and symbolizes productivity, increase, and fruitfulness, as illustrated by the cornucopia full of fruits and vegetable. Her reality gives birth to our natural laws. Through her you obtain the key to physical manifestation and prosperity by knowing that you live in an abundant Universe. With the Empress you are to go and make the world what you want in accordance with the underlying principles of the physical world. Her path shows a process of maturation. Coming from a place of fullness and plenty, her loving generosity has a broad understanding of the external world and the ability to reach inward.

The Empress represents the principle of attraction and magnetism as shown by the Earth hugging the Moon. She draws toward herself what she wants and desires, and gives pleasure to the self through others and beauty. The number three is a creative, joyful, and imaginative energy.

The Empress approaches life through feelings and emotions. Her secret is to get in touch with inner feelings and assert them lovingly in the moment. She connects heaven and earth, spirit with flesh, and can bridge heart and mind, feelings and intellect.

The Hebrew letter for the Empress is *daleth*, which means "**door**" or crossing a threshold or barrier. It is her balanced heart that allows this passage. Yet some writers say this door is the fertile womb, as it is the door to life. A door can also represent protection, preservation, and safekeeping. The Empress has a shield at her feet, along with the Emperor.

On the Tree of Life, the Empress bridges the upper Pillars (Mercy or Form with Severity or Force) and crosses the horizon between **Wisdom** (*Chokmah*) and **Understanding** (*Binah*). This blending of the Father with the Mother principles links the whole **Zodiac** with **Saturn**. Saturn in the Kabbalah represents an ancient yin symbol of fertility, productivity, and manifestation as well as the universal laws at work. The Empress gives forms of nurturing love that positively and dynamically stimulate and generate new possibilities.

Let the Empress inspire you to be compassionate and give of yourself, without losing yourself. Allow her to teach you to open your heart more and love, and come out to create in a place of unity and abundance.

Empress Key words: *Venus; magnetism; love; attraction; creativity; motherhood; fertility; balance of heart and mind; giving and receiving; productivity; imagination; increase; productivity.*

Meditate on how to blend your heart and mind so that you never come from just one or the other way.

Turn on your power of magnetism. See each cell in your body as a magnet, the nucleus of each cell a double magnet, and your heart a triple magnet and literally pull your desires to you.

How can I add beauty and grace to my life?

Am I creating what I truly want?

Where can I enhance my creativity?

How can I nurture myself more as well as those I love?

I am the personification of Love as a creative process and I magnetize grace and beauty in all aspects of my life.

Emperor: Time to pioneer, build, and do, so that you can receive tangible rewards. Trust your own authority and take responsibility to manifest what you desire and find worthy.

8.

Building with the (4) Emperor

Managers light a fire under people;
leaders light a fire in people.

Kathy Austin

The **Emperor** is the fourth principle on the Path of Balance. His active masculine energy flows out into the world, as he is ready, willing, able, and open to conquer and receive the world's rewards. He is the **Pioneer**, **Doer**, and **Builder** whose inner convictions are power, leadership, and responsibility.

As **Aries** is his designator, he is dressed in red, which characterizes being true to himself. The Emperor has learned to live within the present social myths and go beyond them to find his own individual code. His initiative and assertive spirit, undifferentiated by fears, create powerful drives as well as new life. This archetype displays a sense of urgency and immediacy, for he wants things here and now.

His self-directed, active, dynamic, and spontaneous insights are brought into form as he rises against struggle and limitations. The window or picture on the wall shows the fortitude of a climber pursuing a goal.

The Emperor stands in his royal clothes looking dynamic as he carries power and significance with the world. His crown rests on the stool as a symbol of wisdom and prominence. As the authority principle, the Emperor is the archetypical **Father**. Mother is associated with unconditional love, but the Father concept is to accomplish, do well, and be productive. Money and the Father are connected, as the Father provides and supports. He also represents law and order in the Universe and judges, enforces, punishes, and teaches the rules of society.

Seasonally, Aries is the beginning of the Astrological year. In the northern hemisphere, during March 21 to April 19, there are bursts of new life energy sprouting everywhere.

The same protective shield on both the Empress and Emperor links them together. As co-rulers of the Universe, they work creatively as the union of nature and spirit. The Emperor governs with the outer male energy–logic, thought, order, and concrete honest truth. The Empress domain is inner—eros, feelings, and intuition, where sprouts of imagination and ideas grow. Each must be given their time to rule.

Within the Emperor lie great power and the keys to manifestation. Four is the number of foundation, work, and discipline. As well as being practical, disciplined, consistent, and organized, he represents the strength, decisiveness, and determination to come to awareness.

The Hebrew word for the Emperor is *heh*, which means "**window**," and allows light and air into the personality and gives perspective and control. This letter is associated with vision, inspection, and watchfulness. Gifted with sight, he is endowed with original ideas and vision. The Emperor's power of perception also includes rational principles of inductive reasoning, keen mental observation, and analysis.

On the Tree of Life, the Emperor moves diagonally from (the upper sphere on the masculine Pillar of Expansion) **Wisdom** (*Chokmah*) to **Beauty** (*Tiphareth*), which brings the whole **Zodiac** with the **Sun**. This connection is a constituting intelligence, for it comprises the Father principle and its forceful will with a radiant, creative sense of self. Here you learn to blend the Father's dynamic, doing energy with creativity, love, and power. The Lovers sit on the opposite side of the Tree of Life and emphasize the receptive loving side to balance the Emperor's wisdom and force of will.

The Emperor's message is to put yourself out there and take the world in your own hands. When you own your own Father within, you rise up to your own authority and stop giving that role to others. Then you can build the qualities of strength, will, control, protectiveness, and stability inside yourself and manifest a better world.

Emperor Key words: Aries; responsibility; pioneer; doer; authority; builder; power; father; manifestation; beginnings; foundation; leadership; structures; power, taking action.

Meditate on what you want to build or initiate in your life.

How can I own my own authority?

Who do I give my authority away to?

What is important to empower in myself?

What kind of world do I want to live in and how can I move toward that vision?

What can I do to express my innate spirit?

I own my authority and initiate what I want to manifest and produce great rewards in the world.

Hierophant: Listen and trust the deeper parts of yourself. Open to your spirituality and a teacher or inner teacher. You may be resolving a family issue. Listen to your inner child.

9.

Discovering with the (5) Hierophant

A true spiritual teacher does not have anything
to teach in the conventional sense of the word.
The only function of such a teacher is to
help you remove that which separates you
from the truth of who you already are
and what you already know in the depth of your being.

Eckhart Tolle

The **Hierophant** is the fifth step on the Path of Balance. It is where you connect with your inner spiritual teachers. The image is the **Pope**, the **Sage**, and the **Wise One** guiding his children. This archetype has intuitive knowledge that unlocks the mysteries of the collective unconscious. Ruling from the heart, the Hierophant is responsible for giving spiritual counsel to mankind. Called the **Speaker**, the Hierophant is the **Spokesman** for the Gods through oracles and symbols. With the ability to reveal the sacred and secret knowledge s/he bridges humanity and the Divine. The key is to know that this inner space exists in us and to accept that all answers are within.

The Hierophant suggests that you learn to listen to your intuition, so you can manifest from the center your being. The elephants, presented as though they were coming out of his ears, represent listening. As a symbol of great power, they show the gift of hearing, for his talent is clairaudience and heeding the inner voice of the God force within.

The Hierophant is pictured smiling and shows the need for humor and to follow the path that is pleasurable. The snake represents regeneration and the need to shed the old to make way for the new. The orange color represents the healing qualities of the Hierophant.

Taurus, the Fixed Earth sign, is a stable foundation for the Hierophant. It is important that these spiritual principles be brought down to earth and manifest. Applying your inner truth to your daily life will bring the ultimate security and safety.

Seasonally, Taurus is April 20 to May 20 and it is a creative time in nature as "April showers bring May flowers."

Family issues are connected to this symbol, for mother, father, and child are all represented by this archetype. The Hierophant is gifted with children, has a childlike innocence, and has the ability to reach the child within. In his heart lies the child, which tells you that it is the child within that is closest to God. When you honor your inner child, you tap your Divine spark of inspiration, wonder, curiosity, forgiveness, and creativity.

In the Tree of Life, the Hierophant resides within (the upper vertical path on the Pillar of Expansion) **Wisdom** (*Chokmah*) and **Mercy** (*Chesed*). The whole **Zodiac** blends with the benevolent guru, **Jupiter** and creates revelations of the Divine.

The Hierophant offers inspirational wisdom and unconditional love. The Chariot, who sits on the opposite Pillar, understands how to clarify intentions and integrates the Hierophant's generous and compassionate visions.

The Hebrew word is *vau*, and means, "**nail**," or something that joins things together or that others depend upon. It is shown on the staff.

Around the card are the four fixed signs of the zodiac, which include all the elements. They tell you that the laws of the Universe are fixed and what is above is below, uniting the microcosm with the macrocosm.

Five is the number of man and learning through experience. To discover God inside yourself, you are to undergo some uncomfortable confrontations with your own psyche.

Allow the Hierophant to help you listen to that quiet inner voice and develop an inner faith of a better and higher Universal Force that is guiding your life. His message will usher you to your own inner counsel, thus giving you the gift of yourself.

Hierophant Key words: Taurus; Inner Teacher; Spiritual Guide; listening and hearing; intuitively creative; spirit to earth; family; inner child; lessons; wisdom through experience.

Take a mind journey inward. Imagine you are in the country and find a house that has a wise guide. Knock on the door and ask questions. Then go blank and listen to the thoughts that come. Write them down.

Can I awaken my childlike curiosity and notice what am I learning today?

How can I bring my creative ideas into a tangible form?

How can I express blessings and sacredness to my day and family in concrete ways?

I deeply honor my spirituality and intuition and I am inspired to learn and teach.

Lovers: The desire for union within opposing sides is present. You may be coming together and yet looking at what separates you. It's a time of choice. Follow innocence and communicate.

10.

Loving with the (6) Lovers

The best and most
beautiful things in this world
cannot be seen or even heard,
but must be felt
with the heart.

Helen Keller

The sixth step on the Tarot path is the **Lovers**. Here you deal with the **Duality/Polarity** principle of Relationships. The Lovers is a **Bonder** and represents all kinds of love connection—spouses; friends; partners; parent and child; teacher and student, employer and employee, and associations.

The designator of the Lovers is the zodiac sign **Gemini**, the Personal, Mutable Air sign. It symbolizes the "twins and pairs." All relationships and all life stem from the dance of opposite forces, whether you call them male/female, yin/yang, passive/active, or light/dark. Every member of the pair derives its meaning from its opposite. One's awareness of the self is always in reference to that which is the "not self." In the Lovers, you have separation, but with an appreciation and desire to come together.

Seasonally, Gemini is May 21 to June 20, which is a transitional and changing time.

Everything on this card illustrates balancing. The couple reveals the need for devotion or loyal commitment. It also shows compassion, space, and non-restriction, as represented by the

Hermit and the division in the water. There is to be freedom and individuality in their emotional involvement.

The orphic egg is a snake coiled around an egg three and half times, which represents the essence of male and female energies evolving together. It denotes how relationships are constantly changing internally and externally. Full of power and spiritual renewal, they are transformative and regenerative.

The two twin children symbolize how all relationships require a childlike innocence, inquisitiveness, and playfulness. Sitting within the flowers, they indicate the necessity of naturalness, beauty, and goodness.

The lion and the eagle form a pair and also represent your needs in relationship. Leo's lion represents generosity and creativity. Scorpio's eagle portrays involvement and passion.

Smell is the sense connected here, which is associated with perception.

The cupid is a modern day love symbol and signifies eros, or the stimulating and exciting pull toward others, which is how you transcend the isolating and protective ego. There are two kinds of love here, the passionate love and compassionate love, for within both forms of love is eros. Love is the truth of who you are and love is the way to remember that truth. It is more than a noun and a verb. It is consciousness, your Essence and your way of being.

The Hebrew letter for the Lovers is *zain,* which translates as "**sword**" or weapon. It signifies disposing intelligence or the part of the mind that cuts, separates, and distinguishes.

Some old Tarot titles bore the name **Choice**. This path is one of discriminating, setting apart, and seeing differences. The real problem in relationships is the restriction they place on each other and how you cut into each other's liberties and self-expression.

In reality, your relationships are your assignments. They are your karma, processes of growth, and outer mirrors, not ends in themselves. When you look at your relationships as a reflection of your inner balance, you give up blame and projection and make peace with the polarities within. To come together with another in harmony, you first need an inner harmony.

The key to relationships is communication. Gemini is the **Curious Talker.** With clear communication, you can overcome your tendency to constantly separate yourself from your inner guidance. The inner spirit is always hidden from direct view. The path is to bring out your inner feelings and intuition and transform them into a higher state. When the conscious intellect gives direction to the feelings, or when you act on your intuition, you maintain balance in your life. This is marrying your male and female and part of your great work and the way of liberation, for in unity you are greater than yourself.

This symbol bears the number six, which is the highest number of balance. It is the only number that is considered both male and female. It brings both spirit and form to completion. It is the number of responsibility, service, and domestic orientation.

In the Tree of Life, the Lovers card diagonally connects (the upper feminine Pillar of Form) **Understanding** (*Binah*) with **Beauty** (*Tiphareth*). Here you unite the nurturing, receptive, and loving Great Mother aspect of **Saturn** with the **Sun's** visions of harmony, healing, and redemption. All of which are necessary to have satisfying relationships. On the opposite side of the Tree we have the Emperor, bringing in an active dynamic energy, which balances the Lovers' receptive understanding.

Let the Lovers card guide you to see what is going on within your inner relationship. Allow your natural sequence of mental discrimination to follow your intuition. This means to act and speak about your deepest feelings and intuitions. Note that every person you meet is here to relate to as a mirror of an aspect of yourself.

Lovers Key words: Gemini; duality; polarity principle; relationships; attraction; union of opposites through love; mirror concept; discrimination; balance through communication; marriage of male female aspects; choice.

Look at the closest relationships in your life as a mirror of your best qualities and your faults.

Contemplate on the thought, "No one can do to me what I am not already doing to myself."

With a blank sheet of paper, draw two lines vertically dividing the paper in three columns. In the first column, write the name of your mother.

Then quickly without much thought, write three things that you love about her in the second column.

In the third column write three things that bother you about her.

Continue with your father, partner, best friends, and your children.

After you finished glance at the columns to see all your beauty and all your weaknesses.

> How do I come together with others and then break away?
>
> How do I resist when I am in relationship?
>
> Can I own in myself what I project onto others?

All my relationships mirror my inner relationships and reveal my greatness, beauty and my faults.

Chariot: Take time to examine your many possibilities. Make changes and decisions based on your heartfelt feelings. Engage in activities of self-knowledge and quiet meditation.

11.

Contemplating with the (7) Chariot

The only constant is change.

I Ching

The **Chariot** is the seventh step in the Tarot evolutionary path. Here our hero is setting out on a personal journey reflecting and contemplating the potentials of life. The swirling movement shows mental energy, and the need to develop a deep inner life through the mental realm. While he is thinking about moving, a circulating Wheel of Fortune on his lap stimulates his heart and lower charkas to make choices that bring abundance.

The number seven is associated with the contemplative, investigative, observant, and mystical qualities. The Chariot holds this knowledge within himself.

The principle of **Free Will** and **Choice** come into focus, for here you deal with change and its causes. The dark and light horses are facing different directions. Decisions are not easy, for he can see many possibilities. Any decisions made will guarantee changes on every level.

The figures in the field in the background represent the four Fixed signs of the Zodiac and all the elements. The Chariot wants the changes to be grounded, practical, and tangible like the Taurus' bull; creative, self-expressive, and inspirational like the Leo's lion; new, innovative, and progressive like the Aquarius man; and to be passionately involved and have far-reaching perception like the Scorpio's eagle. Once these criteria are met success is assured.

The Chariot's zodiac sign, **Cancer,** is deeply personal, emotional and concerned with home, family and tribe. Its ruler, the Moon, reflects both a deep inner receptive and changeable nature. As the natural emotional gateway to the psyche, the Chariot reveals the need to act and move on feelings. A Cardinal sign, it moves out of itself to set up a situation to which it can respond; thus it is an intuitive outgoing and emotional in drawing energy.

Cancer's symbol is the crab, which is inwardly soft, yet outwardly hard. The crab with its protective shell is pictured behind the Chariot in a steam of water, showing a sensitive, nourishing nature and a need for a safe and supportive environment while breakthroughs and changes are happening.

The Hebrew letter is *cheth*, which means "**fence enclosing a field**" and suggests protection, defense, enclosure and safeguarding the home front .

Seasonally in the northern hemisphere, Cancer initiates the sunny warmth of summer on June 21 to July 22. The golden color around him represents flexibility and inner transformation.

In the Tree of Life, the Chariot travels (vertically from the upper to middle path of the feminine Pillar of Form) from **Understanding** (*Binah*) to **Severity** (*Gerubah*). Blending **Saturn** and **Mars** describes the Contemplative Mover who drives with the brakes on. The receptive Divine Mother merges with the courageous Warrior principle, which is the Goddess Warrior magnetically creating with Love and Presence. On the other side of the Tree of Life, the Hierophant with its benevolent spiritual wisdom integrates the Chariot's courageous intentions of Love.

Tune into the cautiousness of the Chariot, so you can think about plans for movement before you leap. Then when it is time to make a change, you will feel secure and be ready and prepared.

Chariot Key words: Cancer; contemplation; free will; decision; choice; movement; change; causation; direction of the will; combination of stillness and activity.

Take quiet time to be alone and not lonely, so you can ponder what's next. Let your feelings guide your decisions.

What decisions do I need to contemplate to assist my growth?

What changes am I setting in motion?

How can I integrate quiet time and activity?

I contemplate and take responsibility to stimulate change that is motivating for others and rewarding for me.

Adjustment: Time to balance and adjust things. Watch your thoughts and look within for answers. Actively listen to understand how negotiating fits into taking the moderate path.

12.

Balancing with the (8) Adjustment/Justice

The challenge of work-life balance
is without question
one of the most significant struggles
faced by modern man.

Stephen Covey

With the **Adjustment**, you come up with the great Tarot controversy. Aleister Crowley switched its name from **Justice** and its position to the eighth position and the Lust/Strength card to the eleventh position. This exchange had to do with number Eight's position on the Tree of Life. Crowley felt that the Adjustment card should balance the two outer Pillars centrally and connect **Severity** (*Geburah*) with **Mercy** (*Chesed*). We have to adjust to equalize **Mars'** Destroyer with **Jupiter's** Builder and balance letting go and expanding. The Adjustment card has the disciplined intention to support Divine visions.

Eight is the number of power, organization, leadership, and acquisition. The archetypes of Jupiter and Mars signify dynamic abundance, fortunate action, and intentional manifesting.

This path brings the principle of **Alignment** and **Balance.** Astrologically, **Libra** (September 23 to October 22) rules this archetype. This Cardinal (motivated and goal-directed) Air sign has a strong sense of other and strives for unity, fairness, and social duty. The Adjustment has a pronounced aesthetic sense, special awareness, high regard for beauty, and is gifted in healing. Associated with **Pallas Athena** in Greek mythology, she was the **Goddess of Wisdom and Fairness.** Based on the Egyptian **Maat,** she was the **Goddess of Law, Truth, and Justice,** who judged the weight of the heart of the dead.

The mask over her eyes shows she has inner eyes. As you look within and weigh your relative experiences, you can find truth and your center. Going inward is necessary for centeredness and inner balance so that new ideas can be materialized. Adjustment sees all possibilities, yet strives for her interpretation. The balls around her head symbolize the four levels of consciousness—emotional, intellectual, perceptual, and physical.

The Hebrew letter for Adjustment/Justice is *lamed,* which is a verb meaning "**to teach, to instruct**." As a noun, it means an "**ox goad**," and it guides the all-pervading breath of universal energy.

Standing between day and night, our Goddess balances these different levels of awareness on her shoulders. She holds the Ace of Swords in her left hand pointing to her right side. This represents the power of discrimination and directed thoughts, and a creative mind that has a flair for writing. The sword is an emblem of action and searching for understanding. Your thoughts, ideas, and the slightest distraction can disturb your centeredness and balance. Your every thought is creating your karma and life situations.

Upon Libra's symbol of the scales are spheres that reflect the totality of her knowledge. Showing the beginning and the end of a day or initiating and completing. The scales denote the negotiating, arbitrating, valuing, and moderating of your synthesizing mind. As you adjust the workings of fate with your creations, it can be a push and a pull. You will have to deal with cause and effect to set things right. It is by adjusting and balancing that you truly attain the path of moderation.

Invoke Adjustment to bring balance to your life. To make proper decisions, weigh things to see what truly matters and works. Use your mind wisely. Moderate your life by going inside to access your wisdom and then actively expand into your power and manifestations.

Adjustment Key words: Libra; balance; equilibrium; fairness; balance of opposites; centering; writing; healing; law.

Meditate on this card to bring order and dissolve any illusions. Actively pay attention to different sides of your personality; then negotiate with each of them and consciously choose the action to follow.

What do I need to do to be centered?

How can I be more thoughtful?

What throws me off balance and what can I do to restore it?

Is there anywhere in my life that I am not completely truthful?

How can I balance the inner and outer focus in my life?

I am balanced and centered and honor and value my words and commitments.

Hermit: Stop, turn away, and go inward. Be true to yourself and don't compromise what is important for you. You are basically moving forward, but also completing the past. Trust a wise teacher and your inner knowing.

13.

Completing with the (9) Hermit

Your visions will become clear only
when you can look into your own heart.
Who looks outside, dreams;
who looks inside awakens.

Carl Jung

The **Hermit** is the ninth step in the evolutionary journey. He represents the principle of **Completion, Contemplation,** and **Introspection**. His purpose is to withdraw from the outer world to activate the unconscious and awaken the inner self. As you stop your active mind and your busyness, you can give yourself the emotional space to tap into your internal space. The word Hermit comes from a Greek word, which means desert. His gift is being alone, yet not lonely.

The Hermit is on a boat. He has no fixed path, but is a **Wanderer,** for the world is his home. The Hermit embodies the wisdom not found in books.

In the boat with him is a lantern, which shows that his gifts are illumination, inspiration, and hope. This **Wise One,** the **Way Shower,** is a higher authority within that holds the inner light. His rays penetrate spiritual darkness, which symbolize challenging times. Turning inward and solitude are the ways you can renew and secure your inner light. Through introversion you awaken your inner dialogue and creative imagination.

In Greek mythology, Cerberus is the three-headed dog that guards the underworld, which symbolizes the unconscious.

Here two of his heads are looking forward and one is looking back. The Hermit signifies transitions, for he is basically moving forward, but also completing unfinished material from your unconscious past. Nine is the number of conclusions and represents the finishing cycle. It is the number of gestation, preparation, and initiation. It is a magical number, the highest of the single digits, and represents humanitarian service, brotherhood, and universal love.

With the Hermit is the orphic egg, which represents the ever-changing creative energy of the male and female within. Behind him is a wheat field, which represents fertility.

Dressed in a robe of blood red, the Hermit has to be true to himself and navigates you toward an inner perfection. Virgo, his astrological ruler, and its symbol, the Virgin, represents the self-purification process and refining through discrimination. Looking at what is wrong in order to make it right often leads you to a breakdown of the whole into parts, and focusing on details instead of the big picture. The word "Virgo" comes from Latin and means being "self-sufficient." The Hermit symbolizes one who doesn't need anyone or anything to be complete.

Virgo is an earthy, Mutable or changeable sign. Practical and utilitarian, the Hermit methodically and meticulously analyzes, examines, and compares to solve your inner problems. His greatest desire is to be of service. Seasonally, Virgo is the harvest, August 23 to September 22, and time to reap the rewards of our labors.

On the Tree of Life, the Hermit connects (the middle of the masculine Pillar of Expansion) **Mercy** (*Chesed*) to **Beauty** (*Tiphareth*). He joins **Jupiter's** benevolent, grace-filled visions with the **Sun's** high consciousness. Through this generous, compassionate builder, you can manifest your radiant Core. The opposite side of the Tree of Life is Lust, who balances the Hermit with its intentional and determined power and strength.

The Hebrew letter for the Hermit is *yod*, which means, "**opened hand**." This symbol is a tendency or aptitude for power, skill, and dexterity. It also has the religious connotations of benevolence, freedom, and spirit. Its sense is touch.

Open to the Hermit so you can know your deeper self and see your internal light. The light you seek is really your own. When you take time for meditative solitude, you are recharging and allowing your inner parts to speak to you with illuminations and manifestations.

Hermit Key words: Virgo; completion; contemplation; introspection; perfection; service; resolution; wise inner guidance; fertility.

Take alone time for contemplation, inner reflection, and meditation by planning a day of solitude and silence.

Am I being true to myself?

Am I listening deeply to my inner views?

Do I need to complete any unresolved issues?

How can I be of service?

What gives my life meaning?

I go inward and find what has meaning and significance for me.

Wheel of Fortune: Time of great expansion and opportunities. Major changes are happening so stay objective, flexible and keep expanding your creativity. Be positive and expect the best. Expand and open to receive. You are manifesting your goals.

14.

Expanding with the (10) Wheel of Fortune

The secret of true prosperity
is finding our security
through our connection with the Divine,
with the spiritual world.

Christopher Penczak

The tenth evolutionary key is the **Wheel of Fortune**. It represents the principle of **Expansion, Change,** and the **Force of Evolution**. Here you experience the great mystery of life as all things connect and flow in cyclical order in an endless creating and shifting process, both personal and universal.

The three Egyptian Gods on the wheel show you how to create and evolve. The Sphinx is the spiritual lion that faces the rising sun as the guardian of the mysteries. The Sphinx says stay objective and holds a sword to signify discrimination and clear thinking. The monkey portrays that you need to be flexible. It clutches a hook to tell you that you make your own luck. The crocodile represents creativity and has within its grasp an Egyptian Ankh, the symbol of life, showing your need to keep adding new life to your creative endeavors.

In the center of the wheel we have the Sun, the symbol of our individualized essence and origin of all creative energy. It also represents consciousness, awareness, realization, and enlightenment. At the center, you can remain true to yourself as the wheel turns and your life experiences its ups and downs.

Purple is the color of royalty, expansion, and spiritual growth. This is the golden path as **Jupiter**, the planet of abundance, enthusiasm, and expansion, rules it. In Roman and Greek mythology Jupiter/Zeus is the King of the Gods and represents the principle of truth, inspiration, and higher learning. As the **Great Benefactor**, Jupiter is the part of you that is greater than the self that you know. Jupiter represents the step where you open up and take on more of the world and believe in your abilities and yourself.

The Roman Goddess **Fortuna** is connected to this archetype and shows you that you can turn your life into good fortune. If you stay watchful, you see that gifts of abundance come when opportunities are met with preparedness. You can experience joyful breakthroughs and clarity, as you learn to participate in your fate as a collective mover of destiny.

Ten is a number of physical expressions of manifestation and fulfillment. The end comes back to the beginning. What comes up must come down. There is in truth a greater benefit to life's adversities.

The Hebrew letter for the Wheel of Fortune is *kaph*, which means "**grip** or **palm**." This is a closed hand that holds, comprehends, understands, and masters mentally and physically.

On the Tree of Life, the Wheel of Fortune connects (vertically on the masculine Pillar of Expansion from the middle to the lower spheres) **Mercy** (*Chesed*) to **Victory** (*Netzach*). Blending the beneficent planets of Jupiter and Venus brings good fortune and joyful feelings, for you consciously connect grace and pleasure to building and manifesting. The Hanged Man resides on the opposite side (Pillar of Form) and balances the Wheel of Fortune by calling in its intentional, disciplined, Warrior mind.

Open up to the Wheel of Fortune and allow all the goodness of the Universe to flow to you. Believe in yourself. By being open and trusting that you have the power to create and manifest your world with creative abundance, you make your dreams come true.

Wheel of Fortune Key words: Jupiter; breakthroughs; prospects; benefit; luck; creativity; benevolence; prosperity; magnification; abundance.

Count your Blessings. Make a gratitude list.

Contemplate how you experience trust in your life.

Think about what you want to accomplish and what you need to manifest it.

What can I do to add new energy to my creativity?

What is my expectation level?

In what ways am I seeking to grow and change in my life?

How do I connect with something greater than myself?

Through the Infinite power of the Divine, I live in prosperity and abundance.

Lust/Strength: Lust for strength and creativity, for everything is within you. You are overcoming unconsciousness and fears. Look within for your inspiration.

15.

Yearning for (11) Lust/Strength

Ecstasy is what everyone craves—not love or sex,
but enravishment, a hot-blooded, soaring intensity,
in which being alive is a joy and a thrill.

Diane Ackerman

Aliester Crowley renamed the **Strength** card to **Lust**. He felt that Lust was more inclusive, because it symbolizes the beauty and joy produced when you have strength. He also changed its position with the Adjustment/Justice card. His reasoning was based on its placement in the Tree of Life as well as how Lust connects with the master number 11. It is the number of realizations, revelations, and extended vision that draws on the cosmic forces for inspiration, awareness, imaginative qualities, and intuitive abilities.

On the Tree of Life, Lust/Strength traverses (from the middle of the feminine Pillar of Form) **Severity** (*Geburah*) and **Beauty** (*Tiphareth*). **Mars**' courageous intentional Warrior energy connects with the **Sun's** radiant Core self. With the union of love and power, your self-expressive identity and drive are linked with visions of harmony and redemption.

This passionate intentional force is balanced on the other side of the Tree of Life with the Hermit's compassionate benevolence.

Lust rides the beast in its many forms and allows the wild, primitive, and uninhibited forces to move within her and go beyond to the Love and Creativity within. She has strength and passion to manifest her inspired energy. Below her are the dark figures representing fears and unconscious conditioning, yet the ruins in the shadow areas do not bother her.

Here you learn to take conscious control of your inner nature, so you can build strength and experience joy. It happens naturally once you have defined and reshaped the patterns recoded unconsciously. By letting go of defenses, you free your instinctual nature.

Filled with fascination, Lust holds the Holy Grail enflamed, which reveals the inner fire of your wondrous, infinite power of creation. Known as the **Scarlet Woman**, she lusts for her playful passions and Divine intoxications. As the **Goddess of Ecstasy,** she teaches that your closeness to the Divine is related to the amount of joy you have.

Astrologically **Leo**, and its lion symbol, is connected to Lust. Since the ruler is the Sun, this archetype has raw creativity and talent and represents love as a creative process. Leo, the Social, Fixed sign, is the desire of the will to direct your life through intentionality.

Leo's time, July 23 to August 22, is the heat of summer in the northern hemisphere, when the sun is bright. Strong conscious aims and the urge for authority and recognition mixed with the capacity to play give power, dignity, and nobility to the creative process.

The Hebrew letter for Lust/Strength is *teth*, which means, "**snake**" or serpent power, which is also known as the Kundalini power. In Hinduism, it is a form and Force of Divine feminine energy believed to be located at the base of the spine. The snake, as the tail of the lion, symbolizes the healing, regenerative, and transformative power available. Taste is the sense associated with Lust and digestion its function. Lust feeds on itself and is self-sustaining.

Connect with the Lust/Strength card to make love a creative process. Hear her cry: "I lust for my creativity and my personal power." Step into your creative fire and claim your strength to inspire and transform.

Lust key words: Leo; strength; creativity; joyful passions; talent; realizations; self-control; release of the past.

List several ways you can add enjoyment to your day.

Energetically and quietly pour out love to people during your day and notice what happens.

Where do my strengths lie?

What are my inner resources that inspire me to express and create?

How do I seek validation?

How can I open or regenerate my passions creatively and sexually?

How can I infuse my creativity with passion?

What prevents me from having joy?

I find joy in all I do.

Hanged Man: You are ready to face a block, break an old pattern, and embrace a different perspective. Time to sacrifice an ego-centered belief. Surrender without loss, as you are enduring a kind of initiation.

16.

Surrendering with the (12) Hanged Man

The greatest of man's power
is the measure of his surrender.
William Booth

On this twelfth path, the **Hanged Man** is where the **Pattern Breaker** suspends the mind and the will to change your conditioning. Our Hero is hanging upside down suspended in water, which denotes the path of dissolving the ego's restrictive patterns and tuning into the collective unconscious to discover insights with a more impersonal point of view.

Astrologically the Hanged Man is designated to **Neptune**, the **Mystical Escapist**, which can represent great spirituality and creativity or illusions and delusions. In mythology Neptune is Poseidon, the God of the sea, who dives deep beyond rational thinking.

The Hebrew letter for the Hanged Man is *mem*, which means, "**water**." Water is the seed and root of all life. It reflects and mirrors images upside down.

Hanging with her left foot wrapped in a snake inside an upside Egyptian Ankh (the loop with a cross), symbolizes unlimited life force and regeneration. The right foot crosses to form an inverted four, which is the number of solidity and foundation. This archetype also means growth is happening on the inner levels. You are ready to face your limitations, because you see that there are options, answers, and perceptions available for you to consider.

Receiving this card may symbolize a time of inactivity, being immersed in unconscious behavior, and bogged down in feelings. In the background is a grid of small squares, which represent obstacles, limiting beliefs, and inner conflicts. The Hanged Man is hung up, suspended, and made aware of the limitations of his or her normal perception. Once called baffling, this inverse hanging meant to frustrate, confuse, or discourage.

Having a foot in spirituality tells you that faith in the Divine gives you hope. Both the head and foot are awakening to cosmic light, which shows how true surrender to the Divine brings greater awareness, synchronistic flow, and grace. You can sacrifice the small ego for a connection to Divine Will. Carl Jung said, "Sacrifice means to make sacred." A primary step to free those conditioned hang-ups is to surrender the personal will to Divine Will. Real hope lies in faith in the Divine Plan.

On the Tree of Life, the Hanged Man travels (vertically on the lower part of the feminine Pillar of Form or Constriction) between **Severity** (*Geburah*) and **Splendor** (*Hod*). Feelings of futility, disorientation, and uncertainty can exist as this path, for reason is blocked by emotions. As you join **Mercury's** capacity to focus and conceptualize systems with **Mars**' Warrior's ability to set boundaries and intentions, you resolve the dualities of the mind. Once you let go of any useless unconscious patterns, you expand in greater vision, purpose, and illumination. The Wheel of Fortune's benevolent desire to make the world better is on the opposite side of the Tree of Life and balances the Hanged Man. It reiterates that you can expand and take on more.

This is the only card that has a different meaning when it is reversed in a reading. Being upright shows that your grounding and the light of the cosmic energies are more prominent.

Invoke the Hanged Man to look at life from a different perspective. The urge toward higher consciousness comes by letting go and transcending the self so you can invert fear to love, worry to surrender, and frustrations to wisdom.

Hanged Man Key words: Neptune; hung up; suspension; stalemate; surrender; sacrifice; trust; dissolving a pattern; dissolving of the ego.

To transcend and alter your current state of consciousness, suspend your mind and surrender it completely and look at life from a completely different perspective.

Where am I stuck in my life?

Where do I deceive or confuse myself?

What belief or attitude keeps me blocked?

In what areas of my life would sacrifice pay off for me?

What is my level of faith in the unseen and unknown?

I surrender my normal perceptions and my personal will to the Divine Will and enable my life to flow with grace and ease.

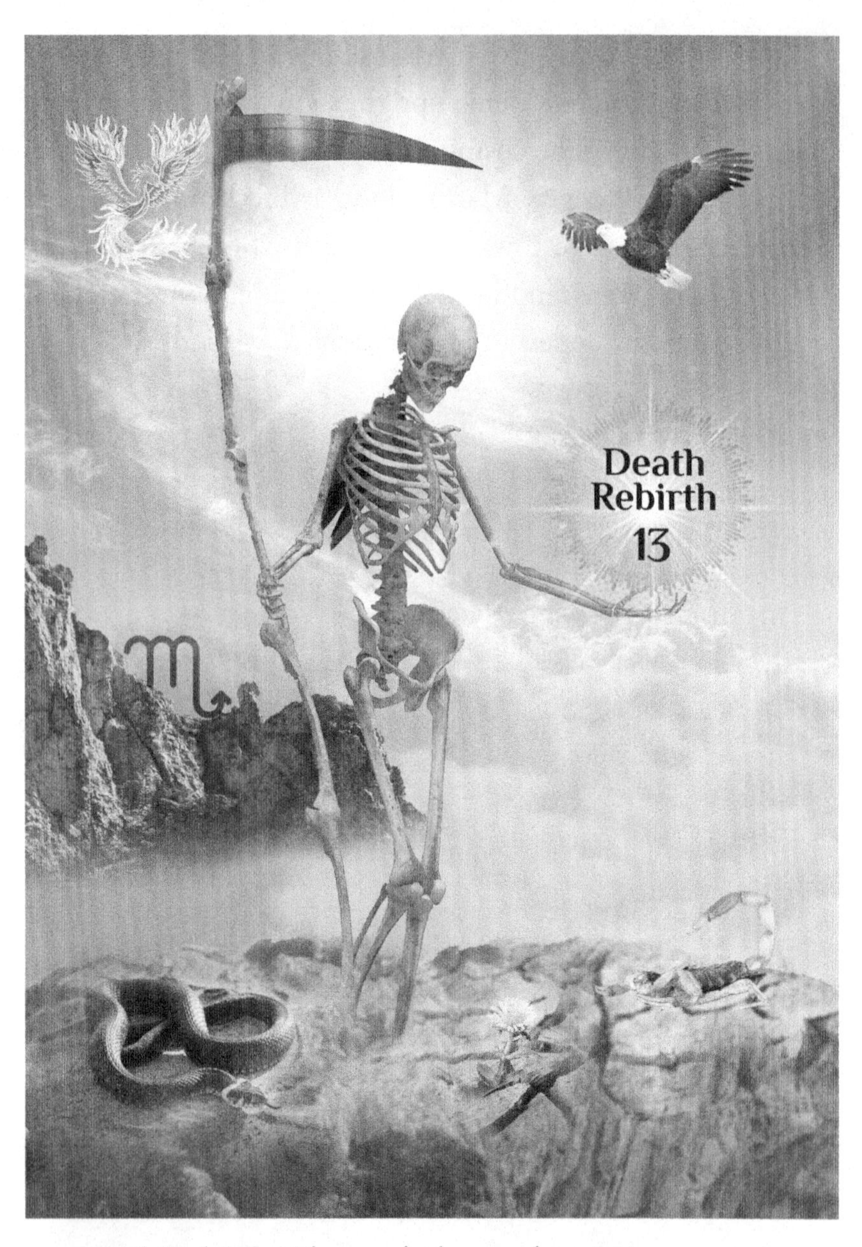

Death/Rebirth: Change is happening. Let go so you can move forward. You are ready to free yourself by cutting away beliefs, concepts, and opinions about things, people and life in general. You are dying to an old identity.

17.

Letting Go with (13) Death/Rebirth

Forgetfulness of your real nature is true death;
remembrance of it is rebirth.

Ramana Maharshi

Death is synonymous with **Rebirth**. It is a radical external process of profound and intense change. This thirteenth path often frightens one upon receiving it, but it represents cutting through limitation at a deep level. In order to have a birth something must die; something has to consciously be let go, eliminated, or rejected. Elimination brings transformative experiences and turnabouts in life; endings bring beginnings.

The skeleton is surrendered. As the basic structure of our body, the skeleton allows movement. The bones of who you are reveal your lineage and your commitment to growth. Holding a sharp sycthe or sickle to cut away and reap the harvest, this **Grim Reaper** looks down in repose and takes stock of things. To the Greeks, Death/Rebirth meant a time to **Decide**.

The sun is beaming behind his head, which is like a halo illuminating an expanded consciousness. On the barren ground there is a snake, which symbolizes regeneration because it sheds its skin and restores a new one. The flower breaking through the dry rock is the sign of new life.

The astrological ruler for Death/Rebirth is the complex and intense Social sign of **Scorpio** (October 23 to November

21). Elementally it is Water, which constantly flows, changes. Whereas Scorpio's modality is Fixed, which is rigid and sustaining. These different inner pulls can create an inner struggle. With **Pluto**, the God of the underworld, as the ruler of Scorpio, this archetype encompasses the mysterious hidden depths. Much of your conditioned patterns have been submerged and operate in the unconscious, but need to be brought to the surface, so they can be faced, cleansed, and changed.

Scorpio encompasses intense urges to identify with Source and uncover its mysteries. Committed to transformation on all levels, it has many symbols. The scorpion is protective and ready to sting during change. The snake shedding its skin represent old forms of the personality peeling away; and after a period of vulnerability, there is a stronger sense of self. The eagle, which soars free and high, shows that with perception and vision, you can stay true to your ideals. The phoenix rises out of the ashes and new life is born. Out of your breakdowns and eliminations, greater parts of who you are can live.

Sometimes it is a passage through the "Dark Night of the Soul," where you experience a crisis. It may feel like danger, but it is an opportunity to let go of old habits, patterns, attachments, and to all that gets in the way of your usable power. All your challenges are for your growth and to learn soul lessons, even if your personality doesn't see this way at the time.

The Hebrew word for Death/Rebirth is *nun* or "**fish**," a prolific animal. The word indicates, "to grow and sprout" and is fertility and generative productiveness.

Motion is the function attributed to Death/Rebirth. It is the second card of motion following the Chariot card.

On the Tree of Life, Death/Rebirth connects **Beauty** (*Tiphareth*) to **Victory** (*Netzach*), (on the lower Pillar of Expansion). **Venus**' devotional love is linked with the **Sun**'s power of creativity and healing. Here the personality bonds to the Higher Self and asks you to give up part of your lower nature. There is power on this path, and with power comes a chance of its misuse, thus it calls for ethics and integrity. On the other side of the Tree of Life is the Devil card, which connects the intellect to your soul nature. You are to balance your heart and mind, and bring love to your will to realize true power.

Invoke the Death/Rebirth card to cut away all that you have outworn so you can be reborn as that which you truly are.

Death/Rebirth Key words: Scorpio; transformation; change; release; cutting away limitations; detachment; loss and gain; decision; regeneration.

Make a list of things and traits that you would like to let go of.

Go into your drawers and closets and give away all and anything you do not want or use anymore.

What do I need to let go of?

Are there any old identities, relationships, lifestyles, or directions that I need to release?

How can I open to new forms of being?

I let go and know that anything that leaves me is finished and I trust a greater good awaits me.

Art/Temperance: Time to bring together polarities. Temper and balance your emotions and perceptions by looking within and creating something new. It is a creative and synthesizing and integrating time.

18.

Integrating with (14) Art/Temperance

Wholeness is not
achieved by cutting off
a portion of one's being,
but by integration
of the contraries.

Carl Jung

On this fourteenth evolutionary key, Crowley changed the name from **Temperance** to **Art**. This archetype is the principle of **Synthesis**, **Integration**, and **Synergy** and it is more than just a tempering of the creative forces.

On the Tree of Life, Art/Temperance (has the royal and central position on the Pillar of Integration) vertically connects **Beauty** (*Tiphareth*) with **Foundation** (*Yesod*). We link the **Sun** and the **Moon**, which describes the alchemical process of integrating the unconscious with the conscious or transforming the lower self into the Higher Self. This is the basis of life, which Carl Jung called the "Process of Individuation."

As we look at the sky we see how the Sun and the Moon incorporate these solar and lunar polarities and create the light and darkness we experience. It also represents the completion and integration of the masculine and feminine within, which is what creates the inner marriage.

With her arms stretched out, Art holds her creations. She stands in between the delicate blending of fire and water or perceptions and emotions. As the **Integrator,** she creates steam or communication and ignites her visions from the arrows of her dreams. This is a challenging path as it takes a perfect balance of fire and water to create steam, which is a source of power. Just like the earth's fertility depends on the sun and the rain, what is needed is equilibrium. Too much feeling will drown out the perception and too much fire will dry up the water. The historical name, Temperance, suggests the need for tempering, modifying, and adapting these forces to equalize them in your life.

The Art card is a higher phase and complement of the Lovers card. The Gemini key shows the principle of separation and duality. The appreciation, desire, and commitment are there to blend, although consciousness is in polarity. The two sides are in opposition, but seeking integration. In the Art card, synthesis and assimilation take place. The initiation started in the Lovers is now purified and transformed. The process is like a beam of light passing through the lens of a camera, directing it to a focal point (Lovers) then re-emerging with the images reversed (Art).

Crowley explained this esoteric process as an alchemical changing into its opposites. Water has become fire and fire has become water. The lion of fiery Leo is now white and the eagle of watery Scorpio is now red. In your life, you can see the yin becomes yang, subconscious becomes conscious, irrationality turns into rationality, repression develops into expression, and the path of least resistance changes into the path of growth.

Art is the **Archer,** like **Diana the Huntress,** Goddess of the Moon. The lunar qualities of receptivity, emotional depth, rhythmic ebb and flow, and sensitivity reside here. These feelings, your dreams and images are integrated within your Core with perceptional visions of harmony, creativity, and healing.

The Hebrew letter for the Art is *samekh*, which stands for "**prop** or **peg.**" It makes a tent or house secure and signifies support, sustenance, and maintenance of your personal life.

The astrological designator is **Sagittarius**, the Universal, Fire, and Mutable sign that constantly aspires toward its goals and visions. It is through your seeking and resolving of your opposites that you express your artistry. Sagittarius is where you awaken your ethical system of beliefs and search for your inner truth. Truth is not concrete; uncovering it for yourself is a relative concept. As you seek your spiritual support, you have to deal with your conscience and morals, resolve your thinking with your beliefs, and strive for the highest level of ethical behavior. Sagittarius teaches you to find your answers within and develop a belief system that fits into a philosophical framework. Jesus spoke of the Law of Attraction when he said. "As ye believe, so shall it be done unto you."

Sagittarius' ruler is expansive **Jupiter** and its expansive season is November 22 to December 21. It includes our holiday of Thanksgiving and many rituals of abundance.

Call upon Art/Temperance to integrate your personality with your spiritual nature. Aspire toward the balance and synthesis of your creative genius.

Art Key words: Sagittarius; integration of opposites; synthesis; synergy; assimilation; creativity; ethical beliefs; support; inner marriage.

Meditate on the different and opposing parts of your personality and then see them as a functioning whole.

Contemplate on the concept of changing into your opposite self.

With your inner eyes visualize a man and woman in front of you sitting on both sides of a scale. Imagine that the woman represents your intuitive, emotional, and receptive side and the man symbolizes your dynamic, energetic, and intellectual side.

Notice if the scale is tipping and which side is calling you to bring it into balance. What part of you needs more expression? Be silent and let an answer come.

Next imagine the two parts are coming together. As you envision them looking into each other's eyes and then hugging, see them blending into a unified whole.

What are my most important visions?

What do I aspire to do, see, or be?

How can I artistically express myself?

How do my beliefs form the framework of my reality?

What practical ways can I change my defensive personality, so I can uncover my actual soulful Self?

How can I bring my unconscious or those hidden parts to my conscious mind?

What do I need to do to integrate my inner and outer?

I creatively express myself through my visions and aspirations. I artfully integrate my subconscious with my conscious mind and creatively blend my masculine and feminine natures into a unified whole.

Devil/Pan: Move beyond self-imposed limitations. Don't take yourself or your sexuality so seriously. If you or anyone demonizes or projects onto you, lighten up and keep a sense of humor.

19.

Humoring with the (15) Devil/Pan

Humor is mankind's
greatest blessing.

Mark Twain

The **Devil**, the fifteenth path, is the most misunderstood card, for it is misnamed. The Devil is Pan, and represents the **Pleasure** principle or appreciating things, having fun, and finding joy in the experience of discovering the Self. In mythology, Pan was half man, half goat who, like the Greek/Roman Dionysus/Bacchus, was a **God of Sensuality**, who frolicked in the fields as the **Patron of Merriment**. During the Dark Ages there was a reaction to the so-called hedonistic activities of Pan, and in order to curtail them, he was labeled evil. During this time, the card was changed into the Devil. As Angles Arrien pointed out, "lived"is devil spelled backward and here you need to face whatever "bedevils" you.

In this rendition Pan is represented by a standing figure that forms a phallic above two globes (testicles). In the East, the male organ is called the lingam, which was a sacred object of worship, with the meaning of transcendental power, infinite potential, and regeneration. Within the circles are two naked couples. These symbols indicate your inner creative potency as well as the principle of sensuality and sexuality. You are being told to accept and enjoy your body as a natural and beautiful part of you. The circles also represent the cell dividing and the beginning of growth. This resonance and the Law of Attraction tell you to go toward what draws and inspires you and to use both your receptive magnetic and initiating dynamic energies in times of beguilement.

The figure in a white sheath has the head of a goat with twisted horns, which symbolize twin spiral staircases to infinity. The two ways out of your relative consciousness are discrimination and devotional perseverance. Pan's grape crown shows your fruitfulness, which is the aspiration of your creative potential.

Pan means pastures, bread, and the breadwinner. The word, Panacea comes from it, which means "all." Crowley called him "**Pan Pangetor**, the **All Begetter**," and saw this archetype as "creative energy in its most material form."

Capricorn is Devil/Pan's designator. It represents the material world in its most exalted form, as it is located at the zenith of the astrological chart. It rules the tenth house of career and purpose and is the Father and authority principle. Its symbol is the goat, which climbs high mountains. It is a productive capacity to follow your joy with step-by-step discipline and steadiness, so you can turn your visions into achievements. Capricorn is the Universal, Cardinal Earth sign that moves out of itself with tenacity and determination to receive tangible rewards in the world.

Your lesson here is developing your will, which is purpose based on intention. It is what gives you the clarity of mind, persistence, and endurance to carry out your purpose and fulfill your unique function. This mastery comes through control, discipline, attention, and action.

The fires are breaking the chains that bind you. **Saturn**, the planet of limitation, boundaries, and forms, rules Capricorn. Here, you are to look at what restrictions or limitations you place on yourself. Your limitations come when you give that authority to someone or something outside yourself and let your "shoulds" and "if onlys" control you. If you do not take responsibility for your own authority, you develop guilt, judgment, and obligation patterns. Guilt says, "If you don't do this you will feel bad." It is a manipulative self-punishment you put on yourself.

Your material attachments will test you. When you activate your higher wisdom, you can see how some of your clinging desires can lead you to fear of loss. Yet when you surrender to the sensuality of this beautiful earth moment-by-moment, you can discover the Divine in every manifestation.

Above the main figure is a hilariously laughing statue, which denotes the principle of **Mirth**. This archetype tells you, "Don't take things so seriously or personally, lighten up, and keep a sense of humor." You are to deal with your life with steadiness and wit. Laughter is a great healing tool for it purifies the subconscious and dissolves the mind's fixations and complexes.

Capricorn is the sign of the perfectionist. You are to watch that you that you don't price yourself out of the market seeking the ideal, which doesn't exist on this material plane. Perfecting is a process, a movement, not a goal.

Capricorn begins the season of winter and is December 22 to January 19, when the light begins to return.

The Hebrew letter for the Devil/Pan is *ain*, which represents "**eye**." Because sight is the most dominant sense most people have, it is linked to self-expression. It also signifies the limitations of what is visible. The message is to go beyond superficial appearances, know that this earth plane is more than meets the eye, and open your inner eyes to a greater vision. The third eye in the center of the goat's face denotes extra sensory perception. The Devil is willing to see the internal as well as the external issues (the other two opened eyes.)

On the Tree of Life, the Devil/Pan connects **Beauty** (*Tiphareth*) and **Splendor** (*Hod*), (from the lower feminine Pillar of Form). You unite the **Sun,** your consciousness of the Higher Self, to **Mercury**, the seat of your intelligence. There is great mystery here as you blend reasoning and mind power to visions of healing, liberation, and the Divine. Crowley said, "In every symbol of this card, there is the allusion to the highest and most remote."

To balance this learning, you can look at Devil/Pan's opposite path on the Tree of Life, which is Death/Rebirth (who's connected to Venus' Victory). You are to bring love and devotion into your intellect. The mind separates and is rigid and judgmental, whereas the heart links and unites. The real marriage is the integration of love and will, or wisdom.

Visually the card shows cosmic energy shining brightly down warming and filling this archetype with insight as well as joyful sensual blessings.

Invoke the Devil/Pan to bring more pleasure, humor and enjoyment into your life, so you do not take things so personally or so seriously. Let the force of your will overcome all fears and attachments. Move persistently and consistently toward what brings you joy, knowing that the journey or process is truly the goal.

Devil/Pan Key words: Capricorn; limitations; sexuality; sensuality; pleasure; humor; procreative energy; will to master; material creativity.

List ten things that bring you pleasure.

Look at how you constrict and restrict yourself.

Ponder the thought of having your feet on the ground and your head in the heavens.

What are the limitations and restrictions I place on myself?

Do I feel any guilt about my sexuality?

What do I do out of obligation or because I will feel guilty if I don't?

What do I appreciate about my life?

How can I bring more humor into my life?

To whom in my life do I give my authority?

With humor, sensuality, and stability, I master my life.

Tower: You are breaking through conditioning to grasp the new; letting go of old ways of being; burning out obstacles; taking a stand; or stimulating growth and healing.

20.

Restructuring with the (16)Tower

Where do we start on the daily walk
of restoration and awakening?
We start where we are.

Anne Lamott

The **Tower**, the sixteenth step on the journey, represents internal changes and deals with the principles of **Renovation**, **Restoration**, and **Restructuring**. You heal and regenerate yourself as you dismantle all the untrue conditioning and everything artificial within your personality.

On the Tree of Life, the Tower horizontally connects (the lower two Pillars) **Victory** (*Niezach*) to **Splendor** (*Hod*). It blends **Venus**' instinctual "gut" responses with **Mercury**'s intellectual replies, and integrates the mind's reasoning power with feelings and heart. To go into love, you have to break down the forms and barriers of the mind.

The symbol of the tower represents all learning, memories, beliefs, accepted values, and material structures that you have built in your personality. It is everything that makes you separate and that you call "I."

Destruction occurs through fire. Fire symbolizes spiritual perceptions that instigate and activate the destruction of all that is obsolete. Four falling figures represent the outmoded conditioning or the emotional, physical, intellectual, and intuitive views that stand in the way of your authenticity. This unlearning of the ego's fixations can bring confusion, but with focus and devotion you create awareness, new life, and healing.

Mars is the planet of energy and action and rules the Tower. As the basic yang or male instinct, it is the function of assertion and the path of pursuing your goals. You take a risk and let your thoughts, words, actions, and expressions follow your feelings.

Crowley subtitled this card, **War**. It is the path to stimulate the Warrior within, which is taking responsibility for your time, intention, and attention. The Warrior's cry is: "I have to be me, I have to do my thing. I direct my desires and passions toward what I desire."

Mars often symbolizes the primal force for survival and the release of anger and frustrations. The key to overcoming anger is to let go of demanding a certain outcome from it. Problems arise from anger's distortions, which are blaming, sarcasm, criticism, violence, vindictiveness, passive aggression, interrogation, manipulation, intrusion, and punishment. These create a chain reaction.

This path has themes of both destruction and creation. There is great healing and regeneration present. The all-seeing eye represents the cosmic third eye of inner wisdom, which show how this archetype is capable of enormously conscious perception once the old forms are gone.

The dove is the bird of peace and compassion. The serpent is the universal symbol of regeneration. Crowley said the dove and the serpent signify the feminine and masculine impulses and two forms of desire. He called them the "Will to Love and the Will to Die." Only by your willingness to let go of the outmoded and to truly love, can you progress to the heights of higher consciousness.

The Hebrew letter is *peh* and means "**mouth,**" as an opening to speak and to receive nourishment. It is a double letter, which gives two meanings; once again these are the destruction of the old and the regeneration of the new.

Invoke the Tower to clear and cleanse yourself of all that is outmoded, so that you can be free to express who you truly are.

Tower Key words: Mars; activation; instigation; stimulation; destruction; creation; renovation; regeneration; restoration; healing.

Write a list of all the people and things that bring you anger. You may want to write a letter to release your resentments without sending it. Pour out any bitterness on the page. Then fold it, and the next day, read it aloud. Add anything you feel that's missing and then burn it.

Change a frustration into a positive affirmation. Pick one each day for a week, light a candle, and sit for 10 minutes focusing on this positive affirmation.

Are there any old outworn thought patterns or beliefs that are holding me back?

How do I assert my desires?

How do I deal with anger?

I break down the old and outworn and experience new life and healing.

Star: Be a star in your own eyes by believing in and trusting yourself. Radiate your vision and confidence. Share your gifts with others and be open to receive. Spend time in self-care; treat yourself with reverence and respect.

21.

Esteeming with the (17) Star

With the realization of one's potential
and self-confidence
in one's ability,
one can build a better world.

Dalai Lama

The Star, the seventh step on the path of evolution, shows the process of openly receiving cosmic inspiration and bringing it to Earth. Ruled by **Aquarius** (January 20 to February 18), this **Humanitarian**, Fixed, Air sign signifies the **Universal Synthesizer, Broadcaster, and Distributor of Wisdom**. Spiritual nourishment is a group event. We are all part of the second coming of the Divine. As the **Water Bearer** who holds bottomless urns, the Star is a Channel of Divine Light. The energy is directed inward as well as outward, showing we are all connected and in a co-creative relationship with the Universe. The Universe flows to and through our inner nature.

As the principle of **Self-Esteem** and **Confidence**, the Star dares to stand on her own ground with trust, knowing that deserving is her Divine right. Robert Wang said, "The Star is the most pure manifestation of the Great Mother at the level of personality and the perfection of the physical form of nature."

Pictured holding two breast-like cups, she receives and brings enriching energy into the world. One cup is gold and the other is silver. These precious metals symbolize riches and wealth. Gold represents perfection in all matter. The golden cup shows how the Universe is inexhaustible and unlimited. Crowley said, "From the golden cup she pours this ethereal water, which is also milk, oil, and blood upon her head." Gold's everlasting luster is soft as well as shiny telling you to be flexible and to galvanize your faith. Silver is a mirror to the soul, helping you to see yourself as others see you. It represents hope, unconditional love, meditation, mystic visions, tenderness, kindness, sensitivities, and psychic abilities.

From the Star the cleansing and healing energies flow from the cosmos to alleviate pain and remove fear on earth. The omnipotent celestial waters have transformed into crystals, showing how emotions can change into accurate perceptions. You have the ability to convert thoughts and feelings into vibrations and create your own reality.

The Star is the symbol of the **New Age Person**—original, inventive, and metaphysical with a strong sense of individuality as well as universality. This androgynous being has both magnetic and dynamic energy, balances the intuitive right-brain and intelligent left-brain, and bridges heart and mind.

The Hebrew letter connected with the Star is *tzaddi,* which means "**fishhook.**" It is a regenerative tool that seeks and draws from the unconscious and the superconscious.

On the Tree of Life, the Star traverses (the lower masculine Pillar of Expansion) **Victory** (*Netzach*) and (the central astral sphere) **Foundation** (*Yesod*). As you blend the **Moon**'s intuitions and instincts with **Venus**'s sensitivities and joyous pleasures, you will heal all your relationships and know exactly what you need to feel secure. The Star utilizes electric and magnetic energy to magically create your dreams.

On the Tree of Life, Star is balanced with the creative Sun card, which has the ability to bring the intuitive to form.

Call upon the Star to truly see yourself in a new light. As you get in touch with your personal power, you can act, set limits, and take responsibility for your sensitivities and the universal healing energy flowing to and through you.

Star Key words: Aquarius; self-esteem; confidence; recognition; universal connection; personal power; interconnection; awakening of consciousness.

Write a list of things you appreciate about yourself.

Examine the balance between how much you give and how much you receive. Consciously be open to receive.

What can I do to care for and honor myself?

Can I instill daily rituals that nourish me?

How can I give to myself?

Can I see how receiving is giving to myself?

How can I receive more universal or metaphysical wisdom?

Is there a group of like-minded people I can join to further my growth?

My connection to Universal consciousness and my recognition of my creative imagination allow me to realize my visions and helps heal and enlighten others.

Moon: There is work to be done and you are revealing the unconscious patterns and habits. Make a decision or choice. By being authentic, you can face and overcome illusions and patterns and transcend karma.

22.

Envisioning with the (18) Moon

How people treat you
is their karma;
how you react is yours.

Wayne Dyer

The **Moon** card, the eighteenth path on the evolutionary journey, shows the long and deep soul journey into consciousness. This card has had much superstition and prejudice connected to it in the past. It was called "the karma card" and signified work to be done in relationships.

Relationships are often called "**Shadow Dancing**," for they mirror what is hidden in your inner reality. Jung called all the unknown, concealed behavior and thought patterns, the shadow. People often do to you what you expect or what you do to yourself. You can't work on a relationship; you can only work on yourself. It is more correctly working on the inner self to bring harmony and balance the male and female within. Relationships mirror your inner reality.

The work of this **Illusion Breaker** is to reveal your patterns and to move beyond old conditioning. In the visual card, the howling dogs represent your instinctual patterns that you carry within you. They guard the journey and can reveal your "Dark Night of the Soul," where you often find the threshold of life. These past patterns are like ruts in a road, or stumbling blocks. The Sanskrit word is *samskara,* which are impressions created from certain actions you have taken that cause your cycle of karma. Just as the physical Moon magnetically pulls the waters of the earth, it receptively induces the tides of your emotions, which subliminally influence your every decision. Upon this path you uncover your unconscious motivations, those remnants from past experiences.

The dark trail behind our couple shows this is a passage of purification, healing, and cleansing. You travel through your feelings and unconsciousness and learn to surrender without loss. The flowing water and the rainbow show the possibility of new life, and also that it is a healing transformation and cleansing process.

When your relationships bring up painful areas, it is a sign that you desire to change and heal. If you surrender, give up blame, stay strong in your heart connections, and open up these tender issues, you can clarify them through verbal interaction. Near our couple are the key symbols of Mercury, which signifies all forms of communication, and Pluto, which denotes power, perception, regeneration, and transformation. You can use your mind to probe the deeper reasons you suffer and create drama. Communication is the key to making changes in your relationships.

The Moon card is designated to sensitive **Pisces** (February 19 to March 20), the last sign of the Zodiac, which collects what the rest of humanity discards. This changeable Water sign has a dreamy, psychic quality, and tells you to trust your intuition to guide you.

In nature Pisces is the season when winter is dying and you anxiously anticipate change as you await the warmth and rebirth of spring. Crowley called this path the "**Gateway to Res-**

urrection, for it is the signpost of a passage of ending one cycle and beginning another."

This archetype is connected with romance, which shows you your projections, dreams, visions, and what intrigues and beguiles you. Basically, romance is like a drug that stimulates your idealistic models and creative imagination. Your challenge here is to consciously choose to be authentic and stop acting from illusions, projections, and obligations.

The Egyptians revered the beetle or scarab, as they considered it sacred and lucky. Dung beetles take their own secretions to lay eggs, which they would roll around in the desert to cool their bodies. This ability to secrete oil was the ability to carry within it the seeds of life. This symbol reveals movement into another world and represents renewal, resurrection, reincarnation, and evolution of spirit. The beetle holding the sun signifies bringing light to the unconscious.

The Hebrew letter for the Moon card is *qoph*, which denotes, the "**back of the head**." This section of the scull holds the parts of the brain that deal with bodily functions. We share this with animals and it stays awake while other parts of our brain sleep. The head means chief, which is the seat of intellectual ability.

Sleep is the function of this letter, and it is where you restore yourself. This is a time of restoration and repair, as well as altered states of consciousness that connect with the deepest Self and the I Am consciousness.

On the Tree of Life, the Moon card bridges (the lower Pillar of Expansion) **Victory** (*Netzach*) to the **Kingdom** (*Malkuth*). When you blend the **Earth** with **Venus**, you can ground your creative and instinctual responses into your body and physical reality. To find universal love, your work is to break free of material illusions of bondage and attachment. As you learn to live and breathe in the Eternal Now, you can embody love and negotiate pleasure and peace in your relationships moment-by-moment.

You ground the Moon card's meaning with the Aeon/Judgment card, which sits on the opposite side of the Tree of Life (at Mercury's Splendor). Resolving relationship patterns and creating real intimacy involves letting go of unconsciousness and being intellectually discerning without judging.

Bring in the power of this mysterious archetype and know that spiritually there are no others. What others are doing to you, you spiritually hired them, to enable you to see these unconscious patterns. It is through your ego's attachments that you bind yourself. Yet when you come from love, you can break these patterns.

The Moon Key words: Pisces; uncovering a relationship pattern; communication; projection; transformation; renewal; authenticity; choices; passage thru the dark phase.

Dream and visualize what it means to express your Soul.

Contemplate a personality of the same sex that irritates you to find your own shadow.

Observe yourself to see if you have any sacrificial patterns in your relationships.

Notice if there are any places where you need to be more authentic.

What are my relationships saying about me?

Do I have any unspoken agreements in my relationships?

Can I see how my glitches in relationship are revealing hidden patterns?

What do I need to communicate to be more authentic?

I communicate and reveal myself honestly in all my relationships, move beyond past patterns, and make authentic decisions and connections.

Sun: Express yourself. You are generating enormous creativity. You may experience a liberating collaboration, finding ways to convey and generate. Bask in your ability to receive recognition, and fulfill your desires.

23.

Creating with the (19) Sun

Creativity is the most important
human resource of all.
Without creativity,
there would be no progress
and the world
would be repeating
the same patterns.

Edward de Bono

The **Sun** card, the nineteenth path, is radiating with the magnificent **Sun**. As the King of our solar system, this life-giving force warms and sustains our world and is the source of all energy, light, and creativity. The Sun is the center of a highly regulated system of planetary bodies rotating around it in perfect cyclical order. Correspondingly, you have the radiant Essence that is at your Core, which sustains your creative force and perfectly moves you toward your evolutionary growth.

Angles Arrien called the Sun card the "cosmic dance of two on the green mountain of creativity" and saw this archetype as the principle of **Collaboration, Teamwork**, and **Cooperation**.

This card portrays two dancers expressing their creativity together on a blooming, fertile hill surrounded by the whole Zodiac. All forms of creative expression through the personality are possible in tangible ways.

The man and woman represent your feminine and masculine energies being integrated in a balanced and creative way. Your dynamic and magnetic sides find forms of creation in the here and now. Here you play in the Divine fields of creative expression. With intentionality and encouragement, this dynamic, radiant energy uplifts and moves you toward a life-giving influence. When the sum of the two is greater than its parts, the result is synergy.

The shape of the mountain suggests aspiration to higher levels of being. The orange flowers signify perception and healing energy. The white lotus shining from above represents Divine Love and Light streaming into the couple and revitalizing them. A new, positive, liberated consciousness is our next stage of development at this time.

The Hebrew letter for the Sun card is *resh,* which means, "**face** or **front**." This is the head and could denote the leader, director, or guiding power.

Crowley designated the Sun card to the **Lord of the New Aeon**, and called it the "**Lord of Light, Life, Liberty and Love**." These qualities sum up the power and regalness of this path as well as give a tremendous forecast for our future. The Light is upon us! As you learn to come from your deep center and allow your light to shine, you can play on the creative mountain and make uplifting choices for the Universe.

Astrologically, the Sun represents your own spiritual Essence wrapped up in ego. It is your tone of Being and shows what you are assimilating and where you are going. It is your future pull. The Sun glyph is a circle with a dot in the center and signifies wholeness. The Sun represents your aspirations and the intention and the motivation to express your personal power. As your desire to be recognized for who you are, it is the light of your personality. The soul moves to Wholeness through the consciousness of the Sun's creative force. It shows your urge to be.

On the Tree of Life, the Sun card connects (lower feminine Pillar of Form) **Splendor** (*Hod*) with **Foundation** (*Yesod*). The blending of **Mercury**'s reasoning mind with the **Moon**'s psychic sensitivities gives us the ability to conceptualize magic through dreaming and visualizing images. There is electrical, magnetic, sexual energy that can be focused. It is the essence of Magnetic Creation, which links mind power or focused intention with attraction.

As you learn to open the formative and emotional realms to the intellect, you differentiate and know when to communicate and when to be silent; when to extend and when to conserve; when to be active and when to be passive. By its position on the Tree of Life, the Star balances the Sun card and brings heartfelt sensitivities to mind.

The power of your sexuality is awakened on the Tree of Life in Foundation, and brings both unusual activity within the body and transformative energy.

Invoke the Sun for co-creative energy with your inner nature or with others. By learning to stay in your radiant center and come from your Source, you can bring vital imagination, creative play, and right and proper choices to the Universe.

Sun Key words: Sun; radiance; creativity; co-creative partnership; collaboration; synergy; awareness; joyful expression; enthusiasm.

Contemplate on who you are. Go beyond your roles to your true Essence.

Describe yourself using emotional and physical adjectives.

Look for where your innermost self is expressed.

Give yourself some recognition and encouragement.

Imagine your heart is a valve of love and light. Each day turn it up a few notches. Gradually increase your capacity to send out brilliant energy shinning from your heart to all you touch.

Feel your heart beaming illumination as if you have the glowing essence of the sun radiating all around you.

Visualize a golden ball of light emanating from your being that surrounds you. Sense the glowing light behind you, beside you, above you, below you, and in front of you and bask in it.

How do I see myself? What words would I use to describe myself?

What is my unique creative expression?

Am I doing what I want to do or am I doing what other's want for me to do?

In what ways do I express my own unique individuality?

How can I convey my need to give light and love?

What is pulling me to be intentional about my creative work?

How do I integrate my personality and my purpose?

What ego patterns are covering my soul?

How can I co-create with like-minded others?

I am fulfilled and co-creating, emanating with the Divine Light, and watching my world blossom.

Aeon/Judgment: Perceive from a greater perspective. Transform criticalness and utilize good judgment. Integrate family and career. You are in a process of deep change. You may be at a crossroads and new life is brewing.

24.

Discerning with the (20) Aeon/Judgment

Transformation literally means
going beyond your form.

Wayne Dyer

The **Aeon** represents changing times and means a long indefinite period, such as an Age. Crowley changed the name of this card to meet the needs of the spiritual evolution of the Universe. Traditionally it was called **Last Judgment**. Some renditions had angels blowing their horns after the dead were resurrected. The Aeon shows a new time and a need to resurrect from the dead ways of the past. You are to die to the past unconsciousness and restore the heights of spiritual inspiration. Aeon is an expansive perspective of looking at the whole and uncovering visions of good judgment and discernment.

Pluto, the mysterious **God of the Underworld** or unconscious, rules this archetype. As the gateway between the visible and invisible, it rarely operates on the surface and is hard to determine by appearances. You are forced to penetrate to the core of your being and hidden truths. You are to rummage around and see what is outmoded and needs to be discarded. Pluto symbolizes letting go of old conditionings and a passage where something expires and is reconstructed. Pluto's energies are transcendental. You can begin to grasp this abstract term through its polarities, such as light and dark, and old and new.

During this death/rebirth, you are to go into the darkness in order to see the light and resolve your past and transcend it.

Pluto is the **Great Destroyer** and **Liberator** and is a **Transformer** and symbolic of the process of a caterpillar turning into a butterfly. In the *Awaken Tarot Cards,* a mother is centered looking at several phases of this deep journey, while the father and child look on. It is the creative process of giving new life to your creativity. The idea of family and being in the world is represented here, and both personal and professional integration are incorporated in this archetype.

Getting this card can often mean it is a time of crisis or a crossroad where you need to make a decision and take responsibility for the reality you are creating. This is an individual process. You are to realize that all that is happening to you is a result of your own inner workings.

The Hebrew letter for Aeon is *shin*, which means, "**tooth**," more specifically the tooth of a serpent. It implies sharpness, biting, or the power to break down the limitations of form, such as teeth breaking down food. Paul Foster Case said, "The fangs of the serpent bring in the ability to kill any falseness of the personality and its separateness."

On the Tree of Life, the Aeon bridges (the lower Pillar of Form) **Splendor** (*Hod*) and **Kingdom** (*Malkuth*). We connect the **Earth**'s sensate plane with **Mercury**'s realm of intellect. Here reason and concepts are communicated in physical reality, and you can ground your mind power. By conceptualizing and making decisions, you can be intentionally deliberate and manifest your will. It is the ego that dissipates the mind with judgments. Avoiding judgment is one of your hardest lessons, for it takes paying attention, monitoring, and balancing discrimination with criticism. You are to let go of the good/bad polarity in your mind that harshly judges.

The Moon card with its instincts to find love and develop emotionally balance this passage, for it sits on the opposite side of the Tree of Life. Our task is to blend heart and mind.

Connect with the Aeon card and look at your urge to procreate something new and give birth to your True Self. Allow the deep transformative energies to show you what you need to release and let go of so that you have more usable power.

Aeon Key words: Pluto; letting go of unconsciousness; discernment; judgment; critical self-analysis; transformation; family; mother; birth to new forms; creativity.

Meditate on your ways of discernment.

Observe your thoughts as if you were a butterfly watching them without judgment. Notice when you judge others or yourself.

How do I go to the depths of my being?

What mental patterns or ways of being no longer serve me?

Is there any place where I see any extremes polarities in my life?

I open to the inner depths and deeply value my creativity that is expressed both in my family and my career.

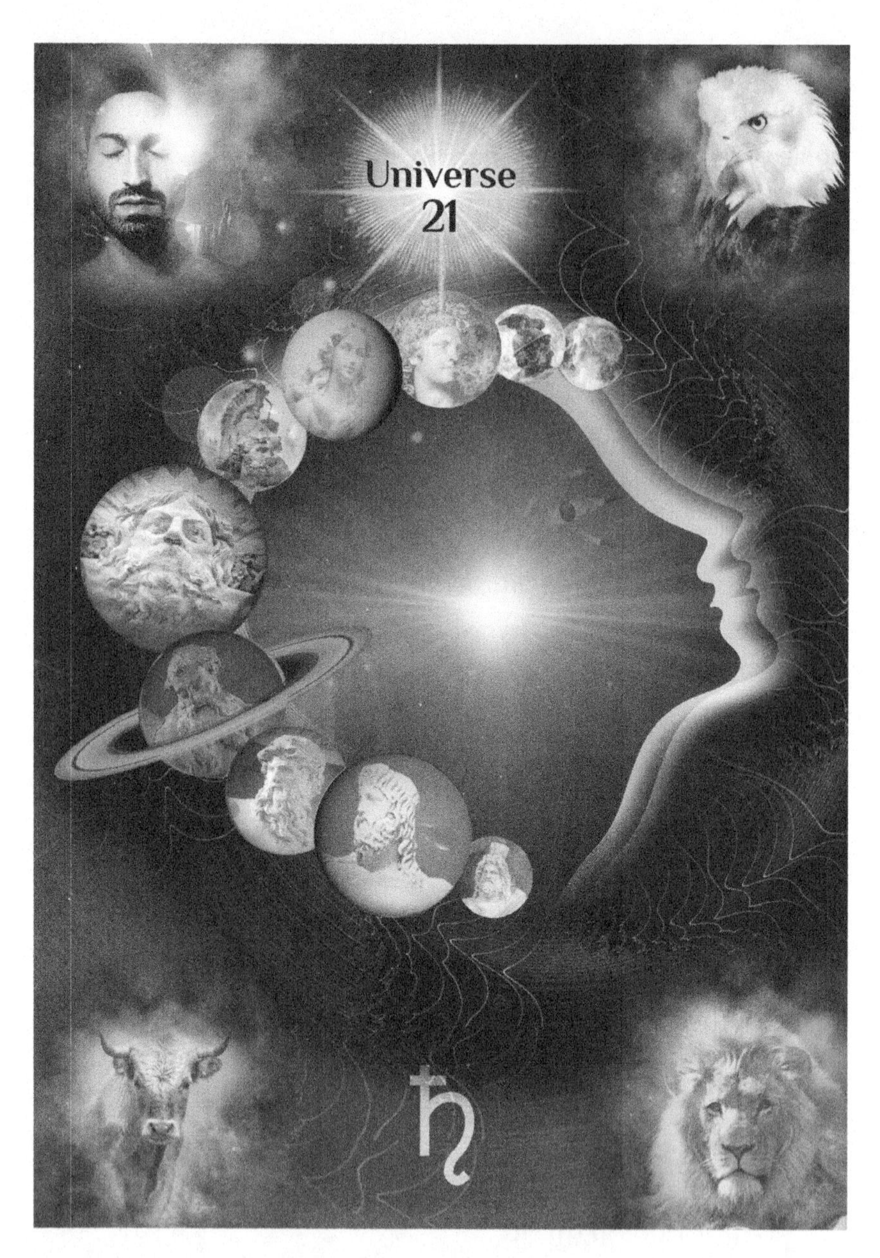

Universe: A goal is reached, and it's time to begin anew. You are breaking through limitations and conditioning and making them work for you. Expand your sense of self and your horizons. Express who you are and your talents in a more concrete way.

25.

Enveloping with the (21)Universe

There is only one corner of the Universe
you can be certain of improving,
and that is your own self.

Aldous Huxley

The twenty-first path is the Universe, which is often called the **World**. Here you have the principle of **Completion**, **Wholeness**, and **Integration**. Often this is the end of the evolutionary spiral, where you begin again with the innocence and ingenuity of the Fool.

This path teaches that the known Universe is more than just matter and energy. Even with the help of our best scientific instruments, most of the physical Universe lies beyond the reach of our senses. It is here we learn the Law of Correspondence, "As above, so below."

Discoveries in Quantum physics state that energy and matter are inter-convertible and share the same consciousness, which is both the source of the cosmos and your mind. The distinction between your inner and outer, mental and physical appears to be one of perception, not value. The earth is also spirit. You are within the Universe and the totality of the Universe is within you. It is also called the Unified Field, which is a living organism and you have access to its phenomenal power and attributes. Jean Houston said, "We and the Universe are inseparable partners in a timeless embrace. We are collaboratively dreaming up the Universe, while the Universe is simultaneously dreaming us up. Buddhists call this co-creation between the Universe and us 'Interdependent co-arising.'"

As a spiritual aspirant rooted in physical reality, you begin the journey from where you are. On the Tree of Life, **Kingdom** (*Malkuth*) is the **Earth** that comprises all that is knowable through your senses. The Universe card connects it (vertically in the lower central Pillar of Integrations) to **Foundation** (*Yesod*).

On this path, all the patterns of consciousness as they are presented in physical form are linked to the **Moon**'s dream world and the magical storehouse of the unconscious. You can manifest your magnetic, electrical and sexual energies to bring form to the hidden collective memories. Metaphysical and spiritual systems, myths, fairy tales, and archetypical models can help you to remember the secrets to creating a better world.

In this rendition, the Universe card is the **Cosmic Mother**. Her head has the solar system around it. Within the planets as the motivational forces are the archetypical principles of the Gods and Goddesses that live within you. This totality of your full individuality shows that you are both simultaneously dynamic and magnetic. It is vital for you to always remember that deep within your center is the Light of your Source.

The Egyptian Eye of Horus is the cosmic eye, which symbolizes the ability to expand awareness and see the truth of who you are and your purposeful visions. When you live with vision and totality, you become at home within yourself as well in the outer world. Cosmic Consciousness is the final seal of the great work represented here.

The Universe card represents the completion or decent of spirit into matter. Here is the doorway through which you begin your ascent toward reintegration. Its ruler **Saturn** governs our physical plane of existence and the sum of our "consensus reality." Yet what most of us agree upon has limited perceptions and is subject to revision.

The Universe has relatively few fixed laws, which are represented in the corners of the card. The symbols of the Astrological Fixed signs are shown to express all the elemental parts of ourselves—physically through the practical energy of the earthy Taurus and the bull; spiritually and creatively through the fiery Leo and the lion: emotionally through watery Scorpio and the eagle; and mentally through the airy Aquarius and the human face.

For the Universe to have meaning, it must have structure. Saturn, as the symbol of boundaries, helps you see your limitations so that you can manifest your purpose. Known as the stern **Father** archetype, this **Task Master** or **Cosmic Cop** will drive you to discover your True Self. With the highest purpose in mind, Saturn frustrates your attempts at self-deception, escapism, and rationalization. Saturn is the **Lord of Karma**, which symbolizes your lessons. Newton's third law best describes karma, "A body in motion tends to remain in motion at the speed and direction to which it is traveling unless acted upon by an outside force." You are being asked to break through your fears and your limitations and all your blocks to achieving.

As the **Provider** and **Lord of Manifestation**, Saturn teaches, "As ye sow so shall ye reap." Your greatest need for development comes in the area of your work. There is a drive within

Saturn to establish secure structures and a lifestyle that has purpose in the world. To build something and finish those tasks that create faith in your ability to succeed completes your manifestations.

The key to Saturn is to be process-oriented, not result-oriented, and to remember that the process is the goal. Through your daily learning and your hardships, you see how life is a continual process of perfecting and everyday becomes a practice of improving. Change involves this constant evaluating, adjusting, and evolving, so you can take practical steps toward your personal contribution to improving the world.

The measure of your life is mirrored in your relationship with the Universe, which is simply your relationship with yourself recreated everywhere. The people in your life are but actors playing out their individual roles for you. All events and how they are ordered in time can be viewed as servants of your will to test you and increase your understanding. The Universe is a hologram and to see a part is to see the whole. Just as the entire story of your body is contained within a single cell, so the story of the Divine is within your being.

The Hebrew letter for this path is *tau*, which means cross, and signifies "**signature** or **mark**." This implies your pledge, security, and guaranty, for it is what you use to validate your agreements and signify your seal of approval. Case called it "the symbol of salvation from death to eternal life."

Invoke the Universe to utilize Magnetic Creation, so you can manifest a world of purpose and inspiration. The myth of the Goddess Warrior on the Hero's Journey is a powerful and integrated model to help you make your mark in the world and leave a signature of Love and Presence in a co-creation dance with the Universe.

Universe Key words: Saturn; completion; cosmic unity; liberation; integration; wholeness; universality; descent of spirit into matter; karma; travel.

Meditate on your life's purpose and visions.

Visualize your creative self-expression being in the greater world.

Explore the different parts of your nature that pull you in different directions.

See the world constantly evolving and becoming better.

What issues in my life need completing?

What part of my nature needs resolving?

Can I see how all my relationships reflect a part of me?

What service can I tangibly contribute to my community, my country, and the entire world?

What is my next step in my growth to open to my purpose and my destiny?

What keeps me from trusting the intrinsic goodness of the Universe?

I am in a co-creative relationship with the Universe. I am in the Universe and the Universe is in me and together we make the world a better place.

Part III

Mental Swords

Don't believe everything
you hear even in
your own mind.

Daniel Amen

Ace of Swords: New ideas or beginnings are brewing. You are clarifying your ideas based on objectivity and logic. You have the ability to bring a concept to earth.

26.

Clarifying with the Ace of Swords

A blade of light dispenses
the dark clouds of the mind.

Aliester Crowley

The **Swords** indicate activities associated with words, ideas, and thoughts. It is the element Air and Jung's Thinking Function. Swords deal with issues that occur at the mental level of consciousness. Astrologically they include the signs, **Gemini**, **Libra**, and **Aquarius**. To control your thoughts is to control your life. This often entails deprogramming yourself, as much of thought is automatic. You have the most lessons to work through on the mental level, such as sorrow, defeat, futility, self-cruelty, and fear of ruin. They are the easiest lessons as they are operating in the mind, and thought can easily be changed. As a general rule you can move through these issues represented by the Swords in days. With each lesson there is an antidote to move through it. It is important to focus on how to eradicate it when you receive an unconstructive card. For example, if the card is showing a scattered mind-set, read it as a need to focus.

The **Ace of Swords** is the highest of mental clarity and perception. The sword is crowned symbolizing intelligence, insight, wisdom, and an expanded awareness. It is pictured on a clear sky eradicating any clouds of confusion or doubt. It representing broad detached thinking. This is the thinking function at its best—quick, concise, inspired, creative, and regenerative. Its wisdom is based on a balance of rationality and abstraction.

It is here that you generate new and original ideas for new beginnings. This is an inventive, imaginative, and analytical mind that denotes writing, investigating, networking, brainstorming, and decision-making.

The Ace of Swords resides on the Tree of Life in **Crown** and signifies excellence, as it is a mind infused with the Divine.

This card can also symbolize people born during Gemini (May 21 to June 20); Libra (September 23 to October 22); Aquarius (January 20 to February 18) that can help you with your ideas or with the clarity of your mind.

Meditate on the **Magician** when the Ace of Swords comes up and you desire clarity of thought, and when you want to bring ingenuity to your ideas.

Ace of Swords Key Words: Air element—Gemini, Libra, Aquarius; objectivity; clarity; rationality; quickness; analytical; wisdom.

Without judgment, notice your mind throughout the day. Then write down the areas of thought and become aware of the workings of your thought patterns.

What new ideas would I like to manifest?

How can I honor and appreciate my mind as a magnificent tool?

My mind is an amazing tool and a clear vessel of wisdom.

27.

Balancing with the Two of Swords

Every breath we take,
every step we make,
can be filled with peace, joy and serenity.

Thich Nhat Hanh

The **Two of Swords** is **Peace**. It represents a meditative mind. A woman resting near water is contemplating and receiving nurturing at a deep level. Two doves flying in the sky signify peace, harmony, cooperation, and unity. This is an integrative mind that can bring resolutions. There might be a decision or choice between two issues, people, or situations that you need to make.

Moon in Libra is the designator, which seeks balance and emotional rapport with others and themselves. Libra (September 23 to October 22) is directed to others, which calls for the need to reflect on your feelings and be adaptable, receptive, diplomatic, and considerate.

This card represents the first 10 days of Libra or the first 10 degrees, which go from 0 to 10 degrees. This gives a time frame and a way to correlate with the astrological chart

Invoke the **High Priestess** when the Two of Swords comes up. Focus on becoming a Peacemaker using **Wisdom** (its Tree of Life position) and a positive will to generate and moderate new possibilities.

Two of Swords: You are seeking mental and emotional harmony at a deep level. Balance your feelings with your mind and contemplate them. You may have a decision or resolution to make. If so, know that peace is the way.

Two of Swords Key Words: Moon in Libra; peace; balance, diplomacy; harmony, companionship; resolution.

Watch your closest relationships to see the inner balance between your feminine and masculine nature or your unconscious and conscious mind.

In what ways are my relationships telling me something about myself?

Where do I go against what I want, and instead do what others want to keep the peace?

What do I need to do to find emotional balance within myself?

Do I ever intellectualize my feelings?

In indecisiveness, can I see my conditional patterns?

I am a reflection of peace and balance.

Three of Swords: Be present here and now to look at your limiting relating patterns. There may a disagreement, separation, or another person interfering. You may be dealing with your shadow and projecting it onto another. There may serious thoughts concerning commitment.

28.

Resolving with the Three of Swords

Every life has
a measure of sorrow,
and sometimes this is
what awakens us.

Steven Tyler

Three of Swords represents a **Sorrow** or conflict. Here you have a limited view or may be ruminating over past conditioning. There may be a difference of opinion, an entrance of another person in your relationship, a loss, or a need to detach from a triangle that is producing sorrow.

The couple is estranged. There may be feelings of rejection, isolation, or inadequacy, as something needs to be resolved. Your relationships are your greatest test of cooperation and compatibility. You are to be more self-sufficient, for another person cannot satisfy all your needs.

The exalted **Saturn in Libra** is the designator, and tells you to look at what is real and valid in relationships. Saturn binds, constricts, limits, and controls as well as brings things to form and manifest. While your attempts to achieve harmony may be frustrated, there is an opportunity to stabilize and bring structure and security to relationships. Relationships, like life, are a never-ending process of improving. As you seek them as choice rather than need, you find more stable and secure structures.

Because Libra (September 23 to October 21) has a desire for harmony and its perspective is to see other sides and possibilities, this card calls for some movement toward others.

The Three of Swords represent 10 to 20 degrees of Libra.

Invoke the **Empress** when you receive the Three of Swords to find **Understanding** of the true reality of what is going on in relationships and how you can compromise, so that you can nurture yourself and others with the power of love.

Three of Swords Key Words: Saturn in Libra; testing, examining, restructuring of relationships; seriousness sorrow; sadness, triads, conflict.

Assess your values and what is important to you about others. Examine how you withdraw or excessively lean on others and what work you need to do in improving yourself and your relationships.

How do I balance getting my needs met with truly giving in a relationship?

Can I see my strong desire for relationship and my equally strong need to be alone?

Does my fear of vulnerability make me controlling?

Can I be disciplined and work on myself rather than being outer directed?

I balance my personal needs with the needs of others and as a result my relationships are grounding and secure.

29.

Opening with the Four of Swords

If you just focus on getting better,
and not being the best,
you have such a good time.

James Acaster

The **Four of Swords** shows that there is a **Truce** and an opportunity for new awareness. Things are opening mentally and are much better. Relationships and communications are improved. Our person is lifting the dark moods into a positive awareness and the whole bright environment ensues.

Jupiter in Libra shows an expansive mindset. Libra (September 23 to October 22) is the sign of negotiation and conflict resolution, moderation, and balance.

Here you have flexibility, cooperation, and an experience of generosity in a judicious way. There is an understanding of the need for harmony, equality, and non-partiality. Angeles Arrien said, "In order for truce to be experienced one must: first, show up; second, pay attention; third, tell the truth; and fourth, not be attached to outcome." Here you have renewal, regeneration, and great expectation in relating.

Meditate on the Four of Swords and invoke the **Emperor** when you want to expand and improve your relating mind and bring in more benevolence, kindness, grace, unconditional love, and forgiveness.

Four of Swords: Things are so much better. There is an opening or conflict resolution after balancing and weighing things.

This card represents the last 10 days of Libra or from 20 to 30 degrees.

The Four of Swords is connected with **Mercy** on the Tree of Life, and adds the ability to actively build encouraging, opportunistic, and fair relationships and mindsets.

Four of Swords Key Words: Jupiter in Libra; truce; betterment; calm; centered; spiritual cleansing; integration; balancing, and expansion of consciousness.

Contemplate your environment and discern how you can create greater peace in it.

What is enhancing or hindering my peaceful clarity?

How can I stay balanced and eradicate any negativity?

How can I serve others while remaining true to myself?

I am in balance and acknowledge all the goodness in my life.

Five of Swords: You may be dealing with negative mental patterns from the past, so decide to release these family patterns. This could be old relationship patterns and your fear of progressing past them.

30.

Moving Beyond the Five of Swords

Any fact facing us
is not as important
as our attitude toward it,
for that determines
our success or failure.
The way you think about a fact
may defeat you
before you ever do anything about it.
You are overcome by the fact
because you think you are.

Norman Vincent Peale

The **Five of Swords** represents negativity from a fear of **Defeat**. The mind is made up of two parts, the conscious and the unconscious. Whenever you are not completely present, you automatically operate from the things you were told in the first years of your life that are hidden deep within you.

This rendition is a despondent person sitting on a swing on the tip of a huge rock which is deep under the sea. Underneath the water, the rock holds a bloody and distorted clock and chain, which represent the conditioning of our past. The feelings of overwhelm are linked to past thinking, which is distorting our present decisions.

Venus in Aquarius is the astrological aspect of this experience. Venus suggests love, creativity, harmony, and the desire to join with another. Progressive Aquarius (January 20 to February 18) is a Fixed Universal sign and can be caught up in an expansive world view to the point of being impersonal and detached. It could be fear of loving because of a belief that it would restrict your sense of freedom. To overcome the fear of starting something new takes getting out of a narrow conventional expectation.

This card represents the first decan of Aquarius or the first 10 degrees, which go from 0 to 10 degrees.

Five relates to the **Hierophant** and to the family, so it could relate to your early conditioning from your parents or siblings before you were five. Bring in this Inner Teacher to support you in reprogramming your mind using affirmations and visualizations.

Because of its position of **Severity** in the Tree of Life, you will need the power of intention and discipline to control your mind. Call on your Warrior for the strength to eliminate any harsh thoughts and to clarify your mental strength. Remember that as long as you remain present, you can think more clearly.

Five of Swords Key Words: Venus in Aquarius; defeat; loss; fear; unconscious thoughts; learning through trial and error.

Think about any negative relating patterns, like freedom and closeness issues.

Contemplate what family dynamics are still being acted out in your mind.

Examine how you balance your need for closeness with your equally strong need for independence. Look for freedom issues that come from old scripts that have you erratically jumping back and moving forward.

How can I give love freely?

How do I experience change?

What negative thoughts keep me from being present?

How can I be completely present and free at the same time?

I am awake to my unconscious thoughts and live in the present moment.

Six of Swords: You have a broad understanding and can perceive on different levels. Be objective and "color outside the lines" for answers and resolutions. You can communicate your ideas in creative and understandable ways.

31.

Integrating with the Six of Swords

The most beautiful thing we can experience is the mysterious.
It is the source of all true art and science.

Albert Einstein

The **Six of Swords** is a balanced, integrated mental nature that has a broad humanitarian perspective. It is the **Science** of our mind. We have a group of six looking at the innovations, integration, and synthesis of cosmic energy. This shows a focused, deliberate, and intentional mind that is rational, objective, observant, and impartial.

Astrologically it is **Mercury in Aquarius**, which is a high-minded, inspirational, visionary mental faculty that can synthesize and unite different perspectives. It is a systematic, creative, and progressive mind that is quick, ingenious, and flexible, with the ability to blend and synthesize many concepts and ideas. Freedom and balance are integrated with an extraordinary exchange of ideas and social awareness. It can also relate to Aquarius people (January 20 to February 18).

The Six of Swords represents the middle of Aquarius or from 10 to 20 degrees.

This card connects with the **Lovers** card, for it compares the duality of opposite thoughts to bring equilibrium to the mind. There is **Beauty** (Tree of Life) to the Sixes, for with it you can balance love and power. The Six of Swords connects your mind to your radiant Core Self to create symmetry, harmony, healing, and compassionate creativity.

Six of Swords: Key Words: Mercury in Aquarius; science; humanitarian thoughts; analytical understanding; all-encompassing vision; objective and creative communication; inspirational and pioneering ideas.

Contemplate where you are narrow-minded and where you are open and innovative.

How can I bring balance and broad objectivity to my mind?

How can I trust my insights and my visions more?

My mind has clear, far-reaching goals and perceptions.

32.

Recognizing with Seven of Swords

It takes but one positive thought
when given a chance
to survive and thrive
to overpower an entire army
of negative thoughts.

Robert H. Schuller

The **Seven of Swords** is a mental state that creates thoughts of **Futility,** ineffectualness, hopelessness, and helplessness. This rendition is a person sitting rather despondently. In her mind is an idea of what she wants, but surrounding that awareness are the symbols of all different kinds of negative self-talk about why "it won't happen."

The planets symbolize the different areas of illusions that the mind takes. The Sun in futility may represent, "I don't deserve" or "I am not good enough." Mars may say, " I don't have the drive or energy." Jupiter could symbolize, "It's too much; I am not equipped to handle it all; or I am not lucky enough." Mercury could express, " If only… or I don't have the ability to communicate or convey it." Venus under ineffectiveness could say, "It would be too good to be true." Saturn might say, "I don't have the time; it will take too long; or I am too old or too young." It could be misunderstanding or negative emotional conditioning that might say, "What is the use?" or "I can't." A feeling of overwhelm brings the need to make a firm decision.

Seven of Swords: Watch your contrary and sabotaging thoughts that tell you, "I can't or what's the use." You know what you want, but you have a "yes, but " going on too. Silence all the contrary conditional thoughts.

Astrologically the **Moon in Aquarius** connects the very personal Moon with the brilliant and unemotional Aquarius. Uranus, its ruler, gives an intuitive, sensitive detachment, yet the inner aspect of the self can be challenged with erratic and unpredictable feelings. What the Moon in Aquarius wants is emotional freedom. Sharing and joining with others in group endeavors can satisfy some of your deepest security needs.

You could affirm that you will be over this sense of futility in seven days or with the help of Aquarians (January 20 to February 18).

This card represents the last 10 days of Aquarius or from 20 to 30 degrees.

The Seven of Swords is connected to **Victory** on the Tree of Life, which tells you to get into the present, where grace and peace reside. Time to contemplate and expand your heart with a sense of joy, as well as to initiate and persist toward what you truly want.

Call on the archetypical energy of the **Chariot** for support, to set things into motion and to generate and motivate positive changes in your life.

Seven of Swords Key Words: Moon in Aquarius; futility; sabotaging thoughts; discouragement; negative mental beliefs; conditional tapes.

Observe your different thoughts that get in the way of what you truly desire.

Contemplate what emotional freedom looks like in your life.

Question your expression as an individual in your environment.

> What are those negative voices in my head?
>
> What are the reasons that keep me from manifesting my ideal life?
>
> Is there a familiar sabotaging pattern in my family of origin?

I clear all negativity and manifest new gifts into my life.

33.

Deciding with the Eight of Swords

A hero is someone who,
in spite of weakness,
doubt or not always knowing
the answers,
goes ahead and
overcomes anyway.

Christopher Reeves

The **Eight of Swords** is an experience of doubting, over thinking, and questioning. The figure, standing near a split in the road, is examining which way to go. The mind is going back and forth in two directions before making a decision. Because of the fear of making the wrong choice, there may be confusion or **Interference**.

Astrologically **Jupiter in Gemini** is the designator, which encourages expansion through communications. Gemini deals with polarity and growth through experimenting. It likes variety and changeable ways. This dual energy encourages indiscriminate thinking, sometimes making it difficult to focus.

Jupiter, a benevolent expansive energy, can represent positive change and expansion. You are being asked to be patient, trust, and allow clarity to come. Consider different possibilities and options.

You can resolve the issue in eight days by yourself or with the help of a Gemini person (May 21 to June 20).

Eight of Swords: There are excessive analytical thoughts or decisions between two issues or people, that have you doubting and moving in different directions. Release any non-trusting thoughts, and focus on what you truly want. Be patient and allow the decision to come.

The Eight of Swords represents the first 10 days of Gemini or the first 10 degrees, which go from 0 to 10 degrees. You can use this for timing or to correlate it to an astrological chart

On the Tree of Life, the Eight of Swords resides in **Splendor**, where there is the power of the mind to focus, reason, and conceptualize. Trust your sincere and impeccable steadfastness to find the right use of your mind.

Let the **Adjustment**, the archetype behind this energy, help you balance and weigh the choices and expand beyond old ways of thinking and being.

Eight of Swords: Key Words: Jupiter in Gemini; interference; deliberating choices; non-trusting; doubt; confusion; over-analyzing; thinking too much.

Observe your doubting mind that makes you indecisive and then just relax and ask for clarity.

Do I ever scatter my energy in just busy work?

Where am I over thinking?

Do I ever give my opinion when it hasn't been asked for?

How do I allow others to interfere with my decisions?

I have clarity and trust myself to find the right answers.

Nine of Swords: Recognize that you are being hard on yourself. Give yourself some loving thoughts and stop all recrimination.

34.

Accepting with the Nine of Swords

Self-love has very little to do with
how you feel about your outer self.
It's about accepting all of yourself.

Tyra Banks

The Nine of Swords represent a negative critic and is called **Cruelty**, which is directed upon the yourself or others. It is shown with blood on the sword and the broken glass. This is a self-critical mind that is on the verge of tears. The feelings are like barren trees in a fog, yet the sun is breaking through. There is hope if you stop and give yourself loving thoughts.

The astrological connection is **Mars in Gemini**. Mars is the motivational force of drive, energy, and assertion. Gemini is a Mutable or changeable sign that signifies duality, going back and forth, and reworking things.

This experience can be energetically charged with a dynamic internal debate or a vicious attack. It is a nervous, excitable, restless energy that needs to focus on and initiate communication. It could be a series of starts and stops and a compulsive need to feel a sense of completion.

This card represents the middle of Gemini and goes from 10 to 20 degrees.

In the Tree of Life, the Nine of Swords dwells in **Foundation**, which is the astral plane that includes your subconscious dreams. You may be remembering a memory or slight in your development that may make you lash out, but also here is an ability to heal and transform.

Invoke the **Hermit,** the Major Arcana behind this energy. Call on his inner light and his wisdom for guidance and support. With introspection and contemplative reflection, you can complete and resolve this pattern within nine days, either alone or with the help of a Gemini (May 21 to June 20).

Nine of Swords Key Words: Mars in Gemini; mental cruelty; self-criticalness; self-accusations; punishment.

Observe the self-critical voices in your head that put you down.

Notice where you first saw an example of this critical thinking given to you, and then quiet it down with love and appreciation.

Where do I beat myself up or think I am not good enough?

How do I wound or punish myself?

What past negative judgments of me by others have I now made about myself?

Can I begin to forgive those that have made these judgment and myself for taking them on?

I love and accept myself fully and am loved for who I truly am.

35.

Healing with the Ten of Swords

Be a force of love as often as you can,
turn away negative thoughts
whenever you feel them surface.

Wayne Dyer

In the **Ten of Swords** we have a destructive mindset that is producing fears of **Ruin** concerning money and the heart. In this rendition, the figure is contracted with lots of mental despair focused at the bottom. There are past fears of emotional havoc and financial concern that are affecting the present. All these negative thoughts, like "things are not going to work out," are disrupting the soul's harmony.

The astrological aspect of this experience is **Sun in Gemini**. This energy has the ability to see all sides, synthesize opposites and paradoxes, and can also manifest as constant nonstop thinking that includes the negative thoughts. Its season is June 10 to June 20, as this card represents the last decan of Gemini and goes from 20 to 30 degrees of the sign.

You may feel ambivalent, split, or scattered and reluctant to reflect on why you feel this way, but that is what is needed now to eliminate this fearful pattern. Call on the support and guidance of the **Wheel of Fortune** to counteract any fears. Get to the truth behind these negative, undermining thoughts with objectivity and flexibility, and then expand into new energy and creativity. Consciously move toward a more positive direction with intention. You can do it within ten days. Believe it.

Ten of Swords: You may be feeling an economic concern or a hurting heart. Focus your energies inward. These may be old fears. Know the possibility of another way to resolve your negative thinking.

The Tens reside in the Earth's **Kingdom** on the Tree of Life and tell you to ground and embody here, so you can complete these lessons.

Ten of Swords Key Words: Sun in Gemini; anxiety; ruin; financial fear; scattered; broken heart; despair; negative thinking.

Contemplate the deeper negative beliefs that are hidden within your fear of not enough love or money.

What do I fear?

Am I afraid I won't be loved?

Do I harbor feelings of "not enough?"

Did my family instill these negative beliefs or was it an experience?

I embrace all good things and am open to the many blessings in life.

Princess of Swords: Use your mind to cut away moods and come back to clarity and your ideals. Move on your convictions and commitment to quality and merit.

36.

Combating with the Princess of Swords

I tend to wear my emotions on my sleeve
and had my share of mood swings.
But it's a powerful thing
when you realize that
you have dominion over
your behavior and your passions.

Matt Dillon

The **Royalty** cards are masters or adepts who personify characters and mediate in their area. They can appear outside as a person or within your own psyche. The Royal Swords are proficient, gifted, and skilled in the cerebral realms for they have learned and conquered their mental challenges.

The **Princess of Swords** is the **earthy part of air**. As a practical thinker, she brings grounding to the mind and can apply her thoughts tangibly and productively. She is the **Mood Fighter** that cuts through all the temperamental feelings that flow into life. Your emotions are like smoke and fog in the air and this archetype has the mental grounding to destroy all that is in the way of clarity.

The Princess of Swords has a connection to the Death/Rebirth card, as she is tied to healing and regeneration. In the I Ching, she is connected to number 18, "**Repair**," which is working on that which is spoiled, as her mind has the ability to see problems clearly. As a true Goddess Warrior, she works on taking direct, assertive action to correct her attitude and makes amends. Here you have mind over emotions.

Representing all the Air signs, Gemini, ; Libra; and Aquarius, she symbolizes incubating your internal seeds and planting new ideas.

The Princess of Swords resides in **Kingdom** on the Tree of Life, which again reinforces the earthy ability to embody the Air element. This archetype could represent a young woman or a part of your inner feminine nature.

Princess of Swords Key Words: Earthy part of air; mood fighter; rebellion; clarity; regeneration; aligning thoughts and actions.

Contemplate how you can fight your negative feelings in a loving way.

What causes my moodiness?

How can I swiftly move out of my emotional waves?

What ideas do I want to practically apply to enhance my life?

I use my mind creatively and constructively and I manifest a great life.

37.

Cutting Through with the Prince of Swords

The creation of something new is not
accomplished by the intellect
but by the play of instinct
acting from inner necessity.
The creative mind plays with the objects it loves.

Carl Jung

The **Prince of Swords** is a mental adept. He represents the **airy part of Air**. This **Limitation Cutter** has the ability to remove mental blocks. The Prince of Swords balances a sword in one hand and a sickle in the other, and is dynamically determined to cut away all restricting thoughts. The three figures show that you need to watch what you hear, see, and speak. Above his head is the illuminating sun that shows your experiences are the result of your thoughts, feelings, and vibrations.

Progressive **Aquarius**, (January 20 to February 18) is its astrological designator and shows you that freedom and broad-mindedness are necessary for creative, enlightened thinking. This rebel with a cause will revolutionize your thinking so that creativity and awareness abound. He's smart, sensitive, intuitive, and objective. He needs to set goals and create the vision that he wants. A **Synthesizer**, he breaks through paradoxes and contradictions to get in touch with the truth. The Prince of Swords represents pulling in on the mental energy to bring clear perception.

Prince of Swords: Cutting away all forms of limitations. There are often three forms that need to be looked upon. You may want to move, travel, or express yourself actively in new and more freeing ways of relating.

This state of mind is like a tree, which branches out and goes everywhere. Mental perception needs to be grounded with constant effort.

He is connected to number 57 in the I Ching, "**Penetrating Influence**," which tells you to move gently, gradually, and patiently for a long-term commitment is required to master all your mental patterns. You are to set visions and goals and concentrate on what you want to create.

The Prince of Swords dwells in **Beauty** on the Tree of Life, which brings in the Sun's vital Essence and provides you balance, healing, and the power of creativity. He can represent an aspect of your inner male or a young person outside you.

Prince of Swords Key Words: Aquarius; Airy part of air; creative; intuitive; objective; freedom; innovation; visionary.

Examine the unsatisfactory and uncomfortable roles you play automatically.

Practice creative visualization and empower what you want more of in your life.

What thoughts or beliefs do I need to let go of?

What are the contradictions and paradoxes in my life?

What beliefs, relationships, and conditioned thoughts do I allow to limit me?

My creative mind is unlimited and I enjoy my self-expression.

Queen of Swords: Cut through the facades or roles of who you think you are. Trust your connection to the Divine Child within you for inspiration. If you need advice or counsel, listen within or seek it from a person you trust.

38.

Unmasking with the Queen of Swords

Every act of rebellion
expresses a nostalgia
for innocence and an appeal
to the essence of being.

Albert Camus

The **Queen of Swords** is the **watery part of Air** and brings emotions into the mind. This adept is a master of rational, objective, and clear thinking. She is a **Mask Cutter** who severs through all defenses and roles she wears.

Mastering the mind enables you to go beyond all your defense mechanisms, and look within for inspiration. The crystal headdress shows the clarity of a far-reaching and supportive mind. She is a keen observer, intensely perceptive, with nothing to hide, as well as foresight and prudence. What's left are the openness, curiosity, and innocence of a child.

The Queen of Swords represents all the **Air signs**: Gemini; Aquarius; and especially **Libra**.

She also represents practical intelligence, which is the attribute of **Athena**, the Warrior Goddess, in Greek mythology. She can symbolize a **Consultant** or **Counselor**, who has the wisdom to give advice or seek it from others. With the ability to evaluate, analyze, and focus on details, she has enormous reflective ability and is an ideal diplomat and practical **Peacemaker** and **Problem Solver**.

In the I Ching, this Air Queen is connected with 28, which is "**Critical Mass**," which shows how in serious situations, she stands strong and certain within. This resilience sees her through any situation.

In the Tree of Life, the Queen of Swords dwells in **Understanding** and incorporates the nurturing Mother Principle as well as the ability to intellectualize and comprehend the universal laws at work.

This archetype can represent the authentic, lucid thinking of an older woman or the feminine within your own psyche.

Queen of Swords Key Words: Watery part of air; clarity; rational; logical; objective; reflection; authenticity; lack of pretense; counselor.

Explore what facade or mask you wear to the world.

How do I hide behind my persona or the role I wear to the world?

How can I embrace my childlike innocence?

I honor my mind, accept myself completely, and remain true to this Self.

39.

Moving with the Knight of Swords

Meaning is essential for life.
Whether it is ultimately up to us
to create our own meaning,
or whether it is our task to discover
some grand cosmic scheme or Divine intention,
the search for guidelines, goals,
and a sense of purpose
is an innate drive in all of us.

Liz Greene

The **Knight of Swords** (King in other decks) is the **fiery part of Air** that gives you passionate fervor behind your thoughts. He is a **Mental Determinate** and similar to the **Chariot**, as he is beginning to move. The propellers on his head show that he is moving on all levels—mental, emotional, perceptual, and physical. This card has the continuing and enduring power of motion applied. The Knight has the water behind him. Here you have the mental over emotions, which means mastering the mental energies, which allow you to move on what you feel. Success comes through continually moving toward your objectives.

The Knight of Swords represents all the **Air signs**: Aquarius; Gemini; and Libra.

In the I Ching, he is connected to 32, "**Continuing**," which shows his endurance and continuing values and traditions. His character is self-perpetuating and self-renewing.

Knight of Swords: Move on your feelings with words or actions. Forge ahead on your plans. Set clear decisive goals and be persistent.

The Knight of Swords resides in **Wisdom** in the Tree of Life, giving it an active and powerful will with flashes of inspiration. Here is the Father principle, which is the dynamic energy of doing. The Knight of Swords is determined, focused, purposeful, and full of certainty.

He holds a sword in one hand and a dagger in the other, which express the receptive and dynamic sides of thinking and symbolizes moving toward unity and balance.

The Knight of Swords could represent an Air sign person or an older man or the inner male within.

Knight of Swords Key Words: Fiery aspect of air; goal-directed; flexible, balanced mental energy; intelligence; ambition; vehemence; determination; purposeful.

Contemplate where you are moving and what you are moving toward.

Look within for character traits that are self-renewing and self-perpetuating.

Do I trust my instincts and move on them?

Does my mind have the staying power to accomplish my goals?

How can I become more committed to focus on my goals?

I move toward my goals with sustained passion and each is being fulfilled.

Part IV

Watery Cups

Water is yielding
but all-conquering.

John Blofeld

Ace of Cups: You are feeling great about yourself and can express love and emotional integrity. You are openly loving and may need to set emotional limits. Believe in yourself and practice more self-love.

40.

Self-Loving with the Ace of Cups

If your emotional abilities aren't in hand,
if you don't have self-awareness,
if you are not able to manage your distressing emotions,
if you can't have empathy and have effective relationships,
then no matter how smart you are,
you are not going to get very far.

Daniel Goleman

The **Cups** deal with your feelings and emotional issues. You respond to and accept or reject these inner subjective, fluid currents that flow through you. Because you live on a planet and in body that are mostly water, your next great lessons are emotional. You have to move beyond disappointment, over-doing, and over-giving to find self-love, share love, and express abundance, luxury, pleasure, happiness, and contentment.

The **Ace of Cups** is the essence of **Self-love.** This rendition is a bride who is expressing an open, caring, and trusting heart, as illustrated by the rose blossom on her chest. It is an inspired love, a spiritual love, a love with wisdom, and a state of emotional honesty and authenticity. It represents knowing yourself, the ability to set emotional limits, and yet not holding back or protecting the self.

The Ace of Cups is a clear and reflective experience, for whatever is inside is mirrored outwardly as shown by the double rainbows. When you open to your emotions, you can be very expressive in love. This is an emotional, balanced energy that can nurture, comfort, and constantly heal and regenerate yourself as well as others, as expressed by the light coming out of the cup and the snakes for its handles.

The Ace of Cups represents the **Water signs** : Cancer, Scorpio, and Pisces. Aces always represent new beginnings.

The Ace of Cups correlates with the **Magician** and its resourcefulness. It has an innate ability to communicate authentic feelings from a place of openness and trust.

In the Tree of Life the Ace of Cups dwells in **Crown,** where the Divine infused feelings bring compassion and excellence.

Ace of Cups Key Words: Self-esteem; self-love; self-nourishment; new beginnings; new love; setting limits; emotional intelligence; clarity; a balance of giving and receiving love.

Contemplate your emotional limits and how easy it is to say "no."

How can I increase my self-love?

How balanced is my giving with my receiving?

I love and appreciate myself, and with my self-love, I have so much love to give to others.

41.

Sharing with the Two of Cups

Kindness in words creates confidence.
Kindness in thinking
creates profoundness.
Kindness in giving creates love.

Lao Tzu

The **Two of Cups** is **Love**. It is a caring, encouraging, and satisfying love. In this card we have an affectionate couple sharing a deep emotional love that is flowing out of them. The waterfalls in the background show how everything is beautiful when you are in love. This loving is expressive and communicative, equal and special, internally and externally felt.

The Two of Cups is **Venus in Cancer**. It is a personal love, but also imaginative, inspirational, and spiritual. Venus is the planet of love, beauty, and creativity. Cancer (June 21 to July 22) is associated with nourishment, comfort, home and family. Here is a need to relate and a real desire to give and receive nurturing, support, and comfort. The tranquility, harmony, and balance of our couple demonstrate a considerate domestic and emotional cooperation. With appreciativeness, protectiveness, and the ability to give pleasure, the Two of Cups is love personified.

The Two of Cups inhabits **Wisdom** in the Tree of Life and brings in dynamic and active expressions of love.

It relates to the **High Priestess**, which is balanced, intuitive, and independent.

Two of Cups: Acknowledge your deep loving nature. Express and receive love equally. You may be experiencing an emotional flow of fulfillment.

This card represents the first 10 days of Cancer or the first 10 degrees, which go from 0 to 10 degrees.

Two of Cups Key Words: Venus in Cancer; sharing love; deep nurturing; receptive love; happy relationships; emotional fulfillment; flowing exchange.

Consciously connect to people in your heart and be open to receive love coming to you from many sources.

How can I express and receive more love in my life?

I love and am loved and open to receive all the good in the Universe.

Three of Cups: You have a rare gift to offer. Communicate your deepest feelings. Express yourself abundantly.

42.

Expressing with the Three of Cups

When you focus on being a blessing,
God makes sure that you are
always blessed in abundance.

Joel Osteen

The **Three of Cups** is called **Abundance**. It's an expansive experience of expressing and communicating fully and joyfully. We have three friends sharing love by chatting deeply, laughing, and celebrating together.

The cup is full of pomegranates, which were what the Egyptians served to their dignitaries, for this exceptional and delicious fruit symbolizes treasures and rare gifts.

The astrological designator is **Mercury in Cancer,** which is communication with feelings. It is a mind that deeply remembers people who were loyal. Cancer (June 21 to July 22) is a sensitive sign, but its modality is Cardinal, which designates movement out of the self to set up a situation to which it can respond. It is expressing loyalty, mentally nurturing, and finding answers by reflection.

On the Tree of Life, the Three of Cups dwells in **Understanding** and you have the influence of the Great Mother's creative, nurturing, and intellectual capacity.

The Three of Cups also relates to the nurturing, creative, and fertile energy of the **Empress**.

The Three of Cups represents the second decan of Cancer and covers from 10 to 20 degrees of the sign.

Three of Cups Key Words: Mercury in Cancer; abundance; artful communication; emotional exchange; rare perceptions.

Consider your gifts and what you have to truly share.

Reflect on how you nurture others with your words.

With whom do I need to share the exquisite feeling of love?

I express my loving self fully, and receive everything I need to feel fulfilled.

43.

Nurturing with the Four of Cups

True success, true happiness
lies in freedom and fulfillment.

Dada Vaswani

The **Four of Cups** is **Luxury**. It is a receptive experience that is nurturing and sumptuously caring. Our figure is experiencing a luxurious bath that is flowing with emotional nourishment and richness. She is feeling emotional satisfaction and fulfillment within and without.

The astrological designator is **Moon in Cancer**, which is its natural placement. It is gifted in self-care and nurturing others. Planets in Cancer (June 21 to July 22) show an eye for beauty.

This changeable energy has an ability to adjust and balance. Cancer is a Water sign, which is receptive. Its modality is Cardinal, which is movable, so this archetype is asking you to take action and set up situations to which it can respond.

Getting this card may mean it is time to initiate some self-care and do something for yourself. It could be telling you to respond to the messages of your feelings. Tune into what you need and listen to what would bring you emotional harmony and accept it unconditionally.

The Four of Cups resides in **Mercy** on the Tree of Life, which brings in benevolence, kindness, grace, encouragement, and compassion to its cultivation of caring.

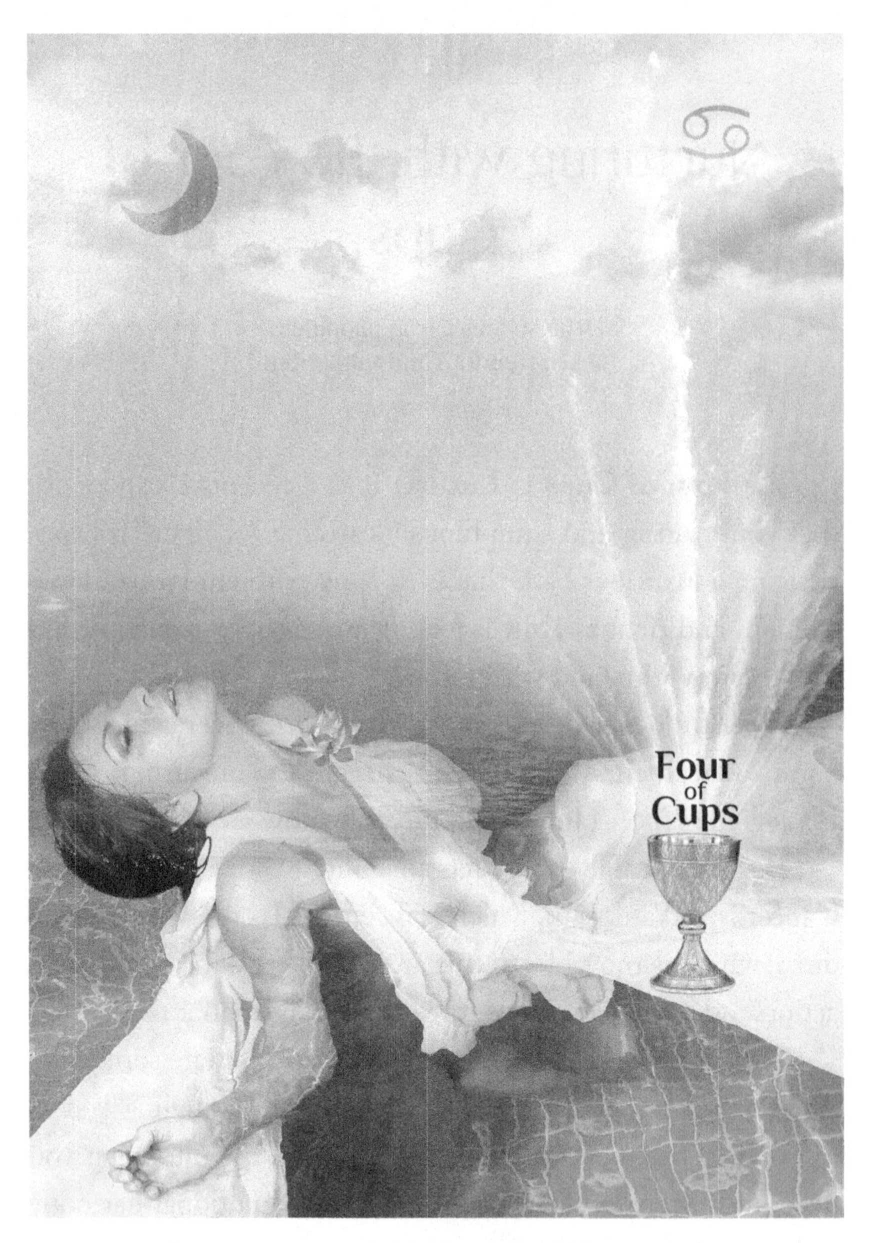

Four of Cups: You are initiating something new for your nourishment. Listen to your feelings and find ways to relish or luxuriate in some self-care.

This card represents the third decan of Cancer, which covers from 20 to 30 degrees of that sign.

In the Four of Cups, this loving generosity is given to the self. It relates to the **Emperor** and the grounding number four, which calls for active doing and structuring to be the foundation of your being.

Four of Cups Key Words: Moon in Cancer; luxury; nurturing; tenderness; emotional self-care; lavish profusion.

Contemplate what you mean by nourishing the self.

Use your daily showers as a ritual of spiritual hygiene or baptism into your greatness.

What personal habit or nutritional supplement do I need to bring into my life?

What can I do to nurture and care for myself?

What could bring me more emotional rapport with others and myself?

How do I give of myself without losing myself?

I nourish myself in many ways, and I feel blessed.

Five of Cups: You need the determination and penetrative focus to move through your emotional vulnerability. Make a conscious intention to release your past hurts.

44.

Overcoming with the Five of Cups

The size of your success
is measured by
the strength of your desire;
the size of your dream; and
how you handle disappointment along the way.

Robert Kiyosaki

The **Five of Cups** is an experience of frustration due to a feeling of dissatisfaction and **Disappointment**. The figure despondently sits on a boardwalk with a spilled cup full of broken glass. This discontentment makes you feel fragile, depressed, and vulnerable. A plant is uprooted, which shows how disconnected you may feel. In the background is a statue of a determined man. There is an ability to transform this excessive emotional and passionate energy into constructive expression.

Mars in Scorpio is the astrological aspect that is aligned with this card. Mars is a driven and assertive energy. Scorpio (October 23 to November 21) rules the hidden depths. It is the ability to take risks and open yourself to others by being vulnerable. It is courageous motivation to remove obstacles, as well as determined and penetrating focus to get what you need.

A disappointment will not stop you; your passionate drive and compulsive desires are too strong, your commitment too deep. This may manifest as a ruthless drive for power or the need to confront a person who you allowed to dominate you.

This energy can be expressed in extreme ways as this raw power is released from the depths of one's being with a boundless potential for either good or bad. There may be a tendency toward self-repression and not being open about one's motives. Motivation can run high plus there is an incredible capacity for self-discipline.

Here you have the instinctual energy to identify with your Source, to act decisively like a Warrior, and both create and experience a rebirth.

This card represents the first 10 days of Scorpio or the first 10 degrees, which go from 0 to 10 degrees.

On the Tree of Life, the Five of Cups inhabits **Severity** and calls for disciplined intentions to move beyond your harsh and judgmental feelings. Be determined and give yourself five weeks to fully overcome this pattern with forgiveness and perceptual awareness.

Call upon the **Hierophant** and draw upon this supportive guide for wisdom, inner strength and spiritual connection. Because the Inner Pope is linked to the family, calling on your inner faith can heal past family issues that make up your wounding.

Five of Cups Key Words: Mars in Scorpio; disappointment; vulnerability; fragility; uprootedness; unfulfilled expectations; family issues; determination.

Purge emotional upsets by sitting down and expressing your feelings in writing. Don't worry about conciseness; just let it pour out of you.

The next day read it and add anything you may want to add. Then burn the paper and release it to the cosmos.

Can I just be with uncomfortable feelings, let them be without judgment, and then let them go?

What deeply moves me enough to go for it and take a risk?

How can I continually build my confidence and determination?

I move through my emotional challenges with determination and penetration and accomplish my goals.

Six of Cups: Great joy, emotional balance, and deep pleasure are available. Enjoy it all and express your gratitude. There is an emotional determination to experience renewal and transformation in a gratifying way.

45.

Pleasuring with the Six of Cups

To give pleasure to a single heart
by a single act is better than
a thousand heads bowing in prayer.

Mahatma Gandhi

The **Six of Cups** is a deep **Pleasure** and a rewarding experience of balance, nurturing, and joy. In this image there is an ecstatic figure in front of a roaring waterfall, fully rejoicing in the richness of her deep feelings. She holds in her hand a lotus to signify an awakened, blossoming energy. In her cup is a coiled snake, which shows renewal and deep, transformative, regenerative power.

The astrological designator for this card is the **Sun in Scorpio**, which represents an intense and creative force and strength in a deeply penetrating way. With personal power, creativity, and the desire to penetrate to the core of oneself, this experience can take you to a state of inner balance, so that you can become more aware of your true Self, rather than of the self that you think you know. Scorpio (October 23 to November 21) is the urge to go beyond the ego and be with someone in a shared mystical experience. A blending of emotional, physical, sexual, and spiritual levels is possible. This intensifies the need to express the Self, to uncover the mysteries of life, and to identify with a healing, cathartic experience in a pleasurable way.

This card denotes the second decan of Scorpio and goes from 10 to 20 degrees of that sign.

The Six of Cups is situated in **Beauty** on the Tree of Life and brings harmony, symmetry, and redemption to the emotional nature. The **Lovers** helps you to see the different parts of you that are brought into balance and harmony.

Six of Cups Key Words: Sun in Scorpio; pleasure; joy; enjoyment; deep transformation; inner balance; vital exchange; lustful bliss.

Contemplate what would bring you joyful regeneration in your body, your mind, and your emotions.

What keeps me from deep and abiding pleasure?

How can I facilitate a profound, transformative and regenerative experience within my intimate relationships and myself?

Because I am in touch with my deeper Self, life is joyful and pleasurable.

46.

Being Moderate with the Seven of Cups

Relationships are the battlefield
where victory comes
by conquering the self.

Unknown

The experience of the **Seven of Cups** is **Debauchery,** negative emotional excess or overdoing. This image is a figure drenched in water and reflecting on some distressing experience. Within her cup is a wilted flower, similar to flowers that have become slimy from having been left too long in water. There is a tendency to react, wallow in the past, indulge in moodiness, or feel sorry for yourself. Sometimes you cope with your uncomfortable feelings through your addictions and indulgences, like shopping, overeating, drinking, drugs, or sex.

Venus in Scorpio is the astrological aspect for this experience, which can bring out the devil or angel in you. You are asked to let go of anything that is superficial, manipulative or self-absorbed, and embrace timeless values such as truth, honesty, and integrity. Scorpio's ruler is Pluto and with this influence, Venus can result in an intense, impersonal, almost compulsive desire to lose the self and annihilate the ego in a climactic experience of passionate love. It can also represent the urge to exert one's full power, break taboos, and dive into the emotional depth and sexual mysteries.

Seven of Cups: You may be overdoing, feeling stagnant, or facing excessiveness or an emotional obsession. Take the moderate path. Stop projecting out there and see how your relationship issues are reflected within you.

There is personal desire for unity of body, mind, and soul, which is misconstrued as a desire to blend and unify with another. Possessive and excessive tendencies need to be transformed into learning how to let go and give of the self.

Like Scorpio (October 23 to November 21), this archetype represents the need to refine the self, and can also have a deeply therapeutic effect that dredges up all kinds of deeply buried emotions. It can be enormously creative and transformative, for once you remove your obstacles and excessive tendencies, you have more conscious usable power.

This card represents the middle decan of Scorpio and covers from 10 to 20 degrees.

The Seven of Cups inhabits **Victory** on the Tree of Life. Here you are taught to honor the Eternal Now with loving presence to resolve all issues. Moderation is the key here and when you purge any selfish power plays, balance your extremes, and expand your heart, you can create a joyful love.

Call on the supportive power of the **Chariot**, which underlies this card, to bring in contemplation and movement.

Seven of Cups: *Venus in Scorpio; debauchery; indulgences; excess, over activity; satiety; jealousy; push and pull in relationships; crisis; overdoing*

Reflect on your relating patterns to see if there are any manipulative, jealous, obsessive, or possessive tendencies or shades of absorption and neediness, so you can eliminate them.

If so, think about how you can heal those tendencies and how you can forgive yourself.

Contemplate the concept of putting together by letting go.

> Where in my life am I excessive or overdoing?
>
> How can I balance any extremes or my need to take on more?
>
> Can I see where I experience simultaneous attraction and repulsion or "I want or like it and I don't" or any propensity to push and pull in my relationships?
>
> How can I purge myself of any selfish, ego-based desires?

I recognize any unhealthy relating patterns and experience an expansion of consciousness and a wider spiritual love.

47.

Balancing with the Eight of Cups

Indolence is the
sleep of the mind.

Luc de Clapiers

The **Eight of Cups** is giving too much and feeling drained, which results in **Indolence** or inertia. This image is languishing in stagnant water, which symbolizes a person emotionally exhausted from overextending and doing for others. The emotional nature needs adjustment, as this is an experience of feeling emotionally depleted and "ripped off." When you get this card, you may be struggling between protecting your own interests and providing help to others. Ask with every opportunity to give to another: "Would I do this if I received nothing in return?"

The astrological significance is **Saturn in Pisces**. Saturn is the Task Master, the "Restrictor" who tells us to restructure. Pisces (February 19 to March 20) can sacrifice the self and surrender the ego to another. A deep awareness and sensitivity to others socially can obligate you and then dissolve your personal ambitions. It is an experience of trying to hold on to water in your hands; it slips through your fingers. There can be waste, as if giving when not asked, or giving what the other person doesn't want or even notice. Give up that sacrificial self immersed in a sense of duty.

Eight of Cups: Ask yourself with every request, “Do I really want to do this?” It is time to set limits and say, “No,” to obligations and replenish yourself. Be wary of over-extension and emotional vampires who drain your energy.

This card represents the first 10 days of Pisces and goes from 0 to 10 degrees.

The Eight of Cups is connected to **Splendor** on the Tree of Life. It grants a gifted intellect, impeccability, steadfastness, and the ability to observe and compute how to balance your giving and receiving. The lesson here is to honor your boundaries and give only what you want to give, not what is expected of you.

Tap into the **Adjustment** card, for with balance, you can change these patterns of over giving, learn to be a practical idealist, and apply spiritual principles to your daily life.

Eight of Cups: Key Words: Saturn in Pisces; indolence; stagnation; over giving; being depleted; slothfulness; apathy; obstruction; confusion.

Contemplate if there is a pattern of over giving and not getting much in return, and if there is, when and who do you do this with, as well as what is underneath it.

Reflect on your life's direction and your degree of self-discipline to accomplish your goals.

Is there anyone I consistently give more to than I receive from?

If so, is it fear, lack of self-worth, or a sense of obligation that has me constantly feeling "ripped off?"

How can I be more determined to set limits and give only my excess, not my core?

Where do I waste energy that causes my vulnerability?

Do I have any past confusion connected to authority figures that has me giving my power away?

Do I ever identify with another's problems?

What challenges my faith?

I am aware of my giving, and balance it with receiving and giving to myself.

48.

Emanating with Nine of Cups

Think of all the beauty
still left around you and be happy.

Anne Frank

The situations around the **Nine of Cups** are tangible expressions of **Happiness.** This image is four friends on a beach jumping for joy, five birds soaring in the sky, and a lotus in the cup. All are expressing happiness and fulfillment, a feeling of being blessed, and deep soul nourishment, inside and out.

The astrological aspect that relates to this card is **Jupiter in Pisces.** Jupiter is the planet of expansion, opportunity, generosity, and abundance. Pisces (February 19 to March 20) is sensitive, fluid, and creative. This highly inspired, optimistic energy has strong imagination, faith, and the ability to touch the hearts of others. This experience encompasses idealism, a free-flowing expansion, great expectations, and the power of positive thinking, which all really work.

This card represents the middle decan of Pisces, which is from 10 to 20 degrees. Knowing the astrological correlation can serve you with right timing and also connecting to your chart.

The Nine of Cups sits in **Foundation** on the Tree of Life, which brings in the magic of dreaming and the utilization of magnetic attraction, so visualize your blessings to bring them into manifestation. Call on the **Hermit** to find your deepest desires, those that illuminate your soul's calling.

Nine of Cups: You know the external reasons for your happiness and fulfillment. Bask in your tangible joy and celebrate it. You are experiencing emotional well-being and expansion.

Nine of Cups Key Words: Jupiter in Pisces; happiness; expansion; gratitude; overflowing joy; blessings.

Count your blessings. Write them down, look at them periodically, and watch them increase.

What truly makes me happy?

How can I express it more tangibly in my life?

When do I feel the bliss of my soul is nourished and I am at peace?

Happiness fills my being and my life.

Ten of Cups: You are feeling deeply satisfied and contented. Trust that everything comes to you at the right moment. Enjoy the fulfillment of being emotionally comforted and gratified.

49.

Radiating with the Ten of Cups

A grateful heart is
a beginning of greatness.
It is an expression of humility.
It is a foundation for the development of
such virtues as prayer, faith,
courage, contentment, happiness,
love, and well-being.

James E Faust

The **Ten of Cups** is an internal contentment that radiates outward. It is an experience of emotional satiety or **Satisfaction** and **Contentment**. This image is a family radiating in the gratification of fulfillment with their devotional and celebratory pose in front of roaring waterfalls with rainbows.

The astrological aspect for this card is **Mars in Pisces**. Mars is the planet of energy, drive, and motivation. Pisces (February 19 to March 20) is Universal and entails a mysterious, compassionate visionary. This vital and expressive energy comes from the unconscious, and there is a deep desire for perfection and fulfillment on the emotional plane. You can become more whole and at one with the Universe through emotional expansion. The outpouring energy of Mars is diverted into many different streams through Pisces, and can flow naturally towards psychic awareness and the transcendence of self. Boundless energy, an imaginative drive, and empathetic action and work combine with a burning need to evolve and progress spiritually. Tapping into one's inner fulfillment and gratification opens new spaces in the outer world, so you can let your light shine, feel good, and be satisfied.

This card represents the last decan of Pisces, which is from 20 to 30 degrees.

The Ten of Cups lives in the **Kingdom** on the Tree of Life, showing us that you are to ground and embody your satisfaction on this Earth plane.

Connected to the **Wheel of Fortune**, you are to keep adding new fire, energy, and commitment to what brings you contentment.

Ten of Cups Key Words: Mars in Pisces; satisfaction; contentment; fulfillment; radiating outward.

Think about what brings you deep satisfaction.

Ponder the idea of feeling a sense of completion within yourself.

Contemplate with an active imagination what you want to make happen, as there is magic and magnetism if you tap into it.

What would I need to feel completely fulfilled?

How can I act upon my conscious ideal to break through any block to my inner gratification?

My life is satisfying and fulfilling.

50.

Detaching with the Princess of Cups

He who would be serene and pure
needs but one thing,
detachment.

Meister Eckhart

The Royal Cups are the masters or adepts that reveal the gifts in our emotional expression of consciousness.

The **Princess of Cups** is the **earthy part of water**. She is a master of emotional objectivity, for she has worked through negative habits of jealousy, possessiveness, and manipulation and is able to express love deeply and with detachment. This is the **Emotional Detacher** and the **Seduction Remover,** as she is free from entanglements and swimming in grace.

The Princess of Cups is immersed in water, and totally serene and comfortable with her abilities. A turtle in a shell signifies loyalty and emotional support and protection. She is committed to growing emotionally. The swan shows emotional security. The dolphin represents her ability to communicate all feelings in a pure and expressive way. The free floating lotus tells us that she is impartial, trusting, and able to let go.

In the I Ching, she is connected with 41, "**Decline,**" which means decreasing her emotional output. The downward arrow shows the need to be emotionally economical and reduce your demonstrative output.

Princess of Cups: Detach from your feelings and look at them from a distance. Gear down any emotional expression now and trust yourself.

The Princess of Cups has been linked to the **Moon** card, due to her emotional testing, but has come out with a sincere and simplified approach.

Princess of Cups represents all **Water signs**: Scorpio (October 23 to November 21); and Pisces (February 19 to March 20); but especially **Cancer** (June 21 to July 22).

This Water Princess inhabits **Kingdom** on the Tree of Life and here you are to embody a clarified emotional state that is free from emotional exploitations and dramas, and to live as a creative being in touch with your body and your emotions.

Princess of Cups Key Words: The earthy part of water; emotional objectivity; detachment; emotional freedom; overcoming jealousy and entanglements; trust.

Ponder where you need to curb your instincts or desires and simply your life.

Visualize yourself emotionally free.

Have I completely eliminated jealousy and possessiveness?

Are there any places where I have an extravagant expression of emotions?

What do I need to do to be completely free of emotional baggage?

I love deeply with detachment and my life is filled with grace.

Prince of Cups: You feel your feelings deeply, but do not drown in them. Feel whatever you are feeling with awareness and objectivity. A lover may be moving toward you.

51.

Aspiring with the Prince of Cups

And ever has it been known that
love knows not its own depth
until the hour of separation.

Kahlil Gibran

The **Prince of Cups** is the **airy part of Water**. He deals with mastering your emotional needs. This image has the Prince happily drenched in water, showing how he can get totally immersed into the emotions, but does not drown in them. His deep desire for body, mind and feeling unified in mystical experience makes him the **Passionate Lover-Boy** of the deck. He has the ability to say, "I love you deeply, but I have the ability to detach and let go." This is shown with the heart cloud and the lotus falling from his hand.

His regenerative and transformative powers are shown through the coiled snake inside his cup.

The Prince of Cups is designated to **Scorpio** (October 23 to November 21), a profound sign with penetrating insight. His social sphere has intensity and tremendous psychological potency, for he comes together for meaningful experience.

In the I Ching, this water Prince is linked to 61, "**Insight**," for he has depth, true character and inner truth to be effective with the minimum amount of words or actions. The Prince of Cups resides in **Beauty** on the Tree of Life, and here you can balance love and power and bring healing and symmetry to your emotional center.

Prince of Cups Key Words: The airy part of water; Scorpio; depth of feeling; desires; loving; transformation; passion.

Ponder your deepest desires—those that are driving your life.

Visualize these desires being made manifest with heart and soul.

Have I let go of and forgiven all my past lovers?

Have I acknowledged my most profound wishes?

I am a lover of truth and awareness and my life is richly blessed.

52.

Reflecting with the Queen of Cups

By three methods we may gain wisdom:
First, by reflection, which is the noblest;
Second, by imitation, which is the easiest;
and third by experience, which is the bitterest.

Confucius

The **Queen of Cups** is the **watery part of water** and here you have a nurturing receptor. She is especially connected to **Cancer** (June 21 to July 22), as she is the **Mother Creator**. The stork flies above ready to deliver its bundle. She is one of the three cards that signify motherhood (along with the Empress and the Princess of Disks) and is gifted with children.

She relates to all the **Water signs**. As the window to the unconscious, she is an **Intuitive** and designated to Pisces (February 19 to March 20) as she wears the **Neptune** symbol and holds a seashell. She is associated with the **High Priestess** for she has great depth of vision to connect all things. A powerful and emotional nature is expressed as seen through her dress made of the sea. Her cup holds a pink lotus, which signifies blossoming love and receptivity.

This Queen is a **Reflector,** for she mirrors her own beauty and the beauty of others. Whatever is reflected from inside is expressed outwardly. She is also related to Scorpio (October 23 to November 22). She connects instinctively rather than on the level of reason.

Queen of Cups: Whatever you feel is reflected outside. Listen to your intuition. Nurture and give birth to your emotional desires.

Feeling and insights come from deep within and are reflected through heightened imagination and inspiration. She receives and transmits insights because she feels a sense of oneness with all.

In the I Ching she is linked with 58, "**Encouraging**," for her joyful uplifting ways of inspiring others.

The Queen of Cups resides in **Understanding** on the Tree of Life, which again gives her the archetypal Mother principle of nurturing and the Creator's ability to bring things into form. Her strong understanding coupled with good will and encouragement gives her an opportunity to communicate emotionally more deeply.

Queen of Cups Key Words: Watery part of water; Neptune; Pisces; reflection; psychic; motherhood; visionary; emotional expression.

Reflect on your inner beauty.

Trust your feelings and let them guide you.

Can I see how my outer reality is a reflection of my inner reality?

How can I show my deepest feelings more freely?

My open receptiveness makes me a clear channel of my Divine Feminine.

Knight of Cups: Look at where you are experiencing an emotional reward, for this is where you will find a deep interchange of like-mindedness.

53.

Mastering with the Knight of Cups

One can have no smaller
or greater mastery
than mastery of oneself.

Leonardo da Vinci

The **Knight of Cups** (or King in other decks) is the **fiery part of Water** and signifies inspired and ardent feelings. This image is a man practicing the art of movement on a beach; in his hand is his trophy cup. He is the **Emotional Reward Maker** and looks for what brings emotional fulfillment. The Knight of Cups is the only Knight without a headdress, which signifies his heartfelt openness. Within his consciousness is a Pegasus, the magical creature that uplifts his familial relationships.

In the I Ching, this Knight is associated with 54, "**Humility**," as he has overcome pompousness, vanity and arrogance, which are represented by the peacock. Here you have an experience of real love, for the Knight of Cups gives of himself without losing himself

Astrologically **Cancer** (June 21 to July 22) is designated to this energy as seen with the crab that crawls on the beach. Cancers love their family, community, tribe, and nation.

The Knight of Cups resides in **Wisdom** on the Tree of Life and brings the outgoing and dynamic Father Principle and male inspirational power to the feeling nature to generate new possibilities in an instant. This is an experience of enormous creativity, inner vision, and generosity of spirit.

Knight of Cups Key Words: Fiery part of Water; emotional reward; capacity for giving; openness; reaching for evolved emotions; spiritual relating.

Think about what service you would do for free.

Contemplate who is your true spiritual family.

How can I enhance and elevate my interactions with my relationships?

In my personal relationships am I truly being perceived for who I really am, rather than my roles?

As I express my true loving nature, all my relationships become rewarding.

Part V

Fiery Wands

Fire refers to a universal radiant energy, which is excitable, enthusiastic, and its light brings color into the world.

Stephen Arroyo

Ace of Wands: You have the insight and ability to burn away obstacles. Something new is about to start. Your enormous vital energy can express your authentic self. Trust your intuition and be aware of your insights,

54.
Perceiving with the Ace of Wands

Changing is not just
changing the things outside of us.
First of all we all need the right view
that transcends all notions
including being and non-being,
creator and creature, mind and spirit.
That kind of insight is crucial
for transformation and healing.

Thick Nhat Hanh

The **Wands** are the **fiery** perceptional and intuitive issues that deal with your inner workings. It is the energy that wants to flow spontaneously with inspiration and self-motivation. Wands are symbols for the spark within, deep inner changes, and the spiritual aspects of consciousness. There are two challenges that stifle our inner fires: strife and oppression. Your innate gifts abound with awareness, dominion, integrity, completion, victory, valor, swiftness, and strength. In timing, as a general rule, Wands can represent months.

The **Ace of Wands** represents an awakening perception and the enormous life force that is within us all. The figure is a sparkling, energizing, and electrifying being who holds a fire-burning torch and is determined to burn out inner blocks, obstacles, and beliefs. Bursting with inspiration, perception, vitality, intuition, and insights, this figure has tremendous cleansing energy. The light from within can be seen shining outwardly. In the

Ace of Wands there is no guarding or holding yourself back or editing your behavior. It is just pure awakened, self-actualized, authentic expression of the Self.

The Ace of Wands signifies all the **Fire signs**: Aries (March 21 to April 19); Leo (July 23 to August 22); and Sagittarius (November 22 to December 21).

The Ace of Wands resides in **Crown** on the Tree of Life and is Divinely inspired. It represents excellence and new insights and beginnings.

Ace of Wands Key Words: Fire; insight; awareness; new beginnings; spiritual perception; energy; authenticity; truth; self-realization.

Contemplate on your inner light. Focus on increasing its volume and capacity each day and shining it outwardly.

What keeps me from listening to my insights and intuition?

I am filled with wonder, curiosity, and new discoveries, which shine through my life. I express this enthusiastic awareness wisely.

55.

Empowering with the Two of Wands

You can have no dominion
greater or lesser
than that over yourself.

Leonardo daVinci

The **Two of Wands** is a state of **Dominion**, which is sovereignty over a dynamic, balanced, and integrated power.

This image has two vibrant horses dancing together in union; they represent power. Above them is the vital, burning sun. Below them are two integrated snakes, which symbolize penetrating, healing, and regenerating energy.

This card represents the male and female energy coming together and in some decks this has been interpreted as the marriage card.

The Two of Wands is designated astrologically to **Mars in Aries**, which is its natural place. It strengthens drive and vigorous potency and is a pioneering and initiating energy. Here is an experience of incisive action and potent force to clear inner obstacles. You own your power, authority, and autonomy in a balanced way and have control over your domain.

Even though Wands generally mean months, Aries (March 21 to April 19) has a sense of urgency, so the timing here is more likely two weeks. This energetic, adventurous, and powerful instigator is the will to do and create something new.

Two of Wands: You have real personal power and energy at your disposal and need to focus. Find your center and you will find your power to begin whatever you want and move in new directions.

This card represents the first decan of Aries which is from 0 to 10 degrees of that sign.

The Two of Wands inhabits **Wisdom**, on the Tree of Life, which reinforces the dynamic Father of inspired doing.

It is connected to the harmonizing and complementary number Two and to the intuitive, balanced, and independent **High Priestess**.

Two of Wands Key Words: Mars in Aries; dominion or mastering a situation; sovereignty; energy; focus; power; Warrior-like; dynamic; pioneer; union; renewal; balance; initiative movement.

Ponder where you want to place your energy and drive.

What do I need to initiate?

How can I instigate more personal power In my life?

I openly express my dynamic energy in positive and pioneering ways of renewal.

Three of Wands: You are true to yourself and will not compromise your virtue and integrity. As you focus on the present and your center, you can unify your mind, your body, and your feelings and operate without restrictions.

56.

Being True with the Three of Wands

I believe it is my nature to dance
to the beat of my heart,
the pulse of my blood and
the music in my mind.

Robert Fulghum

The **Three of Wands** is an experience of being true to oneself with **Virtue** and **Integrity.** This image is jumping forth and dynamically, radiantly, confidently, and honestly expressing herself. This free-flowing spirit has its focus on the present and the freedom of self-expression.

The astrological designator of this card is **Sun in Aries,** which is its exalted position. "I've got to be me. I have got to do my thing! I will not compromise what I intuitively feel or perceive," is its freedom cry. Aries (March 21 to April 19) is an innocent starting quality, optimism for the self, and a pioneering spirit that needs to take action. This vitality operates beyond the analytical mind so your true Awakened Self has free realm.

Three is the symbol of trinity and here you have a union of body, mind, and spirit or an alignment with thoughts, emotions, and actions.

The Tree of Wands resides in **Understanding** on the Tree of Life and the primordial feminine creativity nurtures its inner nature. Linked with the **Empress,** her fertility abounds with the ability and will to bring things to form.

The Three of Wands represents the second decan of Aries which is from 10 to 20 degrees.

Three of Wands Key Words: Sun in Aries; virtue; integrity; honest expression; uncompromising self-confidence.

Contemplate the words, "I have got to be me" and what that means for you.

Ponder a situation where you are coming from your center and living your life with integrity.

Are there any places where I am not true to myself?

Where and how do I compromise my integrity?

Where do I energetically project myself out into the world without fear?

I am true to myself and operate from a centered, integrated place within.

57.

Completing with the Four of Wands

Before we can move forward
in new directions
that have heart and meaning,
it is important
to complete that
which we have set in motion.

Angeles Arrien

The **Four of Wands** is **Completion**, where you end one phase and begin another. This card is a woman sitting before an evolutionary wheel, and in her fingers you see a spark of new life and new fire being created. She is adding insightfulness to her creativity. The Wheel is symbolic of evolving into Wholeness.

Astrologically this card is designated to **Venus in Aries**. Venus is the symbol of love, beauty, creativity, and desire. Aries (March 21 to April 19) is a vibrant initiative power. There is a lot of creative fire, enthusiasm, ardent expression, and vigorous energy where you can move toward your desires and magnetize what you want to you. It is a dynamic attracting force that vitalizes and energizes.

The Four of Wands instills the desire to resolve inner conflicts, such as simultaneously directing the creative force and bringing it to a close, as well as a need for independence and an eager desire to connect with others.

Four of Wands: You are ending one phase of your life and beginning another. This is a transition time, so be spontaneous and adventurous. Look at yourself with wholeness in mind.

This card represents the last decan of Aries which is from 20 to 30 degrees of that sign.

The Four of Wands sits in **Mercy** on the Tree of Life. This position adds generous benevolent vision to your inner evolution and blends it with forgiving kindness and compassionate grace.

The **Emperor** brings inspired doing to give a foundation and structure (from the number Four) to the perceptional changes.

Four of Wands Key Words: Venus in Aries; completion; initiations; endings and beginnings;

Contemplate what needs to leave your life and what needs to be initiated.

Ponder the idea of magnetically and receptively drawing to you your heart's desire

Are there any disparities in my relationships that need to be identified and resolved?

How can I magnetically draw to me what I truly desire?

As I complete old patterns, I am open to creative new ones.

Five of Wands: You feel blocked or limited from a belief like, "If it is not perfect, I don't want to do it." You may be testing yourself in a public situation. Relieve your anxiety by disciplining your creative urge to make things better.

58.

Unblocking with the Five of Wands

Creativity involves breaking out
of established patterns
in order to look at things
in a different way.

Edward de Bono

The **Five of Wands** symbolizes a state of **Strife**, worrying, and hindrance, due to feelings of restriction or holding back your abundant energy or creativity. In the Five of Wands the contracted person stands in a beautiful cathedral with barbed wire and fearful eyes lurking above. There is an abundance of creative energy here, but it is stuck and not moving.

Astrologically **Saturn in Leo** is designated to this card. Saturn is the planet of limitations and boundaries and also of the desire to be perfect. Leo (July 23 to August 22) loves creative expression and power. When the self-restrictive principle connects with the urge for dramatic, creative expression, you have a fear of not being good enough. Frustration, strife, and anxiety generate little vitality flowing, which causes blocks in creativity. Saturn binds, limits, and controls self-expression, yet with time and patience can bring it to manifestation.

The Five of Wands is an experience of repression. Five is the number of change and something must change. It is time to take responsibility for your creativity with focused, consistent directions.

The Five of Wands represents the first decan of Leo, which is from 0 to 10 degrees.

Call on the **Hierophant** as your Internal Teacher to assist you in listening to your own inner voice.

Dwelling in **Severity** in the Tree of Life, it calls for disciplined and intentional determination. As you cut away what is no longer useful, set boundaries, and clarify your strength and confidence, you can trust your inner knowing to lead the way. Then you can reignite your inner fires of creative expression.

Five of Wands Key Words: Saturn in Leo; strife; anxiety; frustration; restriction; restraint; blocked creativity;

Contemplate how you hold yourself back or where you have stuck creative energy.

See if you have inherited any anxious patterns from your family.

Where do I block my intuition?

How do I resist my creativity?

I direct and ground my creative will to the manifestation of my dreams and overcome all obstacles.

59.

Winning with the Six of Wands

If you believe in yourself,
have dedication and pride
and never quit,
you'll be a winner.
The price of victory is high,
but so are the rewards.

Coach Bear Byrant

The **Six of Wands** is **Victory**, a **Breakthrough**, a **Win** of doing what is truly in your heart, intuition, and spiritual nature. The man is happily rejoicing in a triumph and the streamers flow in celebration. Here you have a win-win situation where everyone benefits.

Astrologically the benevolent **Jupiter in Leo** enlarges, inspires, and opens the creative process. Leo (July 23 to August 22) is joyful, creative self-expression and Jupiter is generous, expansive, and enthusiastic opportunities. Recognizing and doing what you love to do is one of life's great rewards.

This card represents the second ten degrees of Leo, which is from 10 to 20 degrees.

The Six of Wands inhabits **Beauty** on the Tree of Life and brings the union of love and power. Your radiant Core finds creative expression and visions of harmony and healing.

The **Lovers** card brings awareness of the different parts and balances and harmonizes the opposites within to create what you truly want.

Six of Wands: You know what you want to do and you are doing it. Congratulations for your inner win, your creative breakthrough, your expansive opportunities, and your inspired triumph.

Six of Wands Key Words: Jupiter in Leo; victory; winning; triumph; breakthrough; expansive self-expression.

Contemplate your highest vision of what you really want to do, then think about your mission statement and write it out.

Where in my life can I expand and open up to my creativity?

How can I improve myself through my creative work?

My creative expression brings me love, growth, wisdom, and fulfillment.

Seven of Wands: You have valor, courage and initiative energy to create something. Move on your creative visions with confidence and trust your intuition.

60.

Daring with the Seven of Wands

Perfect valor is to do,
without a witness,
all that we could do
before the whole world.

Francois de la Rochefoucauld

The **Seven of Wands** represents inner **Valor** or the courage to act on your spirituality with what you value. It moves on its creativity and pursues its goals with intentionality and pleasure. The Seven of Wands has a person courageously and energetically jumping over boulders to new directions.

Astrologically it is the vigorously creative **Mars in Leo,** which is dramatic, loving, and gallantly playful. Here is an experience that is character building, where you can come across with more depth. The changes happen first on the inner and then move to the outer with intentionality.

In Leo (July 23 to August 22) you want to have fun, dynamically express yourself, and be recognized. Mars is the doer, the initiator that directs you to shine, convey your free will, and share pleasure.

The Seven of Wands resides in **Victory** in the Tree of Life and here you learn about the grace of the Present and to bring love and pleasure to whatever you do. By contemplating and initiating what brings creative joy, you can expand your joyful heart. The **Chariot** also reinforces movement after sensing and contemplating things.

The Seven of Wands denotes the last decan of Leo, which is from 10 to 20 degrees of that sign.

Seven of Wands Key Words: Mars in Leo; valor; courage; creative inspiration; active self-expression.

Contemplate your next self-assured actions in your creative endeavors.

How do I actively express my need for recognition?

How do I assert myself and my creativity?

My resourceful self-expression penetrates my life as love in a creative process.

61.

Resolving with the Eight of Wands

A problem which appeared
insurmountable until now
fades meaninglessly
into the background
because of your clarity.

Gerd Zieglier

The **Eight of Wands** is the quality of **Swiftness**. It is when you open your mind to new ways of thinking and perceiving. This rendition is a circle situated on squares. There are blocks or obstacles being resolved and will be overcome as you see things differently.

Astrologically the Eight of Wands is designated to **Mercury in Sagittarius**. Mercury is the planet of your thinking process and communications. Sagittarius (November 22 to December 21) is quick and straightforward. Any obstruction can be resolved with swift, decisive action and by being expansive mentally and perceptually.

Here you can improve and express your belief systems. By examining what you think is truth, you can break down the parts of your conclusions to find your own answers.

With the right use of mind and the aligning influence of the **Adjustment,** you have the ability to see things in a completely new way. You can also manifest empowering and encouraging visions.

Eight of Wands: Meaning: A block or hindrance is being resolved. There is a new way of perceiving something. Communicate directly and be open to taking prompt action.

This card represents the first decan of Sagittarius, which is from 0 to 10 degrees.

The Eight of Wands sits in **Splendor** on the Tree of Life, which brings in sincerity and mental focus to perceptions. Eight is a power and leadership number.

Eight of Wands Key Words: Mercury in Sagittarius; swiftness; expansive communication; direct perception; clearing blocks.

Ponder where you feel blocked and how you restrict yourself.

How do I allow my beliefs to limit me?

How can I move through any hidden block?

What can I do to see things in a new way?

I see clearly as I quickly dissolve all inner obstacles.

Nine of Wands: You may be moving through some dark emotions, but you have amazing inner strength to bring your visions into form.

62.

Strengthening with the Nine of Wands

Stand up to your obstacles
and do something about them.
You will find that they haven't
the strength you think they have.

Norman Vincent Peale

The **Nine of Wands** is inner **Strength** that has vision and foresight. This rendition has a woman standing on her hands in a position of pure strength within a circle of inner fire. The background is darker at the top and lighter at the bottom, which illustrates that you have unlimited spiritual strength that comes from within to move through your personal trials.

The astrological designator is the **Sun and Moon in Sagittarius** and here you deal with inner and outer searching for truth as well as both conscious and unconscious intuitions. Sagittarius (November 22 to December 21) is the Universal and Mutable or changeable sign that inspires you to create higher truths that reflect your values and ideals.

The Nine of Wands signifies the second decan of Sagittarius, which is from 10 to 20 degrees.

Call in the **Hermit**, and go inward and allow him to teach you on the inner, so you can find your innate qualities of goodness, compassion, and inspiration. When you reflect on your inner light, you can know what you truly believe and aspire to be.

The Nine of Wands is connected to the dreamy astral plane, **Foundation** on the Tree of Life, where the secrets of the unconscious live. Here you can tap into the ability to magnetically attract your dreams, make yourself better, and bring magical healing and transformation to the world.

Nine of Wands: Key Words: Sun and Moon in Sagittarius; strength; inner vision and direction;

Ponder on your deepest visions.

How can I become more spiritually aware?

What are the obstacles that hold me back from my grandest visions of my life?

What can I do to improve myself?

I have the inner strength to move through any blocks to my visions.

63.

Overcoming with the Ten of Wands

Oppression does not make for
hearts as big as all outdoors.
Oppression makes us small.
Expressive and silenced.
Deep and dead.

Cherrie Moraga

The **Ten of Wands** represents an inner **Oppression**. Something within is blocking movement on your spiritual and intuitive visions. This card has a colorfully dressed woman traveling in a bleak and obstructed desert wasteland, as shown by the barbed wire. There is spark, drive and desire, but some limiting or repressive beliefs keep her held back.

Saturn in Sagittarius is the Astrological designator for this card. Saturn limits, binds or restricts, but also can manifest and bring to form through persistence and determination over time. Sagittarius (November 22 to December 21) represents a changeable and visionary adventurer. Here you need to restructure what you believe you can manifest.

As you acknowledge the power of words and what you tell yourself internally, you can see how you hold back your enthusiasm as well as your ability to manifest your desires.

Ten is the number of completion. You have to end a deep inner repressive pattern or major belief that is holding you captive.

Ten of Wands: You may have a limiting belief or vision that is oppressing you, or you may be experiencing an inner challenge philosophically, or you may undergoing some frustration traveling.

This card represents the last decan of Sagittarius, which is from 20 to 30 degrees.

Invoke the **Wheel of Fortune** to get more creative movement and optimism. Stay objective, be flexible, and keep adding energy to your creativity in order to fully express yourself. Believe in yourself and your ability to create an enlightened life.

On the Tree of Life, the Ten of Wands inhabits **Kingdom,** which tells you that you are to restructure your perceptions to embody your inner strength.

Key Words: Saturn in Sagittarius; oppression; restrictive beliefs; obstructions; inner blocks to power and vision.

Examine a belief that is holding you back.

Contemplate if you struggle between an inner conviction and a traditional belief.

How do I edit my visions and hold myself back?

How can I release any self-repressive patterns in order to manifest my visions?

I break out of all oppressions and live my visions.

Princess of Wands: You are being liberated from past fears and feel a sense of spontaneity and adventure. Being freed from an internal block, you experience a renewed spirit to be more true to yourself.

64.
Liberating with the Princess of Wands

What a liberation to realize that the
"voice in my head"
is not who I am.
"Who am I then?"
The one who sees that.

Eckhart Tolle

The **Princess of Wands** is the **earthy part of Fire**. As a grounded master **Liberator** of blocks, she is not letting the tiger (which symbolizes fear) affect her. Committed to creating her own beauty, she daringly and boldly dances in freedom to be true to herself. The Princess of Wands signifies courageously and defenselessly moving to free internal blocks. She tells us, "There is nothing to fear."

Astrologically she is designated to **Aries** (March 21 to April 19), which represents independence, self-assertion, and an adventurous individuality. Spontaneously celebrating life with enthusiastic vigor, this self-willed urge for action is an initiating spurt of energy toward a new experience.

In the I Ching, this Fire Princess has 27, "**Nourishing,**" for through the support of her self-perpetuating inner systems, she exercises discipline over her thoughts to break through all fears.

On the Tree of Life she resides in **Kingdom** and embodies a belief in herself and grounds her perceptual shifts to increase insightful awareness.

Princess of Wands Key Words: Earthy part of fire; overcoming fear; free spirit; liberation; new life; self-willed; assertive; inner optimism; breakthrough; independence.

Ponder your greatest apprehensions and then your greatest strengths.

Pay special attention to what you allow to enter into your sphere of influence.

How do I conquer my fears so I can be freer to be me?

How can I exercise vigilant discipline over my thought patterns so I can take my next step?

My fears have been transformed into a liberating strength.

65.
Creating with the Prince of Wands

Creativity is the natural extension
of our enthusiasm.

Earl Nightingale

The **Prince of Wands** is the **airy part of Fire** and a master of moving on his boundless, ingenious, creative expressions. He is the **Artist** and **Designer** of the deck. The Prince holds a fire-burning urn of ideas. A big rose is on his shirt near his heart to illustrate how lovingly creative he is. In the background is the lion, king of the jungle. He has inspired, instinctual power, focused attention, and faith in himself to let his imagination flow. This Prince knows where he's going and has the inner drive to move to manifest creations.

Astrologically the Prince of Wands is assigned to noble and generous **Leo** (July 23 to August 22), the sign that has a sense of drama and flair and a need for recognition. There is a deep passion to express, unfold spiritually, and regenerate.

In the I Ching, number 42, "**Benefit**" is connected to the Prince of Wands. There is great increase and exceptional energy expressed here. It is shown in the visual by the ascending arrow in the background. His expansive state of being absorbed with his creations and his creative synthesis has him associated with the **Art** Card, and also with the **Emperor**, for he knows where he is going and wants to ground his perceptions.

Prince of Wands: You have enormous creative energy and heartfelt generosity, so move on your inspired perceptions and imaginative projects and express yourself.

This card represent the inner dynamic spark, but also a younger man that inspires you to move on your creativity.

In the center of the Tree of Life, the Prince of Wands resides in **Beauty**. He inspires you to bring powerful love to your visions and consciously create with balance, harmony, healing, and redemption from your deep Core.

Prince of Wands Key Words: Airy part of Fire; Leo; abundant innovativeness; increase; creative flow and movement; inspired resourcefulness.

Contemplate how you can empower your creative genius.

Where can I express myself with love as a creative process?

What do I need to do to light the fire of my creativity?

I am in touch with my unlimited creativity and out flows a flood of inspired passions.

Queen of Wands: You are discovering inspiring aspects of yourself. Be proud of where you are and what you have accomplished.

66.

Esteeming with the Queen of Wands

To me, self-esteem is not self-love.
It is self-knowledge as in
recognizing and accepting
who you are.

Amity Gaige

The **Queen of Wands** is the **watery part of Fire**. She is the **Seeker** and **Finder** of the deck, for she knows who she is while remembering the dark places that took her to this knowing. The story goes that once she had dark hair and stood with the panther, but as she began to find herself, her hair changed to brown and her panther turned into a leopard. As she truly knew who she was, her hair turned golden, but she kept her leopard from changing, as the dark spots reminded her of what she had learned along her journey.

As a key to **Self-Esteem**, the Queen of Wands represents mastery of the self. The Pisces' (February 21 March 20) symbol is on her dress, which denotes her intuitive fluidity and movement toward self-actualization. She represents all the perceptual insightful selves—the **Fire signs**—Aries, Leo and Sagittarius, but especially **Aries**, as she represents the journey into Self-knowing.

In the I Ching, she is associated with 17, "**Following,**" for she knows when to act and when to be silent and rest, for she has arrived at a place of seeing. She is a woman of power, strength, and togetherness. She represents your inner feminine of self-mastery, or could be an older woman who gives you insight into your evolutionary journey.

The Queen of Wands resides in **Understanding** on the Tree of Life and brings the powerful feminine creative energy. She is a Nurturing Mother that feeds your inner growth to harvest your potential.

Queen of Wands Key Words: Watery part of Fire; self-knower; self-mastery; self-esteem; transformation.

Contemplate on your steps of self-growth and how you got where you are now.

What can I do to actualize myself this day, this year?

I am the embodiment of an awakened spiritual being.

67.

Revolutionizing with the Knight of Wands

Without continual growth
and progress,
such words as improvement,
achievement, and success
have no meaning.

Benjamin Franklin

The **Knight of Wands** is the **fiery part of Fire** and the master of inner growth and spiritual development. He is the inner **Revolutionary** who consumes all that is obsolete.

The man is a Jedi master holding the Ace of Wands as a fire-burning torch. He knows the power of inner strength to bring insightful awareness and the force of light to burn out all obstacles.

A unicorn flies ahead, which signifies the inspirational and magical power of flight. Here we have the enlightened **Visionary** with the power of insight and evolution. Self-expressive, intuitive, purposeful, and directive, the Knight of Wands dramatically moves on the spiritual quest, eagerly sharing his sacred dreams and foresight to make deep internal and external changes.

In the I Ching, he is linked with 51, "**Shocking,**" for he arouses and stimulates heightened experiences that bring awareness to the inner nature. Related to the **Tower,** he sets intentions and instigates drastic changes.

Knight of Wands: You are insightfully and quickly burning out inner obstacles. Your insight is amazingly perceptive. You are dramatically changing both internally and externally and can assist others with your visions.

The Knight of Wands represents all the **Fire signs**: Aries; Leo; and Sagittarius.

Whether you are male or female, the Knight of Wands is your inner male or could represent an man over 35 who shows you some opportunities for envisioning a greater self or a better direction to follow in your life.

The Knight of Wands sits in **Wisdom** in the Tree of Life and is full of dynamic inspirational revelations and creations. He uncovers deep inner resources combined with an outpouring energy to instantly create new possibilities and give you a powerful will to do good.

Knight of Wands Key Words: Fiery part of fire; inner growth; master of inner goals; dynamic forward movement; revolutionary change; clearing of inner barriers.

Ponder your visions of enlightenment and what needs to be burned away.

How can I bring my insights and inspired visions into reality?

I revolutionize my life and my spirituality by following my inner visions of love, peace and joy.

Part VI

Earthy Disks

An attunement with the earth element indicates
being in touch with the physical senses and
the here and now reality of the material world.

Steven Arroyo

Ace of Disks: You're unfolding on every level—spiritual, emotional, physical, and intellectual. Claim mastery over your life. It's the beginning of a new venture. You are organized, centered, and charged with prosperity.

68.
Unfolding with the Ace of Disks

This symbol is the highest of
the manifestation cards,
it is the capacity
to manifest or produce
what you want in both
internal and external worlds.

Angeles Arrien

The **Earth** element deals with the physical senses, the here-and-now practical realities, and the tangible world of form. **Disks** represent the material issues of health, finances, relationships, creativity, and career. There are two main challenges—worry and fear of failure.

This beautiful planet brings you great physical joys and along the way you will work, instigate change, acquire power, achieve success, be prudent, obtain gains, and accumulate great mental and physical wealth.

The **Ace of Disks** is the highest of the practical experiences. This centered, grounded, healthy, financially stable, and physically successful energy unfolds on every level. The background in the card has natural feathers to illustrate this unfoldment internally as well as externally.

In the *Awaken Tarot Cards,* the Ace of Disks is shown as a woman in joyful pleasure at receiving abundance in the form of coins and diamond jewels that flow like a fountain to her head. She is coming from an actualizing and prospering power to bring the spiritual down to Earth.

Aces always mean the beginning of a venture. The Ace of Disks is designated to all **Earth signs**: Taurus; Virgo; and Capricorn.

The Ace of Disks sits in the **Crown** on the Tree of Life, and is inspired with the breath of God. It is grounded, yet beyond barriers, as it is creativity manifested with compassionate excellence.

Ace of Disks Key Words: Earth element; inner and outer abundance; prosperity; success; fulfillment; integration of body and spirit, heaven and earth; wholeness.

Contemplate your center that connects you within and how you are unfolding.

How can I ground my body and center my visions to make them manifest?

What area of my life do I want to make more prosperous?

I am centered, grounded, healthy, prosperous, and unfolding on every level.

69.

Changing with the Two of Disks

There is nothing permanent
except change.
Heracltus

The **Two of Disks** is an experience of **Change**, a slow, steady, and perpetual change. This image is the yin and yang sign of balance, harmony, and integration, which unifies opposites. The snake symbolizes regeneration.

Jupiter in Capricorn is the astrological designator. Jupiter represents expansion and amplification. Capricorn (December 22 to January 19) is a grounded and stable sign. Here is change that encourages discipline and methodical growth. You can apply your ambitious aspirations and sustained improvements in a responsible and systematic manner.

Within the Two of Disks is an opportunity for transformation in a practical, persistent way.

The number Two brings in balancing and reconciling energy as well as expansive and contracting energy. Together they create self-controlled optimism.

The Two of Disks resides in **Wisdom** on the Tree of Life and signifies inspired and dynamic movement that stimulates new possibilities. On the earth plane, the movement is positive, sure, and steady.

You are to listen to your intuition of the **High Priestess** and balance the changes you make.

Two of Disks: It is the end of the old and the beginning of the new, a sense of urgency, but a needing to wait. The future looks great. Change is happening slow and sure, so open up and be patient.

This card covers the first decant of Capricorn, which is from 0 to 10 degrees.

Two of Disks Key Words: Jupiter in Capricorn; change; transformation; expansive and stable;

Contemplate what needs to change in your life.

How do I deal with change?

How can I balance expansion and contraction in my life?

I am constantly changing and evolving in an expansive and grounded way.

Three of Disks: It's time to work. You have the energy and perseverance to accomplish your goals, if you give them your total commitment. Ask your body, your mind, and your feelings if you have the necessary determination and focus.

70.
Working with the Three of Disks

Great works are performed
not by strength,
but by perseverance.

Samuel Johnson

The **Three of Disks** is asking you to commit in all three aspects—the body, mind, and feeling—and giving things the "**Works**." Here you have a figure working in front of a pyramid, which represents enormous energy. The symbols for the body, mind, and feeling are superimposed within this power structure. You are being asked to prioritize your commitments, in order to have clarity about where and on what you want to focus this disciplined vital force.

Mars in Capricorn is its designator and is the exalted position, which it is the best sign for active and dynamic Mars to be in. Capricorn (December 22 to January 19) is ambitious, concentrated, and tenacious. Together you have a sustained intention that has the determination to break through obstacles. If you know your limits and steadily focus the energy of your mind, heart, and actions, you can use it constructively and tangibly accomplish a great deal.

The number Three is creative, renewing, and expressive. The **Empress**' influence tells you to trust your creative resources and patiently create.

This card represents the second decan of Capricorn, which is from 10 to 20 degrees.

The Three of Disks sits in **Understanding** on the Tree of Life and this primordial loving Mother energy brings things into form. You need to learn to be persistent and disciplined in order to succeed and grow.

Three of Disks Key Words: Mars in Capricorn; work; toil; determination; focused energy moving steadily; duty.

Contemplate and clarify your major priorities and commitments.

What do I need to move through to accomplish?

Am I willing and committed to work hard to accomplish?

What do I need to initiate and move through in a step-by-step manner?

I have the willingness and perseverance to move through anything to achieve my goals.

71.

Empowering with the Four of Disks

The past cannot be changed.
The future is yet in your power.
Unknown

The **Four of Disks** is about personal **Power**, a sustained vital power. It is the receptive contained power of the feminine that knows its limitations and boundaries. This card is a figure holding herself, which represents contained personal power. The castle in the background shows solid, enclosed power or the ability to take care of and empower your own domain.

The **Sun in Capricorn** (December 22 to January 19) is the astrological designator. The Sun represents your vital Essence wrapped in your ego. Ambitious and dependable Capricorn is motivated to achieve in the world. Self-disciplined and willful, this sign is an experience of holding to the practical ambitions and one's personal integrity.

Fours have to do with solidifying and stabilizing structure. The **Emperor** adds a pioneering spirit and dynamic doer to your persistent ambitions.

The Four of Disks sits in **Mercy** and brings the gift of generosity, benevolence, and visions to this grounded vitality. When you add kindness, grace, and unconditional love to your personal power, you have the structures in place that you need to build and manifest.

Four of Disks: You have a contained, persistent, or sustained power to manifest. Know your limits and keep your boundaries. Listen to your heart and empower others and yourself.

The Four of Disks represents the last ten days of Capricorn, which includes 20 to 30 degrees of that sign.

Four of Disks Key Words: Sun in Capricorn; power; integrity; containment; character; boundaries; bringing into form.

Ponder what personal power and having mastery of your own life mean to you.

Are there any blocks to my personal power or anywhere I give my power away?

How can I be more honorable in my character or integrity?

I love what I am doing, living my ideals, and doing my best.

Five of Disks: Stop worrying and let go of those "bogged down" thoughts that repress you. Get into the present and open your mind to what is good and working.

72.

Being Concerned with the Five of Disks

Worry does not empty
tomorrow of its sorrow.
It empties today of its strength.

Corrie Ten Boom

The **Five of Disks** is **Worry**. Worry is negative prayer as it focuses on what is not working. This is a mindset stuck in old habits that feels like constricting thoughts that have a mechanical and grinding effect. It can mean inflexibility, doing too many things, or concern about money or health.

Mercury in Taurus is the astrological significator. Mercury is communication and what you think about. Taurus (April 20 to May 20) is slow and sure, and concerned personally with physical safety and security issues.

This card represents the first part of Taurus, which is from 0 to 10 degrees.

This Fixed sign resists change. There could be apprehension about what you are saying or receiving.

Five is a restless and changeable number. The Five of Disks sits in **Severity** on the Tree of Life and calls for disciplined intentions to move through the harsh, judgmental mind that gets anxiously bogged down in negativity. Trust your inner Warrior to take responsibility for your time and attention and cut away your oppressive and fearful, security-bound ways.

Call upon the **Hierophant,** which is the archetype that can guide you to listen to your intuition and stay in the present with a childlike wonder.

Five of Disks Key Words: Mercury in Taurus; worry; money or health concerns; restrictive thinking; brooding; survival fears; challenging communications.

Observe when your mind goes to worry or negative thoughts and slowly release them.

When you notice your mind is fixed on thoughts of what you don't want to experience, immediately change these thoughts to what you do want to experience.

How do I resist change?

Can I recognize any persistent mental belief that has me stuck in worrying with fear?

Are many of my thoughts in the past with "if only" or the future with "what if?"

My thoughts are free and focused on what is right, good, and working in my life.

73.

Succeeding with the Six of Disks

The foundation stones for
a balanced success are
honesty, character, integrity,
faith, and loyalty.
Zig Ziglar

The **Six of Disks** is physical **Success** or attainment. This figure has reached the pinnacle of a mountain, places the stake, and celebrates an achievement, both internally and externally. The Eastern spiritual symbol of the lotus flower is superimposed on the Western cross. Both denote inner success, which gives you the motivation to make your outer successes possible. The lotus is a sign of beauty and opening and unfolding. The cross signifies integration and synthesis of your experiences.

On the mountain is a circle with a six pointed star; the planets around it reveal how you can succeed. **Jupiter** advises you to expand, be open to opportunities, and positively expect your good to come. **Saturn** instructs you to be disciplined, persistent over time with a step-by-step approach. **Moon** conveys that you are to listen to your true feelings and your truth. **Mercury** tells you to direct and organize your mind and your communications toward your goals. **Venus** shares with you how you should follow your heart and what has meaning for you, and create for the sake of creating. **Mars** motivates you to assertively direct your energy toward your profession and intentions.

Six of Disks: Congratulations, pat yourself on the back and celebrate a success or achievement. You have worked hard for this accomplishment, so take time to enjoy it.

Moon is Taurus is the astrological designator, which is its exalted position, as this stable sign is the best place for the receptive and changeable Moon. Taurus (April 20 to May 20) is the sign of tangible and solid productivity and makes this archetype safe and secure financially and physically.

This card represents the second decan of Taurus, which goes from 10 to 20 degrees.

The number Six is a balanced and abundant energy that has the vibration of Divine inheritance. The **Lovers** brings in the desire to unify and blend all the different parts of you into a whole and complete creative manifestation.

The Six of Disks dwells in the Central Throne of **Beauty** on the Tree of Life, where heaven and earth come together in harmony, symmetry and healing. You can create and ground your visions and actualize your radiant Core Self.

Six of Disks Key Words: Moon in Taurus; success; triumph; achievement; deep inner motivation.

Ponder what success means to you.

What do I need to do to move toward my concept of inner success and outer achievement?

I have inner and outer success as I follow my heart and take practical grounding steps.

Seven of Disks: You are facing your fears and feeling of being constricted physically and financially. Release old memories of failing and apprehensions about how you can handle success. Have courage.

74.

Being Brave with the Seven of Disks

Every adversity, every failure,
every heartache carries within it the seed
of an equal or greater benefit.

Napolean Hill

The **Seven of Disks** is the **Fear of Failure** and also the **Fear of Success.** This figure is traveling over parched land and experiencing a mirage of apprehensive perceptions. Fear is contracting and distorting.

The Astrological significators for this card is **Saturn in Taurus**. Saturn represents your repressions and how you limit and restrict yourself, yet it also wants to bring things into form and manifest. Taurus (April 20 to May 20) is security-oriented, so there is a sense of feeling limited financially or failing to be productive.

The Seven of Disks represents the last decan of Taurus, which is from 20 to 30 degrees.

Face your need for security by looking at how you hold yourself back. The investigative, observing quality of the number Seven may help you. Call on the **Chariot** for the contemplative energy and drive to move out of these apprehensive spaces and transform them into positive tangible outcomes.

In the Tree of Life, all Sevens inhabit **Victory**, where you can tap into the present and your urge to make things better. If you "follow your bliss" and your instinctive gut pulls, you will be able to see, initiate, and persist in what has heart and meaning.

Seven of Disks Key Words: Saturn in Taurus; fear of failure; fear of success; miserly; contraction, physical frailty.

Ponder your deepest fears.

Now imagine what it would be like to be completely free of fear. Imagine you are pulling all the heavy constrictions out of your body and placing them to the side. Sense the lightness you feel without the fear.

As you sense the old fears sitting beside you, imagine them dissolving in the air and dissipating into moving energy and leaving you.

What are my apprehensions telling me about my conditioning?

I have the courage and willingness to succeed as well as to be happy with where I am now.

75.

Being Prudent with the Eight of Disks

Prudence is foresight and farsightedness.
It is the ability to make
immediate decisions
on the basis of
larger-range effects.
John Ortberg

The **Eight of Disks** is **Prudence**, being careful and cautious. This card has a guarded figure and in the background is a tree that is protecting the eight disks.

The astrological designator is **Sun in Virgo** (August 23 to September 22), which is a vitality that is focused on service, improvement, and orderliness. Virgo is the time of harvest. You harvest your power and effectiveness in the world when you gather wisdom, and are being prudent with your energy, time, diet, and organizational skills. Harvest comes from sowing the land and planting the seeds. With attention to the detail, watering, feeding, trust and patience, your creativity will flourish.

The Eight of Disks is connected to **Splendor** on the Tree of Life and brings in mental steadfastness to practical cautiousness.

Eight is a power and leadership number. When you add the **Adjustment's** ability to align and balance and when you add the right use of the mind's focus and reason, you can manifest impeccable creations.

Eight of Disks: Be prudent and careful. "Cover your bases" with practical details, grounded service, and orderiness, so you can reap the harvest of what you have sowed.

The Eight of Disks represents the first decan of Virgo, which is from 0 to 10 degrees.

Eight of Disks Key Words: Sun in Virgo; prudence; carefulness; organizing; protecting; nurturing creations.

Ponder where in your life you need more prudence.

Do I need more attention to details in the area of my diet?

How could I improve on my organizational skills?

I am prudently moving on in my life and receiving a great harvest.

Nine of Disks: You are experiencing gain by being orderly, following your heart, and asserting yourself. Enjoy the benefits of your labors.

76.

Gaining with the Nine of Disks

For everything you have missed,
you have gained something else,
and for everything you gain,
you lose something else.

Ralph Waldo Emerson

The **Nine of Disks** is **Gain** and hitting the mark. The figure is prancing in nature, and feeling advantageous, because she has hit the bull's eye. The target is filled with astrological symbols within colored circles. The planets give you a formula for how you can gain and have physical profits.

The top three symbols denote your dynamic or male energy. **Mars** symbolizes directing your motivation and vital energy. **Saturn** represents persistence, perseverance, and determination. **Jupiter** teaches openness, expansion, flexibility, and a positive attitude.

The bottom three symbols represent using your receptive nature to create gain. **Mercury** is utilizing the power of communication and the mind. The **Moon** is being open to your intuitive nature and trusting what comes from your authentic truth. **Venus** is following your heart and doing what you love and has meaning for you.

The three centers are color coded to represent the qualities you need to unify—blue for wisdom, pink for love, and green for creativity. When you integrate your creative wisdom and love, you reap tangible benefits.

Astrologically **Venus in Virgo** is assigned to this card. Venus represents love, beauty, creativity and what has heart and meaning. Virgo (August 23 to September 22) is a practical, detailed, orderly, and service-oriented sign. If you follow your heartfelt purposes and incorporate your wisdom, you will have substantial physical advantages.

The Nine of Disks represents the second decan of Virgo, which is from 10 to 20 degrees.

Nine is the number of completion, universal love and service. On the Tree of Life, the Nine of Disks dwells in **Foundation,** which is where your deep sensitivities and psychic perceptions are embodied to make things better. You can remember things from the subconscious and ground them into the material world.

Call on the **Hermit** if you need more insight into the internal path of perfection and how you can use this magnetic energy to be more self-sufficient, heal, and transform.

Nine of Disks Key Words: Venus in Virgo; gain; benefit; profit; "hitting the bully's eye;" advantage.

Ponder how you systemize what is in your heart.

How can I be more organized to bring my creative dreams into form?

I am enjoying the fruits of my efforts and appreciate all that I have and do.

77.

Knowing with the Ten of Disks

Learning is the beginning of wealth.
Learning is the beginning of health.
Learning is the beginning of spirituality.
Searching and learning is where
the miracle process all begins.

Jim Rohn

The **Ten of Disks** represents physical and financial **Wealth** and abundance, as well as a wealth of information. Knowledge has been gained and applied. The person looks out on the horizon from a wisdom cave. On the wall is the Tree of Life, which symbolizes a system toward God realization. There is also a treasure chest of riches that has come from the fruits of the mind. It all shows how you have the power to manifest, create your reality, and solve problems.

The astrological designator for this card is **Mercury in Virgo.** It is both its exalted position and its own ruler. Virgo (August 23 to September 22) is where you have a detailed, methodical mind that can organize and find connections. Your communication skills, adroit abilities and inspirations bring riches to you. There are healing gifts shown through the caduceus. You can realize wealth is on every level.

Call on the **Wheel of Fortune** so that the revolving creative changes keep coming. On the Tree of Life, the Ten of Disk sits in **Kingdom**, telling you to embody and ground the changes and to keep producing this wealth of transformational power.

Ten of Disks: You have great knowledge that can be applied to make your life better. Your communication skills and gifts bring you tangible blessings.

The Ten of Disks represents the last decan of Virgo, which is from 20 to 30 degrees of that sign.

Ten is the number of expressed manifestations and fulfillment, and the Ten of Disks wants you to use this wealth for practical service.

Ten of Disks Key Words: Mercury in Virgo; wealth; prosperity; abundance; knowledge; wisdom applied.

Suggestions: Contemplate wealth in your life and in your mind.

Where are you abundant in your life?

How can you make your mind more organized?

I use my mind to bring prosperity to me on every level.

Princess of Disks: New life is brewing. Prepare yourself for this birthing. You may be resolving issues of motherhood or of the offspring of your creativity.

78.

Impregnating with the Princess of Disks

Throw your dreams into
space like a kite,
and you do not know
what it will bring back,
a new life, a new friend,
a new love, a new country.

Anais Nin

The **Princess of Disks** is the **earthy part of Earth**. Full of new life brewing inside her, she signifies the fertile **Pregnant Woman**. She is the third symbol for motherhood, in addition to the Empress and the Queen of Cups. The Princess is the mother of new identity or concepts and grounds practical and innovative energy, for she bears within her the secrets of the future. Behind her is a dense forest telling you that she is coming from her own experience of understanding and wisdom.

The Astrological signs allocated to the Earth Princess are both the springtime **Aries** (March 21 to April 19) and the fall **Scorpio** (October 23 to November 21). She illustrates both an initiative power and a depth of feeling. She is associated with the **Art** card due her creative gifts and **Devil/Pan** for her passionate, penetrating power.

The Princess of Disks may represent a pregnant part of your psyche or it could be a younger woman who is helping you birth new forms.

In the I Ching, she is associated with 52, "**Meditation**," which is keeping still, as she needs to be centered, focus on the present and have an inner perspective in order to maintain objective and inner peace. She tells you not to project too far into the future, and instead apply what you value on the material plane, because the fruits of your labors are ready to be born.

She resides in **Kingdom** on the Tree of Life and her creations are an embodiment of all that she sees, touches, hears, and smells.

Princess of Disks Key Words: Earthy part of earth; Aries and Scorpio; pregnancy; birthing new life; Mother Earth; renewal.

Contemplate what wants to birth itself through you.

What do I need to do to nourish my new beginning?

I am fertile and birthing new life and creative forms into manifestation.

79.

Building with the Prince of Disks

I think of exercise as
the father of the body and
nutrition as the mother.

Mandy Ingber

The **Prince of Disks** is a master **Builder** who is nourished with exercise. He is the **airy part of Earth**. This Earth Prince is a **Sportsman** who is out exercising in the hills among the boulders. He moves surely and steadily through obstacles and nothing is going to stop him.

Astrologically the Prince of Disks is designated to **Taurus** (April 20 to May 20), which is a practical, solid energy that is interested in beauty, secure ventures, and profitable structures. Fruitful forms can be created. In the background are a house under construction and a bull. He is the concrete **Architectural Designer.** Taurus' bull is a symbol of power and determination.

Since the Prince of Disks applies and brings his creative ideas to the material world, there is a connection with the **Hierophant**. Because of his creative movement and great accomplishments, he is linked to the **Wheel of Fortune**.

This enduring and determined energy moves deliberately and steadily through blockages with a well thought-out plan. In the I Ching, he is associated with 53, "**Developing**," which allows a slow cultivation and natural unfoldment of things.

Prince of Disks: You are moving through blocks slowly, surely and steadily, and nothing is going to stop you. Time to take action in the area of exercise, sports, building, or designing.

The Prince of Disks can also indicate moving or traveling. He can be an aspect of your inner male or a younger man who can inspire and motivate you to build, exercise, travel, move, or be active in some other way.

The Prince sits in the creative center on the Tree of Life in **Beauty,** and brings the Core Self's qualities of harmony, balance, healing and redemption into the physical world.

Prince of Disks Key Words: Airy part of Earth; Taurus; Builder; Designer, master of structure; exercise; Sportsman; progressing through barriers; prudent.

Consider what physical activity helps you find satisfaction.

What can I improve with exercise in my life?

What activity could help me realize my true Self?

What new forms are calling me to design or build?

My creative work is developing, nourishing, and fulfilling me.

Queen of Disks: Time to nurture yourself with nutrition. Consider if there is something you need in your diet. Your life is much better and it's time to be persistent with healthy habits.

80.
Nurturing with the Queen of Disks

Nutrition is so important.
It cannot be stressed enough.

Dwayne Johnson

The **Queen of Disks** is the **watery part of Earth**. She is a master **Healer** and **Nutritionist** that improves life through healing with nutrition. She gives great attention, care, and nourishment to the physical body. She may be calling you to add or subtract something from your diet.

The creative Queen sits on the fertile ground, rejuvenated after being through long and barren times, as illustrated by the desolate path in her background.

Her crystal staff and her curled horns show her clarity and extra sensory perceptions. Her crown filled with peaches and a pineapple shows her fruitfulness and ability to renew. The goat beside her symbolizes her procreative power and ability to generate new life.

Astrologically the earth Queen is designated to self-controlled **Capricorn** (December 22 to January 19) and self-motivated **Aries** (March 21 to April 19) as shown by her horned crown. This Earth Queen is someone who is persistent, tenacious, and determined, who independently initiates new ventures in her self-care. This master of the body is committed to a natural environment, and is tied with the **Universe**.

Her creative and fruitful motherly instinct connects her with the **Empress.**

In the I Ching, she is associated with 31, "**Attraction**," as mutual attraction creates all things; for while she serves others, she allows others to influence her.

She can be a part of your inner feminine or she can represent a dynamic, directed woman over 35 who motivates you to take care of yourself and eat healthily.

The Queen of Disks resides in **Understanding** on the Tree of Life and again illustrates the nurturing Mother who creates and wills things into form. She asks you to be reasonable and agreeable adding the power of love to discipline and persistence with your diet choices.

Queen of Disks Key Words: Watery part of earth; Capricorn; Aries; fruitful; nutrition; nourishment; self-care; triumph over the barren past.

Ponder what is your best diet. Think about intermittent fasting, as it is healthy and doable.

What food or nutrient is my body telling me I need?

In what ways do I neglect my bodily needs, and what can I do to remedy this?

I nourish my body with the right diet and self-care and it blesses me with healthy energy and vitality to live in grace and joy.

81.

Healing with the Knight of Disks

Love and help others to rise to the higher levels
simply by pouring out love.
Love is infectious and the greatest
healing energy.

Sai Baba

The **Knight of Disks** is the **fiery part of Earth**, a master on the physical plane, yet bound to spirituality. As the **Healer** or **Doctor** of the deck, he is dedicated to the self-purification processes. This earthy Knight has diagnostic ability that can pertain to the body and the material realms.

The Knight of Disks is the **Harvester** and a **Producer of Life**. He walks with practical determination through the fertile land, where grains have been gathered and bundled. The wheat gives him an association with the **Hermit**.

He makes his inner wealth tangible and visible. His shield with the lion emblem is resting. It represents creative renewal and gives him a connection to **Leo**. He is in a time of replenishing through nurturing as he walks toward the sun. His horse is tired and getting nurtured. His prospects look positive. The antlers on his head symbolize expanded perceptions.

Astrologically all the **Earth signs**, Taurus, Virgo, and Capricorn, are assigned to this Knight. Earth signs gives it grounding, practical know-how, and tangible skills. He is the **Manifester, Financier,** or **Investor**.

Knight of Disks: The future looks good, but it is going to take some time. This is the healer. Be of service, as your work will reap the harvest. You will manifest and reap what you have sowed.

In the I Ching, the Knight of Disks is connected to 62, "**Conscientiousness**," which tells you that when you deal with the world and responsibilities, you are to have self-control and attend to details. As you cultivate your inner development, you are to maintain humility and dignity.

This archetype can represent the dynamic, grounded aspect of your psyche or an man older than 35 who helps you heal, manifest, and reap your reward.

The Knight of Disks, resides in **Wisdom** on the Tree of Life, and brings in the dynamic, inspirational Father energy that positively activates new possibilities. You have an outpouring of vital willpower that can be grounded and embodied to bring inspirational changes in the world.

Knight of Disks Key Words: Fiery part of Earth; Leo; Taurus; Virgo; and Capricorn; financial abundance; healing; harvest; toil; work.

Contemplate what is the positive outcome of your labors.

Focus on what you are learning.

What is my inner healer/doctor telling me to do to improve my health?

What do I need to do to reap my harvest?

My labors will succeed and bring me health, wealth, and happiness.

Part VII

Integrating Tarot

The Tarot map indicates interrelationships among different ways of being in the world.

Judith Rozhon

82.

Decoding the Path

Symbols are creative ideas, like keys,
they help to 'unlock' unintelligible connections of facts
and, thus enable man to penetrate deeper into the mystery of life.

M.L. van Franz

The main themes you are learning to embody are: balance; motion or initiating new things; creativity; healing; transformation; and self-actualization. You are to embark on the spiritual journey and awaken the Adventurer and Liberator of your fears, the (0) **Fool**.

You step on the Path of **Balance** with all the resourceful tools to create masterfully with the (1) Master Communicator, the **Magician/Magus**. To tune into your inner feminine is to awaken the Independence Intuitive Inner Knower, the (2) **High Priestess** and bring insight and balance. Tapping into your inner masculine is to know the (5) **Hierophant**, your Inner Teacher. You personify your outer female as you open to the (3) **Empress**, the Magnetic Mother and flourish in the fertile garden and creative resources within you. When you awaken your outer male, the (4) **Emperor**, you epitomize the Pioneer, Builder, and Doer. You balance the duality in your nature within your relationships, the (6) **Lovers**.

You set things into **Motion** by contemplating and choosing how and when to move, the (7) **Chariot**. You are to balance, adjust, and weigh your issues and your inner polarity with the (8) **Adjustment/Justice**. As you look within and are true to yourself, you continually move forward, but deal with the past, the (9) **Hermit**. When you open up and stay objective, flexible, and keep adding new creativity, you magnetize abundance with the (10) **Wheel of Fortune.** As you lust for your creativity, you do not let unknown fears get you off track, the (11) **Strength/ Lust**. You have to cut through the obstacles and look at things from a different perspective, the (12) **Hanged Man**.

Creativity, **Healing**, and **Transformation** or the Death/ Rebirth issues are your next type of learning. You need to let go of the old forms and allow them to be regenerated into the new with the (13) **Death/Rebirth** card. As you balance and integrate your emotions and perceptions, new life is initiated, (14) **Art/Temperance**. A sense of humor and looking at how you limit yourself helps you not take things so seriously, the (15) **Devil/Pan**. You are to instigate the elimination of any old forms, so that perception and healing can occur (16) **Tower**. The more you change your emotions into perceptions and trust yourself, the more self-esteem you have to bring universal energy to others and yourself, the (17) **Star**. As you communicate and break through old patterns, you have the ability to choose and be authentic, the (18) **Moon**.

Self-Actualization happens when you have enormous energy to express, and it is the creative dance of co-creation and collaboration that allows it, the (19) **Sun**. The passage of integration occurs through time with discernment and good judgment, (20) **Aeon/Judgment**. You are to expand your horizons and know that your inner world reflects the outer world, (21) **Universe**.

The Minor Arcana covers life's experiences as your challenges and opportunities through the four elemental levels.

On the **mental** journey, you are to learn how to use your mind as a masterful tool and overcome habitual beliefs as seen through the **Swords**. Things often start with the clarity of an idea (Ace). The workings of the mind are designed to enable you to find peaceful balance (2); clarity and openness (4); and a broader perspective on life (6). The Swords, also known as the mental realm, hold the most lessons. You are to move through your trials that you created from: your sad disagreements (3); your defeating attitudes (5); a sense of futility (7); a doubting deliberation (8); self-cruelty (9) and negative fears around love and money (10).

You master the mental realm when you act on your inspired thoughts (Knight); move through the mundane to innocent perceptions (Queen); cut through paradoxes to get to the truth (Prince); and control your emotional waves with the Mood Fighter (Princess).

The **Cups** deal with the **emotional** realm. Your thoughts and unconscious programming constantly stir your emotions. Your challenges are to master your emotional disappointments and vulnerability (5); indulgences and overdoing (7); and over giving (8). You have a great capacity to be and express love (Ace); to share love (2); and to communicate your emotions deeply and uniquely (3). You are to nurture yourself with self-care (4); find great pleasure in life's gifts (6); experience inner happiness (9); and emanate contentment (10).

You master your emotions when you detach from them (Princess); feel passionately and perceptively (Prince); reflect others and your own beauty (Queen); and are able to see the emotional rewards in life (Knight).

The Wands reveal when your inner fires, spirituality, intuition, and awareness, are ignited. You see that insight (Ace); personal power (2); integrity and self- expression (3); the ability to initiate and complete projects (4); and an inner knowing of doing what you want to do (6); valor and courage (7); new ways to perceive (8); and an internal strength (9) are all available. There remain two challenges that can smother your inner fires: fear of not being good enough, which creates the attitude "If it's not perfect I don't want to do it" (5) and oppressive beliefs (10).

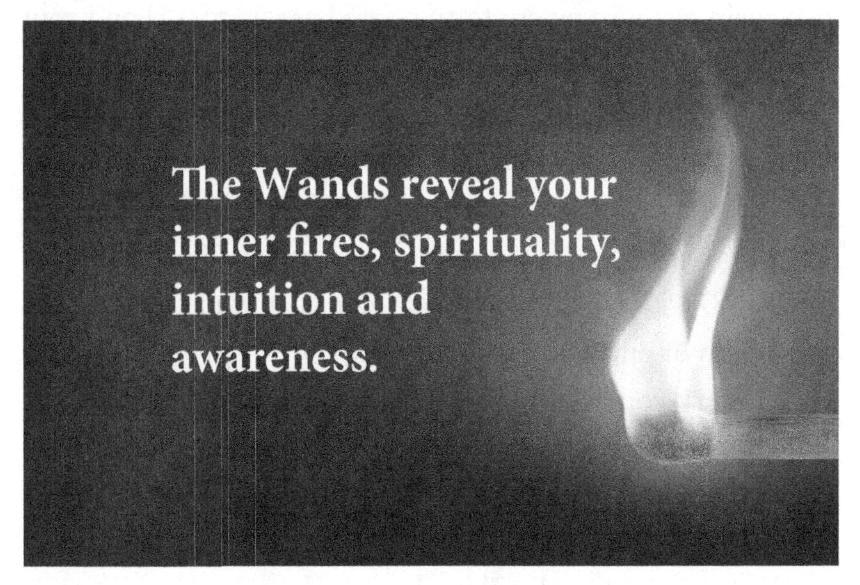

You master your perceptions with the ability to perceive and burn out the obstacles (Knight); doing your inner work and knowing and esteeming yourself (Queen); being creative (Prince); and liberating yourself from your fears (Princess).

Concerns of the **physical** and **financial** go deep into your body and your lifestyle and are revealed through the **Disks**. The two main lessons you are to transcend are worry (5) and your fear of failure (7). You have access to a great unfolding abundance (Ace), and if you are patient and expansive, you become open to change (2). If you are determined, willingly work (3) and are open to your personal power then in a slow but sure way (4), your success is assured (6). You have to be prudent and careful (8) and accept the physical gains (9); while you tap into the wealth of practical knowledge (10).

Mastery comes as you can experience your Inner Healer and Manifestor (Knight); activate your creative Nutritionist (Queen); exercise your Builder (Prince); and empower and impregnate new life (Princess).

The path within the Tarot is a complete guide to understanding your life process and how to grow and enhance it.

The Tarot archetypes give me a map of the evolutionary journey.

83.

Blending with the Major Arcana

The Tarot embodies symbolic presentations of universal ideas,
behind which lie the implicits of the human mind,
and it is this sense that they contain secret doctrine,
which is the realization by the few of truths
embedded in the consciousness of all.

A. E. Waite

The universal maps of Tarot and Astrology communicate life's energies and hold the keys to your evolutionary journey. It is a perfect blend, as the Tarot's twenty-two Major Arcana fits with the Astrology's ten major planets and twelve zodiac signs.

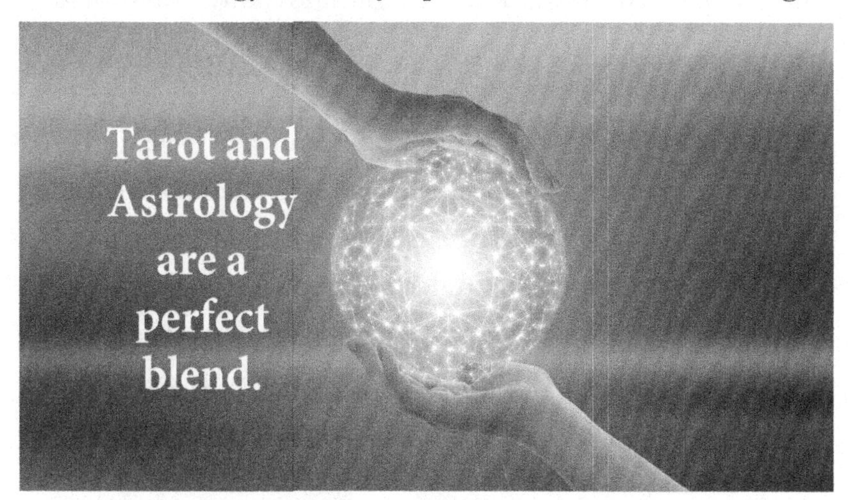

Here is a brief summary of the twenty-two Major Arcana cards as they reveal your learning:

You start and end with the (0/22) **Fool** who is designated to **Uranus.** This androgynous being is ready, willing, and able to hear the Call and to embark on the Great Adventure. Uranus is the **Rebel Genius**, the **Revolutionary Changer**, and your attunement to truth, originality, experimentation, and freedom. The Fool is a **Universal Soul** who tells you: "Take a leap of faith and move beyond any fear. Dare to be! Honor your uniqueness. Glorify yourself and be all that you are. Trust that you have within you all that is necessary to break free and achieve your goals. Believe it and it is yours. Dare to know and evolve."

The (1) **Magician** or **Magus** is **Mercury** and advises you to apply the right use of mind. Mercury is your creative skill or intelligence, the ability to convey information, reason, discriminate, and agree through objective and clear understanding. This **Gifted Communicator** and **Master of Symbols** is both personal and social and says, "Look beyond your conventional thought patterns toward the magic and power of thoughts. Keep your mind proactive. Be intentional and make choices. Communicate timely and with humor."

The (2) **High Priestess** is the **Moon**, the **Psychic Inner Knower**, which is responsive, sensitive, and adaptable. Moon is your personal need to nurture and be nurtured and your urge for inner contentment. Her reflections are: "Meditate and withdraw to hear your intuitive knowing. What do you see? What do you perceive? What do you feel? You know. Listen. Do not become your feelings, but pay attention to their messages."

The (3) **Empress** is **Venus**, your generous **Creative Giver**. A **Heartfelt Earth Mother**, the Empress shows you how you desire, express love, affection, find similarities, and show appreciation; as well as how you share with others, and find beauty. She is an **Allowing Lover** and a **Fruitful Creator**. She loves for its own sake. Her motto is: "Love and allow. Accept what

Is. Trust your enormous creative resources. Create for the sake of creating."

The (4) **Emperor** is the Fire sign **Aries**. Dynamic, assertive Mars rules Aries, whose symbol is the ram and reveals an independent, pioneering, and initiating spirit. Being personal and Cardinal, it is a self-willed urge for action and release toward new experiences. This **In-Charge Leader** directs you to: "Pioneer. Build. Do. Initiate. Assert, and take the world in your hands. Rise to the occasion and become your own authority."

The (5) **Hierophant** is the Fixed Earth sign **Taurus**. Ruled by Venus with the symbol of the bull, personal Taurus strives for comfort, security, and beauty. With the depth for appreciation that relates to physical sensations, it can be steady, retentive, and possessive. The Hierophant is a **Sage**, the **Pope**, and **Spiritual Teacher** who wants to instruct you to: "Listen to your inner Sage. Bring in the sacred. Trust your innocence. Manifest by applying your inner knowing and faith to a better and higher life."

The (6) **Lovers** are designated to the Air sign **Gemini**, which is a Personal Mutable sign. Ruled by Mercury, its symbol is the twins. It is a curious, changeable, friendly and relational energy that likes to observe immediate perceptions and verbalize the connections. Through this **Bonder** you are taught: "Combine your heart and your head. Watch how you restrict your self-expression. Look at relationships as a mirror and an aspect of yourself."

The (7) **Chariot** is connected to the sensitive Water sign **Cancer**, which is a Personal Cardinal sign. It is motivated to move outside and set up a situation to which it can respond.

Ruled by the changeable Moon, it is moody, imaginative, and nurturing. There is a focus on the home, family, tribe, or nation. It is reserved and instinctively protective like its symbol the crab. This **Contemplative Mover** declares: "Set something in motion. Choose what has heart and meaning by following your feelings. Get in touch with your personal power and set your intentions."

The (8) **Adjustment/Justice** is connected to the Air sign **Libra**, which is ruled by tactful Venus. Social and Cardinal, Libra is oriented toward others and moves toward harmonizing differences for the completion of the personal self. Its symbol, the scales, shows the impartial adjusting and balancing of opposites. This **Equilibrator** decrees: "Balance, weigh, be fair, simplify, and seek equilibrium."

The (9) **Hermit** is assigned to the Earth sign **Virgo**, which is ruled by Mercury. Social and Mutable, Virgo is helpful, detailed-oriented with a need to serve, analyze, and discern so that life can have order and be systemized. Its symbol, the Virgin, shows the need to perfect. Virgo observes what is wrong and how to make it right. This **Way Shower** directs you inward and says: "Take alone time. Contemplate. Introspect. Be true to yourself. Strive for meaning and to make things better. Choose life from a sense of completion."

The (10) **Wheel of Fortune** is connected to expansive **Jupiter**, which rules the Universal Fire sign, Sagittarius. Optimistic and hopeful, Jupiter is the urge to develop and be more than the self that you know. This inner **Guru** is your faith, openness to grace, and reliance on a higher power. The **Wheel of Fortune** is your **Creative Enhancer** who teaches you to: "Be objective, open, and keep adding new fire to your creativity. Connect with your patterns and beliefs. Follow your visions and believe in something greater than yourself."

The (11) **Lust/Strength** card is connected to the creative Fire sign **Leo** that is ruled by the Sun. Social and Fixed, Leo represents sustained warmth and vital radiance and is dynamic, playful, and self-expressive. Like its symbol the lion, Lust/Strength is the urge for recognition. This **Creator** directs you to: "Take conscious control of your creativity and your strengths. Express, play, and move beyond the unconscious to Source."

The (12) **Hanged Man** is connected with the nebulous Lord of the Oceans, **Neptune**, and ruled by the Universal, Mutable water sign Pisces. Neptune is the **Mystical Escapist** and the urge to rise higher in consciousness. It is an attunement with spirituality, an all-encompassing compassion, and the living of an ideal. It also has self-destructive, non-committal, and evasive tendencies. The Hanged Man is the **Pattern Dissolver** and illustrates: "Surrender and look at life from a different perceptive. Explore your ego patterns and emotional wounding, so that you see your hang-ups."

The (13) **Death/Rebirth** card is the Water sign **Scorpio**, which is ruled by Pluto. Scorpio, a Social, Fixed sign, is a penetrating drive to delve into the depth of emotional power. It is the **Catalytic Transformer**, the **Eliminator**, and **Renovator** who eradicates and restores. Scorpio has several symbols: the scorpion that crawls on the ground and bites; the snake that sheds its skin; the eagle that flies at a high attitude, which gives it a broader perception, and the Phoenix, from out of the ashes new life is born. Death/Rebirth says: "Let go and cut away the apparent limitations in your life and whatever is outworn and no longer needed. Penetrate to the roots of your psyche and uncover the mystery of your attachments."

The (14) **Art/Temperance** is connected to the Fire sign **Sagittarius**. Jupiter rules Sagittarius and its symbol is the Archer. This Universal and Mutable sign shows a restless, uplifting, enthusiastic spirit that is striving for knowledge. It is concerned with beliefs, generalizations, and ideals. This **Integrator** says: "Integrate your passions and your creativity. Blend your motivations with your emotions, your dynamic side with your receptive side, and your mind with your heart to create something. Examine your belief systems, for they become your truth."

The (15) **Devil/Pan** card relates to Capricorn, the Earth sign, which is ruled by Saturn and whose symbol is the goat. Capricorn is a both a Universal and a Cardinal sign, has a practical, persistent, and impersonal determination to build and get things done. This is a self-controlled, cautious, reserved, and **Ambitious Climber** that moves and perfects. Ironically, Capricorns are known for their humor. This **Merrymaker** enjoins you to: "Enjoy yourself. Lighten up and don't take yourself so seriously. Look how you limit yourself and apply yourself to strengthen your own will."

The (16) **Tower** card is designated to the motivational and initiating planet **Mars**. It rules Aries, which is the dynamic, courageous, impatient, and willful **Driver**. In the Tower your motivation to do, act, and assert a personal aim is stimulated. This **Renovator** reveals: "Be encouraged to release and clear away your conditioning and all unhealthy habits and patterns so that you can renovate your life. Be vigilant of your mind and motivations."

The (17) **Star** is associated with the air sign **Aquarius,** which is ruled by Uranus and is symbolized by the Water Bearer. Universal and Fixed, this highly individualistic and freedom loving sign represents community, group evolution, and a detached coordination of people and concepts. This **Universal Channel of Wisdom** and **Self-Esteem** teaches: "Believe in yourself and your power and ability to manifest. Change your emotions into perceptions. Feel your connection with all humanity and trust the flow of the Universe."

The (18) **Moon** card is linked with the idealistic Water sign **Pisces,** which is ruled by Neptune. Collective and changeable, Pisces is symbolized as two fishes swimming in opposite directions, which denotes counter pulls. It represents inspiration and idealism as well as escapism and vulnerability. Here is a soul yearning to transcend, one that has healing compassion for all that suffer. This is the **Authentic Smasher of Relationship Patterns.** The Moon card expounds: "Break through your illusions and ideals. Explore your shadow and the unconscious patterns that come out in your relationships. Wake up from your trances. Communicate and use your mind power to create the reality you want."

The (19) **Sun** card is connected to the luminary **Sun,** which rules the Social, Fixed, and Fire sign Leo. Astrologically the Sun is your Essence wrapped in your ego. As the outpouring of love, creativity, and spirit, your individual self is your basic drive to be and to express. The Sun card is the **Co-Creator, Collaborator,** and **Synthesizer.** This **Radiant Life Force** tells you to: "Shine and express yourself and your intentions, join with others, and co-create with the Divine on this abundant earth."

The (20) **Aeon/Judgment** card is associated with the primal **Pluto**. Pluto is your **Rota Rooter**, a racking ball that has a powerful drive to renew and transform through letting go. It is the need to face the depth of your obsessions, compulsions, and desires and transmutes them through effort and intense experience. This **Evolutionary Changer** teaches: "Refine yourself by taking the time to penetrate into your unconscious family patterns so you can transform them."

The (21) **Universe/World** card is related to Saturn, Capricorn's ruler. Saturn is your defensive **Taskmaster**, the archetypical **Father**, who rules our consensus reality. It is how you restrict, control, bind, limit, and bring to form and manifest through disciplined effort and an acceptance of duty and responsibility. The **Cosmic Being** instructs you to: "Cut through your limitations. Branch out into the world. Strive to be better. Practice economy and conserve resources. Keep giving structure to your intentions. Recognize the existence of Spirit within the laws of the Universe. Harvest what you have sowed."

The Major Arcana are the universal principles you possess and encounter. Their themes teach you to balance your heart and your mind, your conscious and unconscious, your feminine and masculine parts, and your inner and outer natures. As you set things in motion and initiate new things, you can express your creativity. You heal and transform by dying to the old ways and being reborn to who you truly are.

The Major Arcara with its astrological correlations gives me a Divine Curriculum.

84.

Connecting with the Hero's Journey

Like the eye, Tarot is a vehicle
for awareness and facilitates our sight.
It is a magnifying glass that shows what is apparent,
but undeveloped within an individual.
Akin to the x-ray, it reveals what is hidden but not obvious.
The telescopic properties enable us
to see far into the unconscious.
It gives a wide-angle, fish-eye view
that allows us to picture
all the elements of the Universe.
Like the hour-glass, it provides time perspectives.
It is microscopic as it can be applied in depth
to any one aspect of our lives.

Angeles Arrien

The Tarot is a fascinating road map of the spiritual path and connects with Campbell's Hero's Journey.

In Part I, you "Separate from the Past" to hear the "Call to Adventure" through the (0) Fool who is ready, willing and able to venture forth into the Spiritual Quest.

You deal with your "Refusal to Return" as you learn to handle the challenging cards in the Minor Arcana. Your ego's fixations and your emotional wounding are often reflected in all your relationships, the (6) Lovers, as they become a mirror of your inner journey. "Supernatural Aids" come from many places, but especially through your own intuition, the (2) High Priestess. As you can release old ways of being you let go and regenerate,

(13) Death/Rebirth. You can heal your "Belly of the Whale" as you surrender old emotional patterns, the (12) Hanged Man.

"Crossing the Threshold" of consciousness comes by setting things in motion the (7) Chariot; after introspection, perfection, and contemplation, the (9) Hermit; and utilizing the tools of Magnetic Creation of attraction and intention, the (10) Wheel of Fortune.

In Part II, there are six "Initiations:" "The Road of Trials" teaches you the power of your mind, the (1) Magician, and to be proactive or focus positively.

You are to love and allow or "Meet the Goddess" through the (3) Empress and overcome the "Temptress" or the temptation to control, manipulate, struggle, and create drama.

You "Atone the Father" through the (4) Emperor and learn to own your authority and be responsible for your time, attention, and intention.

"Apotheosis," or making life sacred, comes through your inner spiritual teacher, the (5) Hierophant.

You can become the change that you want to manifest with the (8) Adjustment/Justice, by adjusting and balancing all the different pulls within and without, as well as by looking within for inspiration and the creative spark, the (11) Lust/Strength.

You give back what you have learned through Part III, "The Return. You experience the "Refusal to Return" until you integrate your creativity into a synthesized synergy, (14) Art/Temperance. You have to look at your limitations and learn to laugh at yourself with the (15) Devil; clear out and regenerate the old forms with the (16) Tower.

"Magical Flight" happens with the (17) Star, as you tap into the universal flow and move beyond any obstacles from past relationships or patterns, the (18) Moon.

You will be "Rescued from without through co-creation, collaboration, and cooperative teamwork and partnerships with the (19) Sun.

"Crossing the Return Threshold" is an integration and transformational process of the (20) Aeon.

You "Master Both Worlds" with the (21) Universe and expand to deal with your wholeness of being a spiritual soul walking on the earth plane. "Liberation" or being free from all the personality games encompasses the whole path.

The Minor Arcana gives you your life's opportunities and challenges, as you have lessons mentally, emotionally, perceptually and physically. It is here that you can expose how you "Refuse to Answer the Call," and dive into the "Belly of the Whale."

The passage through the signs gives you the pattern. Cardinal signs in each suit start or initiate, then you center and stabilize through the Fixed signs, and finally you change and give out the qualities through the Mutable.

You have the most negative lessons in the mind, for it is commonly described as a monkey and a chatterbox. Remember the mind is a great tool, but a poor master. The early Swords are Libra, which tells your mind to initiate peace (Two); consider the other (Three); and be open to negotiate (Four).

Through Aquarius, you learn to break out and revolutionize negative mental patterns of fear of defeat (Five); and futility, (Seven); and ground the broad, high-minded consciousness of scientific and humanitarian understanding, (Six).

The mutability of Gemini teaches you to gather knowledge, but to watch out for becoming scattered and overextended. You have to overcome the doubting indecisive mind (Eight); self-cruelty, which has turned criticalness on itself (Nine); and the despair of an overactive, fearful mind (Ten).

The Water element covers your emotional initiations and your lunge into the "Belly of the Whale." Our bodies are mostly water and we live on a planet that is mostly water, so our feeling waves are important lessons. The Cardinal water sign, Cancer, teaches you to give nurturing self-care and to set up a situation that can get you a response. You are to give love and be Love (Two); communicate from your heart and bestow encouraging feelings (Three); and provide self-nourishing fulfillment (Four) so that you can share with others.

Scorpio, the Fixed Water sign, deals with deep inner current and the process of letting go. You are capable of deep and abiding pleasure, as it is your birthright to revitalize and regenerate yourself (Six). You have to learn to deal with and let go of disappointments and vulnerabilities (Five), and addictive habits of debauchery or overdoing and overreacting, depression, and general moodiness (Seven).

The Mutable water is the fluid, sensitive Pisces. You have to dispense with the pattern of indolence or over-giving or doing for others while sacrificing yourself (Eight). Great outer abundant happiness (Nine) and inner emotional satisfaction (Ten) are your Divine right.

The Fire element is your spirit and intuitive life force. With Aries, the Cardinal Fire sign, you have the initiative power of an independent dynamic spirit. You learn that the spark within is balanced and integrated with a sense of sovereignty and dominion (Two). You need to be true to yourself and act with virtue and integrity (Three); and continually complete what you initiate so you can move in new directions (Four).

The Fixed Fire sign, Leo, wants to emanate dynamic creative expressions. You often have to deal with strife, anxiety, or frustration due to fear and holding yourself back (Five). When you open to an inspired expression of your vital inner force, you experience an inner victory (Six). What you have to do is dare to be all that you are by centering in valor (Seven).

The Mutable Fire sign, Sagittarius, has an aspiration to grow and venture into expansive and higher consciousness. You have to open to new ways of seeing things (Eight) and disperse with any inner blocks, old beliefs, and oppressions (Ten). You can move through any dark places with your inner strength and vision (Nine).

The Disks deal with the Earth element, your physical, practical, and financial issues, which include the health of your body and your money. The Cardinal Earth sign, Capricorn, is a slow, sure, prodder who is climbing a mountain to achievement. It initiates by way of a willingness to patiently change (Two) and being determined to work and commit body, mind, and feelings to move through any obstacles (Three). Once you know your limits and boundaries, you can apply forceful sustained power to manifest (Four).

The Fixed Earth sign, the security-minded Taurus, is persistent and resistant to change. You have to overcome how the mind ruminates on worrisome concerns (Five) and deep fears of failure and inadequacies for success (Seven). Great physical and financial success is available to you when you stabilize the productivity of Taurus to manifest (Six).

Virgo, the Mutable Earth sign, is an orderly, industrious, and service-oriented sign that practices to make perfect. You are to be prudent and take care of the details in order to harvest your gifts (Eight). You gain and benefit in life when you organize your creativity into systems that work (Nine). Wealth and abundance can be yours if you use communication skills in methodical ways and align your mind with the abundance principles (Ten).

The Tarot, like Astrology and the Hero's journey, is a magnificent map and symbolic of all the laws operating in life.

I find great richness and guidance knowing the different and interrelated paths of evolution.

85.

Connecting the Numbers

We are all affected by vibrations
that govern the Universe.
Finding the vibration of numbers
gives us a chance to take
our place in the world.

Florence Campbell

Numbers are symbols and have a basic quality, with many layers and meanings. Symbols do not do anything or make anything happen—they are guides that announce the nature of things.

Aces are always positive and represent beginnings, the primal essence, and the highest of the element. The number one is an original, creative, pioneering, individualistic force that is yang or active and dynamic. All **Aces** relate to the (1) **Magus**. On the Tree of Life, Aces reside in Divine Crown and are infused with the spark of Divine Light and thus represents excellence.

Two represents balancing, harmonizing, and reconciling. It is feminine, receptive, magnetic, adaptive, and cooperative energy. There is duality and polarity. The Twos deal with moving toward something, as they have the Cardinal modality. In the Tarot, all the Twos are positive. We have peace (Two of Swords, Moon in Libra); love (Two of Cups, Venus in Cancer); dominion (Two of Wands, Mars in Aries); and change (Two of Disks, Jupiter in Capricorn). All the Twos have a connection with the (2) **High Priestess,** and to a lesser degree to (11) Lust/Strength and the (20) Aeon/Judgment. In the Tree of Life, the twos reside in the sphere of Wisdom and represent a positive outpouring energy that stimulates new possibilities.

Three is a creative, joyful, renewing, and outward expression. The qualities of three are imagination, enthusiasm, and inspiration. In the Tarot, the Threes deal with the dynamic, moving quality of the Cardinal signs. Sadness is a challenge that symbolizes a difference of opinion or the entrance of another person (Three of Swords, Saturn in Libra). All the other Threes are constructive. There are mental abundance (Three of Cups, Mercury in Cancer); virtue and integrity (Three of Wands, Sun in Aries); and commitment to work (Three of Disks, Mars in Capricorn). All Threes associate with the (3) **Empress**, and to a lesser degree the (12) Hanged Man, and the (21) Universe. In the Tree of Life, the Threes dwell in the sphere of Understanding, the great Feminine Sea of Consciousness that wills to form and compensates, forgives, and reasons with the power of Love.

Four has a practical, stable, industrious, and concentrative vibration. Four deals with systematic order, and solid, economical, pragmatic, and dependable energy. Four also deals astrologically with the motivation to move of the Cardinal signs. On the Tree of Life, all the Fours connect with Mercy, the generous, benevolent Father force that builds a container and framework for grace, compassionate power, and manifestation. In the Tarot all the Fours are opportunities. We have truce (Four of Swords, Jupiter in Libra); luxury (Four of Cups, Moon in Cancer); completion (Four of Wands, Venus in Aries); and personal power (Four of Disks, Sun in Capricorn). All Fours connect with the (4) **Emperor** and to a lesser degree (13) Death; and the (22/0) Fool. This means that there is a call to ground and initiate change in the Fours.

Fives have a progressive, freedom loving, versatile, adaptable, and changeable vibration. They are active, adventuresome, enthusiastic, hasty, unstable, and restless; yet have to deal with the rigidity of the Fixed signs. In the Tarot all the Fives represent challenges and lessons to learn. In the Tree of Life, all Fives are placed in the sphere of Severity with the Mars Warrior. There is a call for intention, boundaries, and discipline to clarify and destroy all that is counterproductive. We have the defeat patterns (Five of Swords, Venus in Aquarius); emotional disappointment (Five of Cups, Mars in Scorpio); perceptional strife (Five of Wands, Saturn in Leo); and physical worry (Five of Disk, Mercury in Taurus). All Fives have the special support of the inner wisdom of the (5) **Hierophant**, and the (14)

Art/Temperance. Listening and integrating change are what all Five's need to invoke.

Six is a balanced, humanitarian, artistic, protective, and providing frequency. It has the meaning of Divine inheritance, righteousness, and compassion. In the Tree of Life, the central sphere of Beauty hosts the Sixes, where we can express our radiant Core Self with symmetry, harmony and the power of creativity. All the Sixes are favorable, and in the Tarot deal with the sustaining and stability qualities of the Fixed signs. We have scientific knowledge (Six of Swords, Mercury in Aquarius); emotional pleasure (Six of Cups, Sun in Scorpio); inner victory (Six of Wands, Jupiter in Leo); and success (Six of Disks, Moon in Taurus). All Sixes have a vision of balance and redemption and relate with the (6) **Lovers** card and to a lesser degree the (15) Devil/Pan.

Seven has a philosophical, investigative, researching, and observant quality. It represents analytical seeking and thinking as well as contemplation, melancholy, mysticism and spirituality. In the Tarot, Sevens also deal with the inflexibility and stability of the Fixed signs. In the Tree of Life, Sevens deal with Venus' sphere of Victory. It is the pleasure principle with the ability to initiate instinctual gut responses and negotiate relationships with diplomacy and peace. We have three Seven challenges in Tarot: mental futility (Seven of Swords, Moon in Aquarius); emotional debauchery or overdoing (Seven of Cups, Venus in Scorpio); and the fear of failure and success (Seven of Disks, Saturn in Taurus). Courage and valor are our initiative gifts (Seven of Wands, Jupiter in Leo). All Sevens associate with the (7) **Chariot** and to a lesser degree with the (16) Tower.

The Sevens call you to restructure, instigate change, and stimulate the Warrior within.

Eight is a power number, authoritative, efficient, materialistic, and dependable with organized, executive, and leadership ability. It also has the frequency of frankness, impatience, and over activity, as well as the flexibility and changeableness of the Mutable signs. In the Tree of Life the Eights dwell in Splendor, Mercury's sphere, and have a receptivity to language and mental systems, as well as the power to focus, reason, and conceptualize. There are two challenges: the interfering, doubting mind (Eight of Sword, Jupiter in Gemini) and indolence or overdoing (Eight of Cups, Saturn in Pisces). The two constructive opportunities are perceptual swiftness (Eight of Wands, Mercury in Sagittarius); and prudence (Eight of Disks, Sun in Virgo). All Eights relate with the (8) **Adjustment/Justice** card and to a lesser degree the (17) Star card. The Eights call you to weigh matters and realign in a way that values and respects the personal self.

Nine is the number of completion, universal love, and service. It is an imaginative, intuitive, humanitarian, inventive, and charitable number. It also has the adaptability of the Mutable signs. In the Tree of Life the Nines dwells in the astral sphere of Foundation. Ruled by the Moon, it provides cyclical, magnetic, and electrical energy within the magical storehouse of dreams and the unconscious. The challenge is self-cruelty (Nine of Sword, Mars in Gemini). The opportunities are external happiness (Nine of Cups, Jupiter in Pisces); inner strength (Nine of Wands, Moon in Sagittarius); and gain, such as possessing and hitting the mark of achievement (Nine of Disks, Venus in

Virgo). All Nines are associated with the (9) **Hermit** and to a lesser degree the (18) Moon card. The nine calls for completing and being authentic.

Ten represents physical expressiveness, manifestation, and fulfillment. It has the changing, completing energy of the Mutable modality. In the Tree of Life the Tens sit with the Earth in the sphere Kingdom of physical creation and embodiment. There are two challenges: thoughts about financial and romantic ruin (Ten of Swords, the Sun in Gemini) and perceptual oppression (Ten of Wands, Saturn in Sagittarius). The gifts of the Tens are emotional satisfaction and contentment (Ten of Cups, Mars in Pisces) and wealth through knowledge (Ten of Disks, Mercury in Virgo). All the Tens relate to the (10) **Wheel of Fortune** and encourages you to call for objectivity, flexibility, and change.

Astrology, Numerology and the Tree of Life added together reveal an amazing amount of information. Numerology is entertaining, thought provoking, and incredibly accurate and easy. I will be offering a summary in *Awaken the Inner Archetypes*. Considering the numbers that make up the cards gives more meaning, which your intuition can draw upon.

I find meaning in the numbers, systems, and positions that add depth to the archetypes.

86.

Glancing into the Tree of Life

The Tree of Life is a diagram
which shows the ten
fundamental aspects
of the Life-power and their
relationship to each other.
It is also the key to the Tarot.

Paul Foster Case

The Kabbalah is an ancient, mystical system of knowledge whose structure provides the path of the Tarot. It is often spelled *Qabalah*. The word comes from Hebrew word *qabal*, which means, "to reveal or receive." It is a complex, multi-leveled formula. Often it is considered the secret wisdom and the steps to God-realization. A part of both Christian and Judaic traditions, it has been suggested that you do not study this subject until after you are forty, for you need maturity to understand it. I studied it briefly in the 1970's and found it involved and complicated as it has four different layers. References to it were in my scores of notes on the Tarot, and I found the information insightful and important in this rewriting. Here is a concise review to help you understand the structure of the Tarot.

The Tree of Life is the geometric structure within the Kabbalah. Its diagram is made of ten spheres (*sephiroth*), which are Divine emanations that channel influences into and out of the world. These stages show how you symbolically relate to the Creator.

There are three vertical pillars and seven horizontal planes of existence, which are the ten spheres that correspond to the numbered cards (Ace through Ten). The twenty-two paths between the spheres stand for the Major Arcana.

Here is what each of the three pillars represent:

The **masculine** right-hand pillar is called the **Pillar of Mercy,** or **Expansion**, for energy flows and is positive. It is more giving and holds the spheres **Wisdom, Mercy**, and **Victory**.

The **feminine** left-hand pillar is called the **Pillar of Severity, Constriction,** or **Form** for it is yin, more passive, and represents constriction and restriction. It has more to do with receiving and contains the spheres of **Understanding, Severity**, and **Splendor**.

The central pillar is the **Pillar of Harmony** or **Integration**, where these energies come into balance. It is more unifying and includes **Crown, Beauty, Foundation**, and **Kingdom**.

The planes show the stages of your spiritual descent and are similar to your bodily wheels or centers, shown through the Chakra system. From top to bottom they are:

7th Chakra or Spiritual Center: 1) **Crown**

6th Chakra, the Third Eye or Intuitive Center: 2) **Understanding** and 3) **Wisdom**

5th Chakra, the Throat or Expression Center: 4) **Mercy** and 5) **Severity**

4th Chakra, the Heart Center or the Higher Self: 6) **Beauty**

3rd Chakra, the Solar Plexus or Power Center: 7) **Victory** and 8) **Splendor**

2nd Chakra, or the Sacral or Emotional or Astral Center: 9) **Foundation**

1st Chakra or the Root or Physical or Survival Center: 10) **Kingdom**

Here is a brief look at the spheres within the Tree of Life with key words and phases that are not an exact fit to the ruling planets:

1. **Crown** (*Kether*) is the top and is the breath of God, the Creator, the Infinite, the All That Is. The Divine is where the first motion begins and to which we return. This is the state of Being that dissolves all barriers, the Nothingness that is above creation. Most hidden, it represents excellence and absolute compassion. This sphere has no astrological symbol. Its color is white and its symbol is the crown. All **Aces** are assigned here. From here we have the (0) **Fool**, the (1) **Magus**, and the (2) **High Priestess** at the height of the spiritual journey.

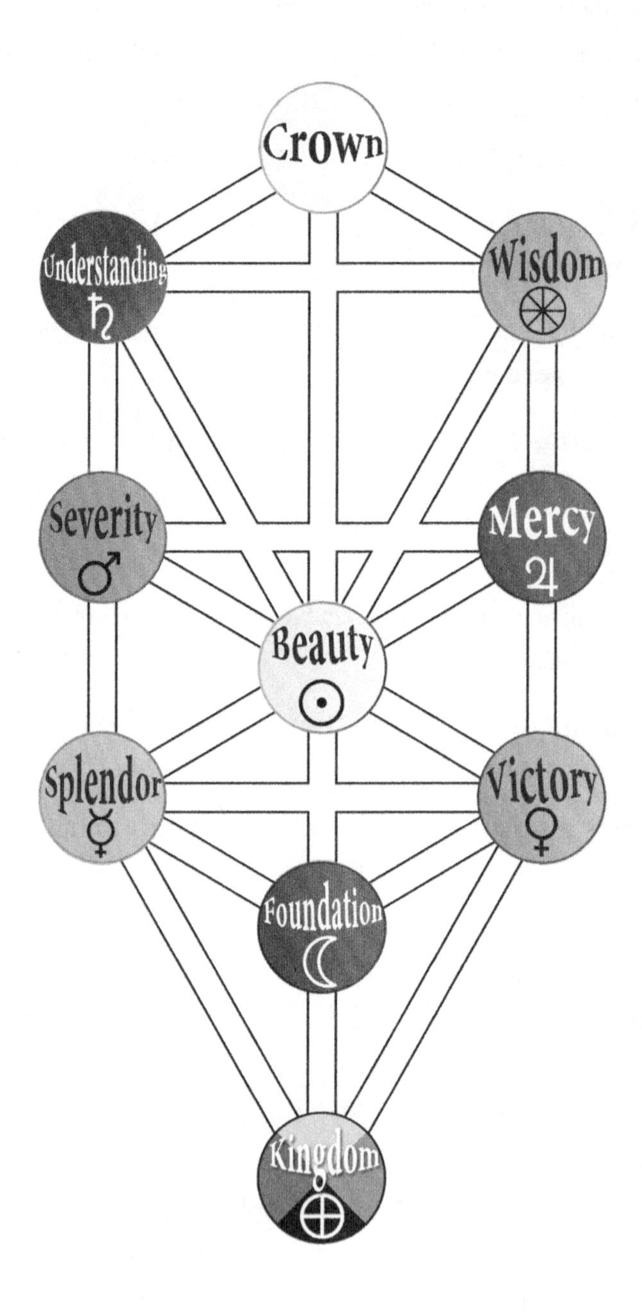
Crown
Understanding
Wisdom
Severity
Mercy
Beauty
Splendor
Victory
Foundation
Kingdom

2. **Wisdom** (*Chokmah*) is the Divine creation, the flash of revelation and inspiration. It is the Father principle, which is a positive, active, stimulating, and forceful will. This dynamic outpouring of energy is the doing state that generates new possibilities in an instant. The whole **Zodiac** is represented here. Its color is grey and its symbol is the phallus. The (0) **Fool**; the (3) **Empress**, the (4) **Emperor**, and the (5) **Hierophant**, come from Wisdom. The four **Twos** and the four **Knight/Kings** reside here.

3. **Understanding** (*Binah*) is the primordial feminine womb of energy, the Mother, the passive, the yin and the great sea that wills things to form. Connected to **Saturn**, it is the ability to see the Universal Laws at work, so that they are comprehensible. Although Astrologically Saturn is the archetypical Father, there is an ancient harvesting aspect that deals with the all-inclusive production of nourishment. Saturn helps you in the Understanding of your soul, as well as shows you the necessity for practices, discipline, persistence, and focus in order to succeed and grow. Here you compensate, atone, and reason with the power of Love. Its color is black and its symbol is the womb and the triangle. The (1) **Magus**, the (3) **Empress**, the (6) **Lovers**, and the (7) **Chariot** connect here. The four Threes and the four **Queens** originate from Understanding.

4. **Mercy** (*Chesed*) is overflowing generosity, benevolence, unconditional love, vision, and the intention to emulate the Divine. Astrologically it is designated to expansive and abundant **Jupiter**. Mercy is the receptacle of all kindness, grace, forgiveness, and compassionate power. Here is an active and powerful force that builds, structures, and manifests. Its color is blue, its

symbol, the square and the equal armed cross. The (5) **Hierophant**, the (8) **Adjustment/Justice**, the (9) **Hermit**, and the (10) **Wheel of Fortune** flow from Mercy. All the **Fours** are connected here.

5. **Severity** (*Geburah*) is the power of intention and discipline. The Hebrew word translates as "heroism," "bravery," or "valor." As the Warrior King and astrologically **Mars**, it resonates with strength, courage, power, energy, action and force, yet can be judgmental and harsh. On the feminine Pillar of Constriction and Form, it destroys all that is useless. It clarifies as well as sets boundaries. Here you deal with an ability to respond, judge, and determine. There are four Major Arcana that deal with this determination (7) **Chariot**, the (8) **Adjustment/Justice**, the (11) **Lust/Strength**, and the (12) **Hanged Man** course from mighty Severity. All four **Fives** reside here.

6. Right in the heart of the Tree of Life is **Beauty** (*Tiphareth*), which is the union of love and power, heaven and earth. Astrologically it is designated to the luminous **Sun**, from which you identify and express your radiant dynamic Core. This central sphere has been called the Throne of God and relates to the consciousness of your True Self. It represents symmetry, harmony, compassion, and the power of creativity. Here you have a vision of balance, healing, and redemption. Its color is yellow; its symbol, a rose cross. In the Tarot, the four **Sixes** and the **Princes** connect with Beauty. There are eight Major Arcana that emanated from this central light: the (2) **High Priestess**, the (4) **Emperor**, the (6) **Lovers**, the (9) **Hermit**, the (11) **Lust/Strength**, the (13) **Death/Rebirth**, the (14) **Art/Temperance**, and (15) **Devil/Pan**.

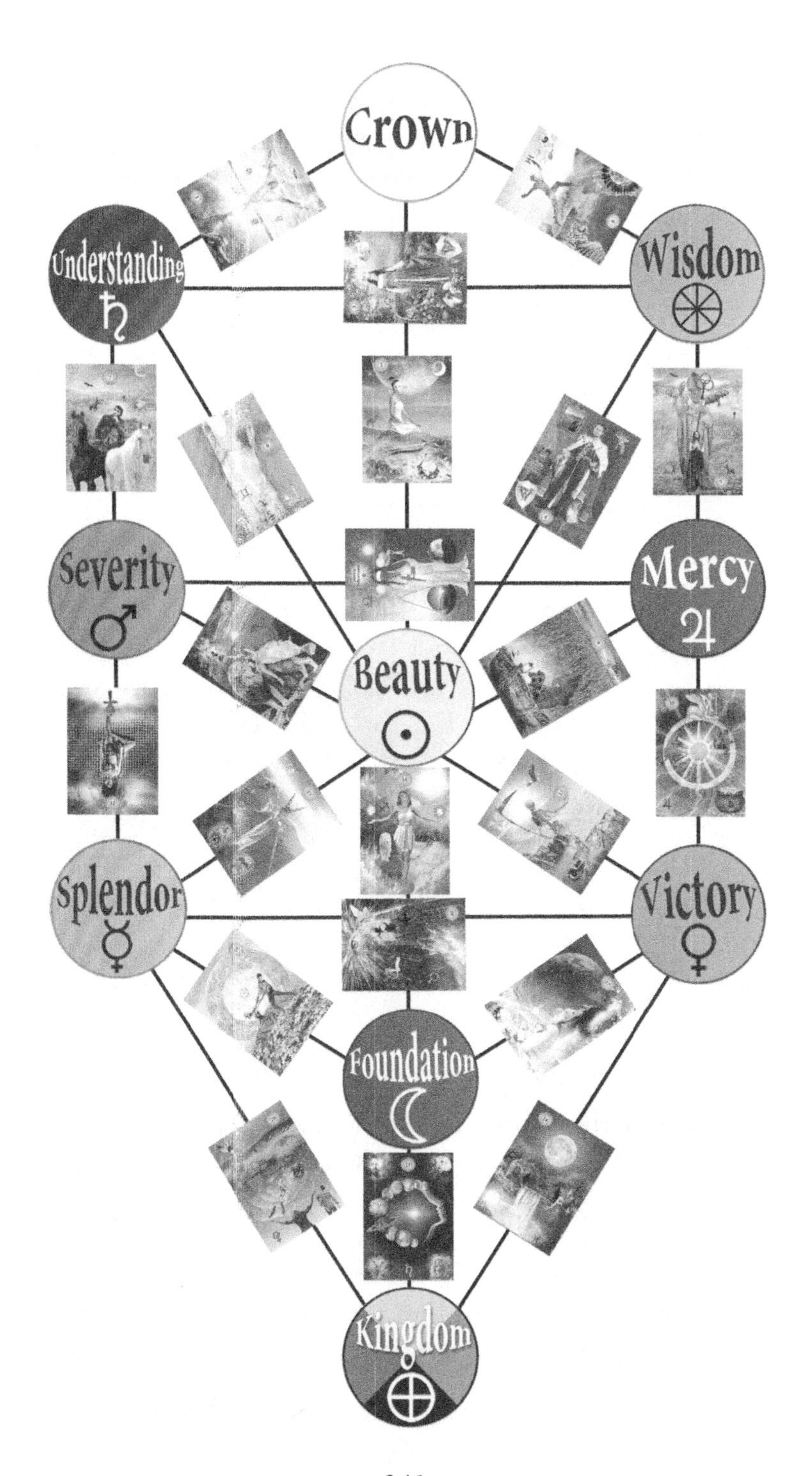
Crown
Understanding
Wisdom
Severity
Mercy
Beauty
Splendor
Victory
Foundation
Kingdom

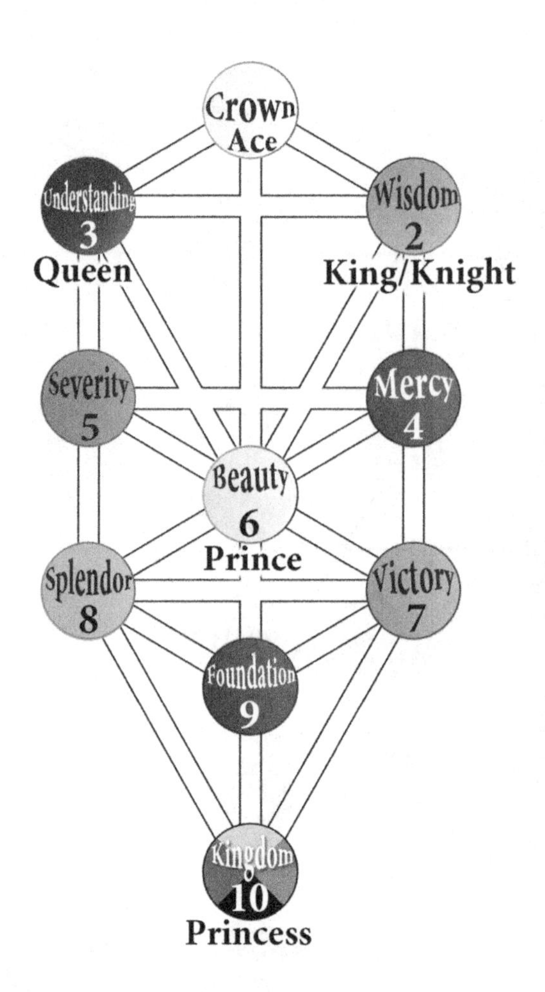

7. **Victory** (*Netzach*) is often called Eternity, for it has the active grace of the Now. It is the urge to repair or make the world better. Astrologically it is **Venus** and the sphere that gives love, pleasure, sensuality, and instinctual "gut" responses. With the ability to sense, feel, create, contemplate, initiate, and persist, it oversees peace, diplomacy, negotiations, and relationships, nature, and the arts. Here you expand your heart and sense of joy. Its color is green and its symbol is the rose. The five

Trump cards that connect to Victory are: (10) **Wheel of Fortune**, the (13) **Death/Rebirth**, the (16) **Tower**, the (18) **Moon** and the (19) **Star**. All the **Sevens** relate here.

8. **Splendor** (*Hod*) is astrologically **Mercury** and represents language, all forms of communications, visual images, and commerce. It includes systems, science, and magic or mind power with ability to observe, focus, reason, compute, and conceptualize. It has the receptivity of sincerity, impeccability, and steadfastness. Here you learn right use of mind. Its color is orange and its symbol, religious verses. There are five paths that link to Splendor: the (12) **Hanged Man**, the (15) **Devil/Pan**, the (16) **Tower**, the (19) **Sun** and the (20) **Aeon/Judgment**. All the **Eights** correlate with this sphere.

9. **Foundation** (*Yesod*) is astrologically the **Moon** and represents the cyclic energy of matter. This sphere includes the secrets of the subconscious and is the magical storehouse of dreams and images that underlies the material world. It is the ability to remember, to know, and to utilize attraction and sexual energy. Here you develop your astral light or your intuition and psychic sensitivity, which is both electric and magnetic energy. It governs hidden memories, transformation, and healing and knows exactly what it needs to feel secure. It is here in Foundation that the sleeping "kundalini serpent" lies dormant within you, which is the symbol of your creative fire and a source of your sexuality. There is magic in your sexuality if you discipline and harness it. Its color is violet and its symbols are perfume and sandals. The (14) **Art/Temperance**, the (17) **Star**, the (19) **Sun** and the (21) **Universe** connect with Foundation. All the **Nines** connect here.

10. **Kingdom** (*Malkuth*) is the place on which you live, breathe, see, touch, hear and smell. Astrologically it is the **Earth** and encompasses the entire physical creation. It is your body and ability to ground and feel embodied. Often the Earth is considered our classroom, for here we deal with our life's lessons. Its colors are crimson, olive, russet and black. Its symbol is the double cube. From the Kingdom, we have the (18) **Moon,** the (20) **Aeon/Judgment**, and the (21)**Universe**. All the **Tens** and the **Princesses** reside here.

This mystical symbol of the Kabbalah contains the laws for all creation. This Divine model is a primary structure for the Universe. Like its symbol, the tree is light at the top and then gets more grounded and dense at the bottom. It stretches from the Creator, which is above, and descends to our physical existence, which is below. Even though our discussion went from the highest to the lowest, you start your journey where you are and move from the Earth to the Creator and back again. The information within the Tree of Life is a revelation and type of spiritual light.

I embrace the archetype of the Tree of Life, which adds depth and insight to my knowledge of the Tarot symbols.

87.

Finding Ways to Understand the Archetypes

The seat of the soul is there,
where the inner and
outer worlds meet.

Novalis

To truly understand the symbols, it is wise to summarize them and to look at them in different ways. Here are some names for these Universal Spirits and the archetypical journey. The **Major Arcana** are the universal patterns in life:

The (0) Fool is the Courageous Adventurer; Iconoclast; Wanderer; Messenger; Rebel with a Cause; and Revolutionary Liberator.

The (1) Magician is the Magus; Juggler; Gifted Communicator; Master of Symbols; and Transformer.

The (2) High Priestess is the Psychic Inner Knower; the Intuitive One.

The (3) Empress is the Heartfelt Earth Mother; Allowing Lover; Creative Giver; and Fruitful Creator.

The (4) Emperor is the Pioneer; Doer; Builder; Authority; In-Charge Leader.

The (5) Hierophant is the Spiritual Teacher; Pope; Inner Guide; Sage and Spokesperson of the Gods.

The (6) Lovers is the Relationship Maker; Bonder; Dualistic Relater; and Inner Mirror.

The (7) Chariot is the Contemplative Mover and Traveler.

The (8) Adjustment/Justice is the Balancer and Fair Simplifier.

The (9) Hermit is the Way Shower; and Inner Director or Inner Investigator.

The (10) Wheel of Fortune is the Flexible Optimist, Creative Enhancer, and Opportunist.

The (11) Lust/Strength is the Inspired Creator and Strong Expresser.

The (12) Hanged Man is the Pattern Cutter; Block Dissolver; and Mystical Escapist.

The (13) Death/Rebirth card is the Catalytic Transformer; Renovator; and Eliminator.

The (14) Art/ Temperance is the Creative Integrator and Synthesizer.

The (15) Devil/Pan is the Humorist; Prodder; and Sensual Merriman.

The (16) Tower is the Instigator; Eliminator; Renovator; and Restorer.

The (17) Star is the Universal Channel of Wisdom and Self-esteem; Humanitarian Broadcaster.

The (18) Moon is the Authentic Breaker of Relationship Patterns.

The (19) Sun is the Co-Creator; Collaborator; and Synthesizer.

The (20) Aeon is the Changer of Times; Transformative Evolutionary.

The (21) Universe is the Expansive Encompassing World Being.

Royalty Cards are the masters, inner teachers, and reveal the areas of your gifts.

Swords, the mental level of consciousness, deal with your thinking, reasoning, and analytical issues.

Knight of Swords: Mental Pursuer; Determined Accomplisher.

Queen of Swords: Mask Cutter; Authentic. Defenseless Resolver.

Prince of Swords: Limitation Cutter; Eliminator of Restrictions; and Creative Mover.

Princess of Swords: Mood-Fighter; Positive Reframer.

Cups are indicative of your emotional fluidity and feeling tones.

Knight of Cups: Emotional Winner; Optimist for family and creativity.

Queen of Cups: Reflector; Mother Nurturer; committed to being true to yourself.

Prince of Cups: Passionate Lover; strong fervent nature that does not drown in feelings.

Princess of Cups: Detached Lover; has overcome jealousy and possessiveness.

Wands deal with your inner resources, perceptual nature and spirituality.

Knight of Wands: Revolutionary; Evolutionary; Bringer of positive change,

Queen of Wands: Self-Explorer; Seeker/Discoverer; Committed to knowing and being who she is.

Prince of Wands: Gifted and expansive Creator.

Princess of Wands: Liberator of fear.

Disks symbolize the practical, physical environment, your body, health, finances, and home and creativity.

Knight of Disks: Doctor; Healer; Harvester; committed to a sound body, mind and spirit.

Queen of Disks: Nutritionist; Naturalist; committed to healthy nourishment.

Prince of Disks: Builder; Architect; Exerciser; Sportsman.

Princess of Disks: Pregnant; Gifted; loaded with ideas, concepts or creative children.

The Tarot is deeply connected to Judaism. The letters of the Hebrew are designated to each of the Major Arcana. The letters are nouns and are actually labels that add to the pictures and their meanings. Paul Foster Case says that the Fool stands alone, but the others relate to powers, laws and conditions Here is a list to see the whole picture:

Card	Image	Meaning
0 Fool	ox	manifesting
Powers and Potencies		
1 Magician	house	that which goes on within us
2 High Priestess	camel	resourseful self-sufficient
3 Empress	door	caring protection
4 Emperor	window	watchful sight
5. Hierophant	nail	joins together
6 Lovers	sword	discrimination
7 Chariot	fence	safeguarding
Symbols of Laws and Agencies		
8 Adjustment	ox goad	guidance
9 Hermit	hand	skill dexterity
10 Wheel/Fortune	grip palm	comprehension
11 Lust	snake	transformative power
12 Hanged Man	water	reflective mirror
13 Death/Rebirth	sprout	generative productivity
14 Art	prop peg	support sustenance
15 Devil/Pan	eye	sensory perception
Conditions and Effects		
16 Tower	mouth	opening to speak
17 Star	fishhook	tool to draw the unconscious
18 Moon	back of head	bodily functions
19 Sun	face front	guiding power
20 Aeon	tooth	breaking down
21 Universe	equal cross	mark, signature

There are different ways you can distinguish and quantify the Tarot journey.

The **Transformers** are: the revolutionary (0/22) Fool, the expansive principle of motion and change (10) Wheel of Fortune; the regenerative (13) Death/Rebirth; the restructuring (16) Tower; the shifting (20) Aeon/Judgment.

The master **Communicators** are: the (1) Magician; the (6) Lovers who balances through communication; (17) Star, the universal broadcaster.

The **Intro-specters** are: the intuitive (2) High Priestess; the wise, intuitively creative (5) Hierophant; (9) pensive Hermit; the surrendering (12) Hanged Man; the (18) Moon who reveals our unconscious patterns.

The **Creators** are: the fertile (3) Empress; the talented (11) Lust; the integrative, synergist (14) Art/Temperance; and the co-creative (19) Sun.

The **Movers** are: the pioneering (4) Emperor; the changing and traveling (7) Chariot; the aligning (8) Adjustment/Justice; the (15) Devil/Pan moving from limitations; (21) Universe/World has to do with branching out.

In the next chart there is a summary of the Major Arcana card with the path on the Tree of Life and its planetary rulers (when applicable). Crown, which is above rulership, is denoted as Spirit. While you read the words together, spend some time thinking of the blending of these combinations. Just the words together can give you valuable insight into the meaning of the card.

Card	Path	Planetary Path
0 Fool	Divine Wisdom	Spirit Zodiac
1 Magician	Divine Understanding	Spirit Saturn
2 High Priestess	Divine Beauty	Spirit Sun
3 Empress	Understanding Wisdom	Saturn Zodiac
4 Emperor	Wisdom Beauty	Zodiac Sun
5 Hierophant	Wisdom Mercy	Zodiac Jupiter
6 Lovers	Understanding Beauty	Saturn Sun
7 Chariot	Understanding Severity	Saturn Mars
8 Adjustment	Severity Mercy	Mars Jupiter
9 Hermit	Mercy Beauty	Jupiter Sun
10 Fortune	Mercy Victory	Jupiter Venus
11 Lust	Severity Beauty	Mars Sun
12 Hanged Man	Severity Splendor	Mars Mercury
13 Death	Beauty Victory	Sun Venus
14 Art	Beauty Foundation	Sun Moon
15 Devil/Pan	Beauty Splendor	Sun Mercury
16 Tower	Splendor Victory	Mercury Venus
17 Star	Victory Foundation	Venus Moon
18 Moon	Victory Kingdom	Venus Earth
19 Sun	Splendor Foundation	Mercury Moon
20 Aeon	Splendor Kingdom	Mercury Earth
21 Universe	Foundation Kingdom	Moon Earth

Another way to look at the Major Arcana is their motivation.

The (0) Fool, (1) Magician; (2) High Priestess; (3) Empress and (4) Emperor or the first five cards deal with the desire to assert a **Willful self**.

The (5) Hierophant (6) Lovers; (7) Chariot; (8) Adjustment; and (9) Hermit deal with Stillness and Motion, and seek a **Social self.**

The (10) Wheel of Fortune; (11) Lust/Strength; 12) Hanged Man; (13) Death/Rebirth; and (14) Art/Temperance recognize harmony with universal forces, moves to a **Conceptual self**.

The (15) Devil/Pan; (16) Tower; (17) Star; (18) Moon and (19) Sun desire effectiveness, and connect with work and **Universal powers**.

The (20) Aeon/Judgment and (21) Universe/World aspire toward a universal self and link with **Collective work.**

Another process that James Wanless wrote about are the different life principles, like a sense of self; community; government; and adaptability. He designated the Major Arcana cards to these areas of life.

The (1) Magus; the (2) High Priestess; the (7) Chariot; the (11) Lust/Strength; and the (17) Star represent a **growing sense of Self**, with direction, intuition, motivation, assertion, and esteem.

The (3) Empress; the (6) Lovers; the (12) Hanged Man; the (18) Moon; and the (19) Sun deal with a **sense of Community or mutual commonality,** through love, meeting of the minds, sacrifice, recognition, and interdependence.

The (4) Emperor; the (8) Adjustment/Justice; the (10) Wheel of Fortune; (15) Devil/Pan; and the (20) Aeon/Judgment deal with **Governing, decision-making**, life enhancing, working, and virtuous actions.

The (0) Fool; the (5) Hierophant; (9) Hermit; (13) Death/Rebirth; (14) Art/Temperance; the (16) Tower; (21) Universe cover **Adaptability** and produce a willingness to change, learn, adjust, let go and create new life.

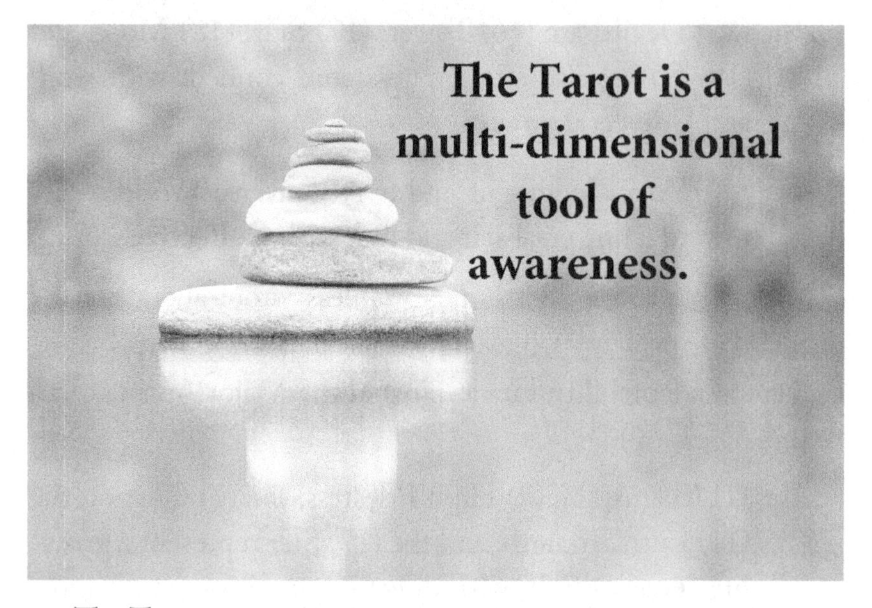

The Tarot is a multi-dimensional tool of awareness that you can use to integrate yourself through its steps.

All the categories of the Tarot images give me insight into their meaning.

Part VIII

Incorporating Tarot

The images of the Tarot are a mirror of the images in our souls.

Gerd Ziegler

88.

Finding Your Life Profile

Symbols are not truth in themselves;
rather they are intended to guide the mind
toward the attainment of truth.
Remember that this system is merely a tool;
the ultimate objective is to express the energy that we are.

Jack Schwartz

The Tarot archetypes are all our collective experiences, initiations, and the universal principles on the path toward higher consciousness. Here are some insightful ways to personalize the Tarot Journey:

To calculate which Tarot archetype is your lifetime significator is quite simple. All you need is your birthday. Then you can reference the numbers that correlate with the Major Arcana cards and then with the planetary archetypes.

Add the day, month, and year of your birthday together.

Then reduce that number to up to 22 and then to a single digit.

For example, if your birthday is March 28, 1944, when you add it together it reduces to a 22, then to a 4. This correlates to the Fool and the Emperor.

Month	3	
Day	28	
Year	1944	
	1975	= 1+9+7+5=22 2+2=4

The double digit is the Personality Card.

The single digit is your Soul Card.

Next notice to which planetary family your personal lifetime card relates.

In this example the number 22 relates to the Fool, which is the Personality Card and the Soul Card is the Emperor. The Fool is connected to Uranus, and the Emperor to Mars.

Some of us will have a Soul Card and a Personality Card; others will have one for both.

For example, if your birthday is May 20, 1954, again add your day, month, and year together and then add horizontally to a single digit.

Month 5
Day 20
Year 1954
1979= 1+9+7+9=26 2+6=8

The example above has a sole focus of the Adjustment/ Justice, but because of the great controversy of how Crowley switched the two, I would also include the Lust/Strength archetype, which many traditional decks consider being numbered 8.

In general, if your answer adds up to 23 or more, you have a single digit and your Soul Card and the Personality Card are the same. When lifetime symbols are singular, it designates that you have come in with a single purpose and carry a specific archetype.

The following list shows how to quickly find your Zodiac Cards. When you examine what planet and sign are deeply important in your life, you can use them as a growth tool.

Card	Planet/ Motivation	Sign/Attitudes
0 Fool	Uranus	
Path of Balance is about harmonizing.		
1 Magician	Mercury	
2 High Priestess	Moon	
3 Empress	Venus	
4 Emperor		Aries
5 Hierophant		Taurus
6 Lovers		Gemini
Path of Life Lessons and Opportunities is about motion and initiating new creativity and cause and effect.		
7 Chariot		Cancer
8 Adjustment		Libra
9 Hermit		Virgo
10 Wheel of Fortune	Jupiter	
11 Lust/Strength		Leo
12 Hanged Man	Neptune	
Path of Rebirth is about healing and transformation.		
13 Death/Rebirth		Scorpio
14 Art/ Temperance		Sagittarius
15 Devil/Pan		Capricorn
16 Tower	Mars	
17 Star		Aquarius
18 Moon		Pisces
Path of Actualization is becoming whole and unified.		
19 Sun	Sun	
20 Aeon/Judgment	Pluto	
21 Universe	Saturn	

Angeles Arrien taught how to find your Inner Teacher through the Royalty Card. For some supernatural reason, it is a way to perceive helpers and directions on the journey.

Write your full name given at birth.

Count the letters in your name.

If the letters add up to more than 16, then reduce to a single digit.

Disks	K 1	Q 5	Pr 9	Ps 13
Swords	K 2	Q 6	Pr 10	Ps 14
Cups	K 3	Q 7	Pr 11	Ps 15
Wands	K 4	Q 8	Pr 12	Ps 16

Swords, Air or mental consciousness, are intellectual, conceptual, progressive, observable, relatable, and diplomatic.

Cups, the Water element, are subtle, sensitive, intuitive, available, emotional, and imaginative.

Wands cover the Fire element and are noble, inspiring, visionary, and creative. With courageous daring there is fertility, passionate action, and vivacious evolution.

Disks, as the Earth element, are grounded, reliable, productive, capable, and concerned with material wealth and bodily health.

Knights/Kings deal the fiery part of the element. These adapts or teachers are about taking your male authority, leadership, and command so you can dynamically move ahead.

Queens are the watery part of the element and add compassion, sustenance, and enduring, matriarchal power to the reverence of feminine magnetism.

Princes are about the airy part of the element and represent movement. They are questing for honorable goals. These travelers are looking for inspirational service and fulfilling a need or a cause.

Princesses are the earthly part of the element and deal with grounding and liberating the element. Here is a messenger and impulse for new power, skills, artistry, efficiency, and service.

What is my Personality Card?

Who is my Soul Card?

What is my Zodiac Card?

Who is my Inner Teacher or Master Dignitary that is calling me to develop, utilize, express, and direct my life?

What element is calling me to learn, express, and reveal my purpose?

With this knowledge you can ponder on your particular helpers that describe the principle reason you are here and what you are to embody.

Knowing who are my special teachers adds more to the understanding of my purpose and myself.

89.

Understanding Your Yearly Growth Cycle

Everything that is in the Universe
is existing in accordance
with a cycle of rhythm and a cycle
of progression distinctly its own.

Spencer Lewis

To find your yearly growth card, add your birthday to the present year. Take the day and month with the current year. The growth year goes from birthday to birthday.

For example, if your birthday is December 30, add that to the present year.

Month 12
Day 30
Year 2020
2062= 10 (2+0+6+2=10).

In this example, it is a Wheel of Fortune year. You do not reduce this number for the growth year, unless it is above 23.

> What is calling you in your Growth Card for this Year?

After you calculate the growth year, you'll see that the (0) Fool and the (1) Magician are never Growth cards. Both are universal principles of the Divine spark and communication skills that are innate in all of us.

In the (2) High Priestess year, it is time to be independent within relationships; to take inner time to nurture yourself; and to listen to and develop your intuition.

The (3) Empress year is a time to celebrate your creativity; enhance your beauty and magnetism; enjoy pleasure and beautiful things; deal with pregnancy and nurturing others; blend your heart and mind; and relate to women or feminine side.

The (4) Emperor year is a time to pioneer and build your identity in the world; establish groundwork or a secure base; restructure things by being assertive; and resolve issues relating to men or your dynamic side.

In a (5) Hierophant year, time to learn and teach; listen and speak; work with social structures and systems; resolve a family issue; and act intuitively.

A (6) Lovers' year brings an awareness of relating; the coming together or breaking apart of a deep love relationship; and making choices and accepting responsibility for them.

The (7) Chariot year is a time to set things into motion; prove yourself in the world; and take care of yourself and others. Contemplate where you want to be and progress toward it. You may move, travel, or have changes in your home.

The (8) Adjustment year is a time to consider contracts, legal, and financial matters, balance partnerships, and harmonize with others, while being true to yourself.

The (9) Hermit year is a completion time. It is the ending of a cycle. There is solitude; introspection; learning by experience or with a role model; seeking; and improving.

The (10) Wheel of Fortune is a year of major changes in many areas. It is an expansive, lucky time, full of fate, fame, and fortune, so be flexible, open to opportunities, and keep adding creativity.

The (11) Lust/Strength year is a time to feel your innovative power; express your creativity and strong passions, and may call upon your endurance and strength.

In the (12) Hanged Man year, you can break old patterns; handle your hang-ups, overcome self-sacrifice, martyrdom, and addictions, and see things in a new way.

The (13) Death/Rebirth cycle calls for cutting through limitations, and letting go so that new life can be born. It is a time of regeneration, research, and examining things to their full depth.

The (14) Art/Temperance year is an integration time of creative flow. Time to develop health and healing practices, and to incorporate new philosophy and beliefs.

The (15) Devil/Pan year calls for looking at how you limit yourself; use humor and lighten up, question authority, and express strong sensuality.

The (16) Tower year tells you to let go of all those parts of your personality that no longer serve you, so that a healing can take place. It is a cleansing time in your body, diet, and home.

The (17) Star year is a time of recognition and achievement; and listening to ideals and your intuitive flow.

In the (18) Moon year, you are learning to have authentic communication with important people in your life; healing karmic relationship; dealing with imagination and dream work.

The (19) Sun year is filled with co-creation and collaboration; recognition and achievement of a goal, and a sense of worth.

The (20) Aeon/Judgment year is a time for deep transformation, dealing with criticism, evaluating, breaking through old beliefs; giving up your judgments, and expanding your horizons.

The (21) Universe/World year is the time to branch out and take on more of the world, expand your limitations, and feel a sense of endless potential.

When your growth year is the same as your Soul or Personality Card, it is an important time to get on track. I call it a "car wash year," as it reminds me of how when you have your car washed in a drive through, if you are off track, your car will be yanked and put back on track.

Finding my cycles allow me to have a special teacher for the year.

90.

Drawing a Daily Spread

Your daily life is your
temple and your religion.
When you enter into it
take with you your all.

Kahlil Gibran

In the following chapters are some sample readings. I urge you to make up your own readings. They can be as simple as: "What is my present issue?" "What can I do about it?" "How can I get what I need?" My friend Nelise Carbonare does Tarot readings and uses a time frame, in which each card represents a month. She goes back and forward in time with the present at the center of her semicircle. You may want to use the questions presented after each card's commentary as a reading. After you think about the question, pull a card for it and receive more meaning to your answers. There are endless possibilities.

It is wise to tune in each day with the cards. When you do this, not only do you have a daily mirror to reflect on, but it is also a good way to gradually learn the meaning of the cards. I started out with just three cards that represent the body, the mind, and feelings and suggest you stay with these three if you are just starting out with the cards.

1. How is my body doing today?

2. What is my mind thinking today?

3. How am I feeling today?

Daily

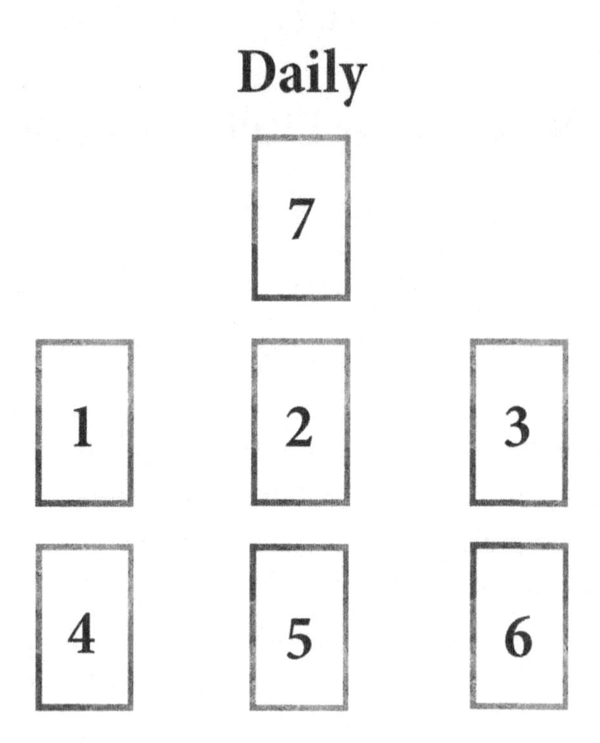

Later I used seven, adding an inner and outer body, an inner and outer mind, and inner feelings and outer feelings and one for the spirit.

4. What is my inner body doing or drawing toward me?

5. What are my inner thoughts or self-talk?

6. What am I feeling on the inner? What feelings am I drawing to me?

7. What is my Soul or spirituality telling me today?

Let your imagination soar with the different kinds of readings, all aiming to add more purpose and meaning to your life.

I tune into my day and easily find ways to improve it.

91.

Using the Astrological Reading

The unfailing concurrence of
stellar configurations and
sublunary events compelled my unwilling belief.

Johannes Kepler

The astrological houses are a great and comprehensive spread. Using this framework is my personal favorite choice for reading, as it covers our personal, social, and universal approaches to life through each of the elements. This complete layout mirrors all aspects of life.

1. What is my persona, my outer covering (the mask I wear to the world)? How do I come across to others? How do I go about getting what I want? How do I protect myself? How do I promote myself?

2. How do I personally deal with money and resources, my security and safety needs? What is necessary for my survival and sustenance? What is my attitude toward my body? How do I receive sensual gratification?

3. What is my lower mind's thinking process or day-to-day communication like? What am I learning? How are my daily short journeys?

4. What are the conditions in my home or the quality of my nest? What is my emotional past saying to me now? What is my emotional foundation?

5. How do I express myself creatively? What is happening with my children? How do I play and socialize? How do I

receive pleasure? How do I receive recognition or ego gratification?

6. What are my health habits? How can I repair or do maintenance on my life? What is going on in my work or service? What needs to be adjusted?

Astrological

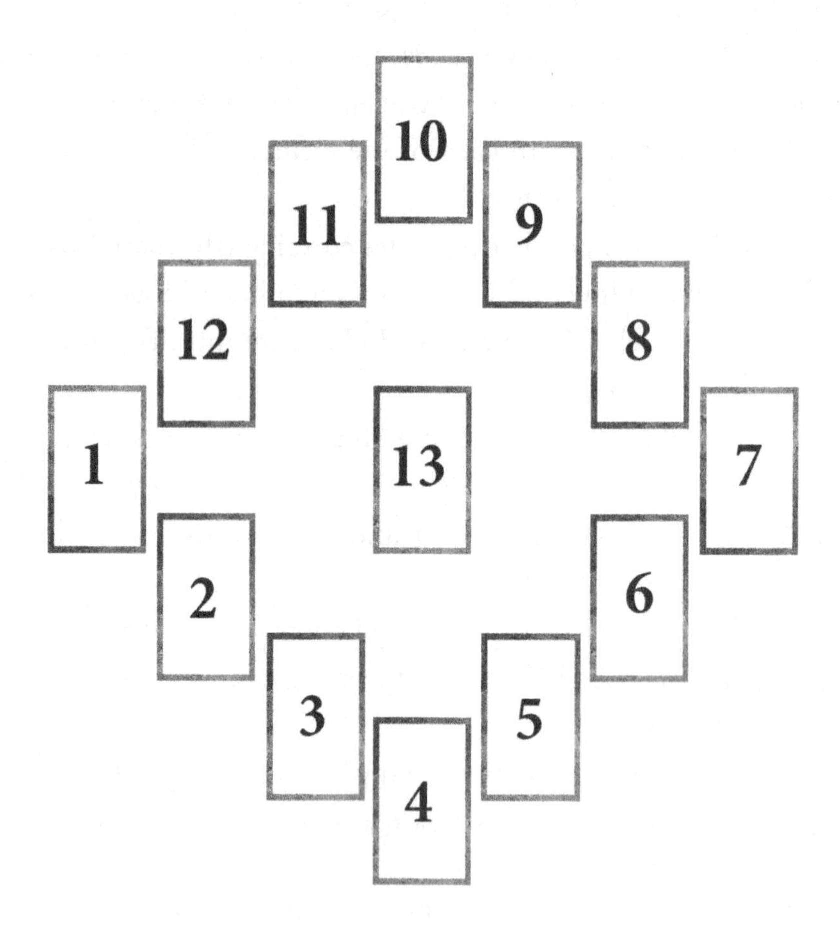

7. What is happening in my relationships? What qualities am I attracted to? How do I wish to complete myself? What is within me that I see projected outwardly?

8. What needs to be integrated? What is calling me, but may be painful if I do it and painful if I don't? What is the area of my life of maximum crisis and upmost growth? What must die to be reborn? How am I dealing with my personal dragons or my sexuality?

9. What is going on in my faith, my consciousness, my philosophy, and my beliefs? How am I searching for wisdom? Am I thinking of long journeys or publishing?

10. What is my purpose? What is going on in my career or public life? What is my public image? What are my future intentions?

11. How am I being received in the world? What is going on in my friendships, my community, and my groups? What are my collective aspirations?

12. What is hidden within my unconscious? What is in my closet or treasure chest that will manifest later? How am I paying for karma now? How am I repressing or undoing myself?

13. What is my Soul telling me now? What am I learning spiritually?

Let's take this Astrological wheel of insightful information one step further. When you place an image of the Tarot card that correlates to each of your planets and signs in the houses of your birth chart, an amazing map of your personality and potential is revealed. This exercise takes some knowledge of Astrological symbols, and many of you may need help to superimpose the Tarot cards on your chart to gain greater meaning about your life path. As a beginner, you could start with a list of the names of your planets in their sign to link some Major Arcana cards together. For example, if you have your Sun in Aries, that would blend the Sun card and the Emperor. If you have the Moon in Sagittarius, you would link the High Priestess and the Art/Temperance cards. Venus in Taurus combines the Empress and the Hierophant. Reading one as a motivation and the other as an attitude can bring awareness to you.

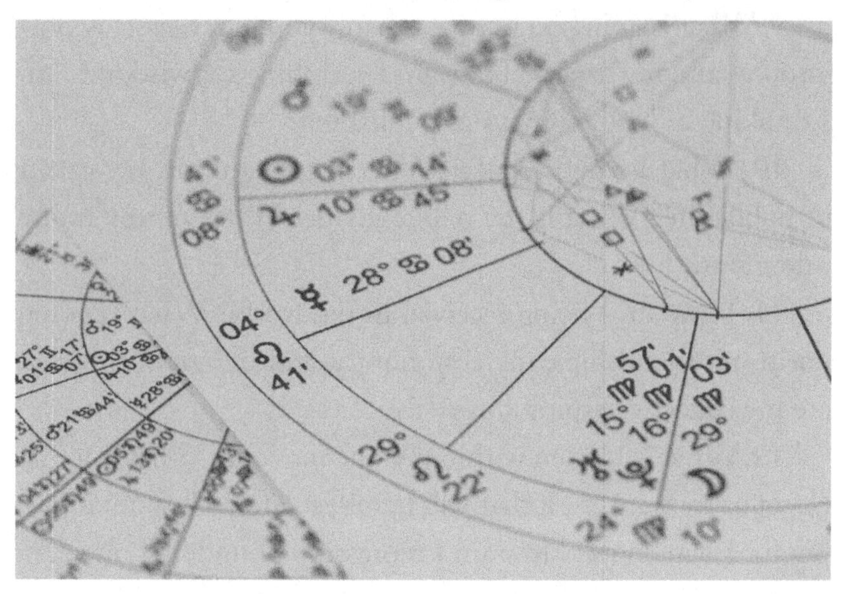

To get your astrological chart, all you need is your birth date, time, and place. There are many free websites to get it. Here is one site on the Internet: https://astro-charts.com/tools/new/birthchart/

Place an image of the Tarot cards that correlate to your planets and signs in the houses.

Notice the archetypes that are closely interacting and blending their energies together. What are they saying about you?

Whatever archetype is on your ascendant shows you qualities of your persona and within the 1st house reveals your individuality (9 o'clock position on the wheel).

Whichever archetype is on or in the 2nd house is teaching you about security and what you value (8 o'clock position on the wheel).

The archetypes that describe your daily communication patterns are in or on the 3rd house (7 o'clock position on the wheel)?

Whatever is within or on the cusp of the 4th house describes your home and fundamental nature (6 o'clock position on the wheel).

Which archetypes show you how to procreate, play, and express yourself is in and on the 5th house (5 o'clock position on the wheel).

Whichever symbols vacate on or in the 6th house are showing you how you work, problem solve, and stay healthy (4 o'clock position on the wheel).

The Tarot symbols in or on the 7th house will give you insight on how you relate to others (3 o'clock position on the wheel).

What you need to integrate and let go of is shown through the images in and on the 8th house (2 o'clock position on the wheel).

The archetypes in or on the 9th house illustrate your philosophy and higher learning (1 o'clock position on the wheel).

Whatever symbols are on or in the 10th house reveal your purpose and career (12 o'clock position on the wheel).

The archetypes that are connected to the 11th house express your friendships and money made from your career (11 o'clock position on the wheel).

Whichever archetypes are in or on the 12th house illustrate your reclusiveness and hidden treasures (10 o'clock position on the wheel).

While you look for the predominant mythos in your life you can also see an overview of what you need to do to progress on the spiritual journey. Their sacred and secret teachings are the bridge between humanity and the Divine.

Astrology and Tarot are amazingly insightful to help me understand who I am and what is happening in my life.

92.

Exploring a Whole Person Spread

Individuality is only possible if it
unfolds from wholeness.

David Bohn

This classic Celtic cross spread is made of ten cards and is a general review of what the emotional, physical, mental, and spiritual issues that are going on with you. I received this rendition from Angeles Arrien.

1. What are my heart or emotional concerns of the past?

2. What is the heart of my emotional opportunities or concerns in the present?

3. What is my conscious mind aware of?

4. What are my subconscious mind's areas of concern and hopes and desires?

5. What is pulling me in the area of work, service, or creativity?

6. What am I doing, deciding, or acting upon in the area of responsibility?

7. What is a possible outcome concerning my work or creativity?

8. What is the quality of my relationships with friends, coworkers and intimates?

9. What are my hopes and fears?

10. What is my expression or what do I want to release?

Whole Person

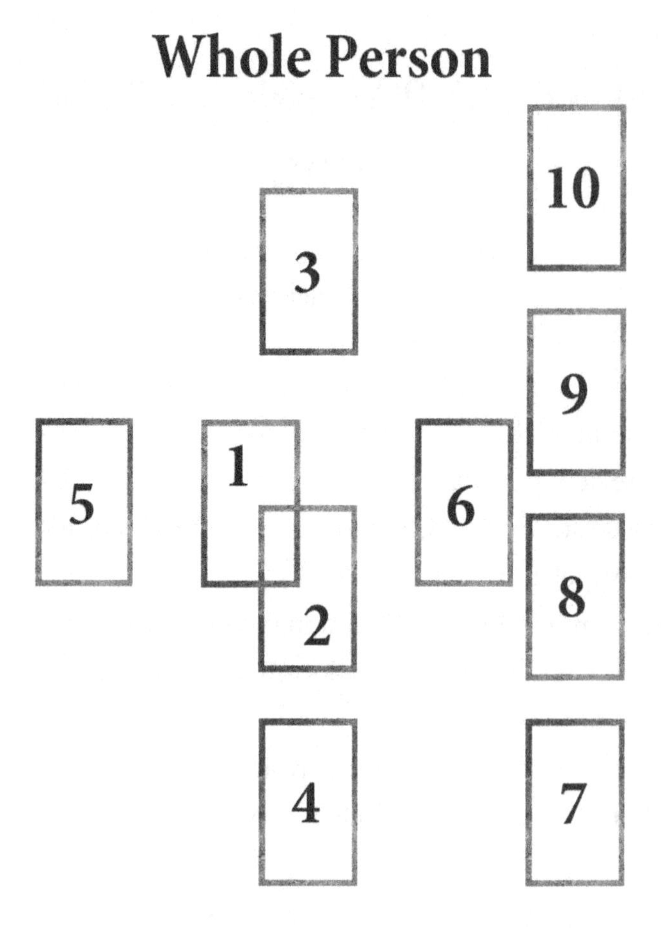

This Celtic Cross Reading has been a classic for most Tarot readers, as it answers a range of questions to ponder. I have found that the more you blend the question with the answer from the Tarot symbols, the simpler it will become for you to discern the answers to them.

I find creative ways to reflect my energy and my life is enhanced by it.

93.

Discovering with the Path of Balance

Life is like riding a bicycle.
To keep your balance,
you must keep moving.

Albert Einstein

The Path of Balance was taught by Angeles Arrien and gives you an opportunity to see how balanced you are and how your inner and outer feminine is working with your inner and outer masculine.

1. Magician: What is in my mind and how am I communicating?

2. High Priestess: What is my inner feminine, intuition or my self-esteem saying?

3. Empress: What is my outer female expressing or how well do I give and receive love?

4. Emperor: How is my inner male—my personal power, energy, leadership, and ability to lead and initiate doing?

5. Hierophant: What is my inner masculine learning and teaching within?

6. Lovers: How well do I maintain balance in relationships?

Being balanced in life is important. It gives us equilibrium and stability and makes us effective, which is why the integrative archetype of the Goddess Warrior is such a powerful model to emulate.

Path of Balance

I am balanced and aware of how I am integrating my inner male and female.

94.

Learning with the Chakra Reading

Every natural fact is a symbol
of some spiritual fact.

Ralph Waldo Emerson

Chakras are your bodily energy centers, which are where you both receive from the cosmos and transmit and connect with other people. It is beneficial to tune into the body's inner chakra wheels to see how well they are functioning.

1. Root: What are my survival issues? What is my root or body's foundation? What are my issues relating to money, health, and possessions?

2. Sacral: What am I feeling emotionally, sexually, and instinctually?

3. Solar Plexus: What is my sense of power, my self-assuredness, and my level of endurance?

4. Heart: How loving and trusting am I?

5. Throat: How open are my communication channels?

6. Third Eye: What is my intuition saying?

7. Crown: What is my spiritual connection?

With this inquiry you can scan your body and see how you are doing and what area needs tending. You could add meditation to the areas that need tending and actually visualize the energy opening and spinning the chakra wheels to clear any blockages.

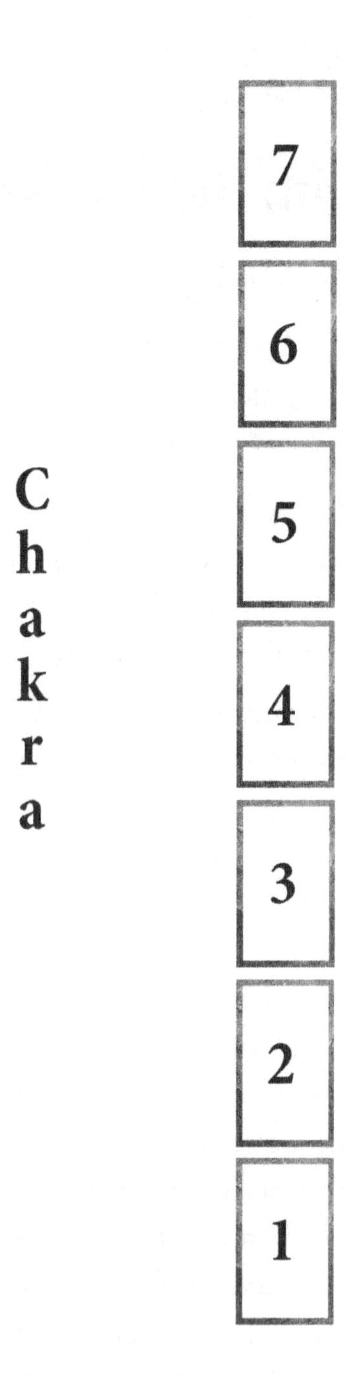

Using the Tarot gives me a window into my inner workings.

95.

Looking with the Relationship Spread

Love will find its way
through all languages on its own.

Rumi

It is often helpful to have ways to assess what is going on in your relationships. In this relationship spread, both partners are to answer the questions. I often use two decks, one for each person, but it is not necessary.

Here are some sample questions. Be creative and if you can think of your own questions you want to ask, please include them.

1. What are my current feelings, reactions, or issues with this person?

2. What am I giving to this person?

3. What am I receiving from this person?

4. What is going on deep inside me concerning my feelings about this person?

5. How do I communicate to this person?

6. How is the physical connection between us ?

7. How are our souls connecting spiritually?

8. What am I learning with this person now?

9. Where does this relationship seem to be going in the near future?

10. What is our higher purpose for being together?

Relationship

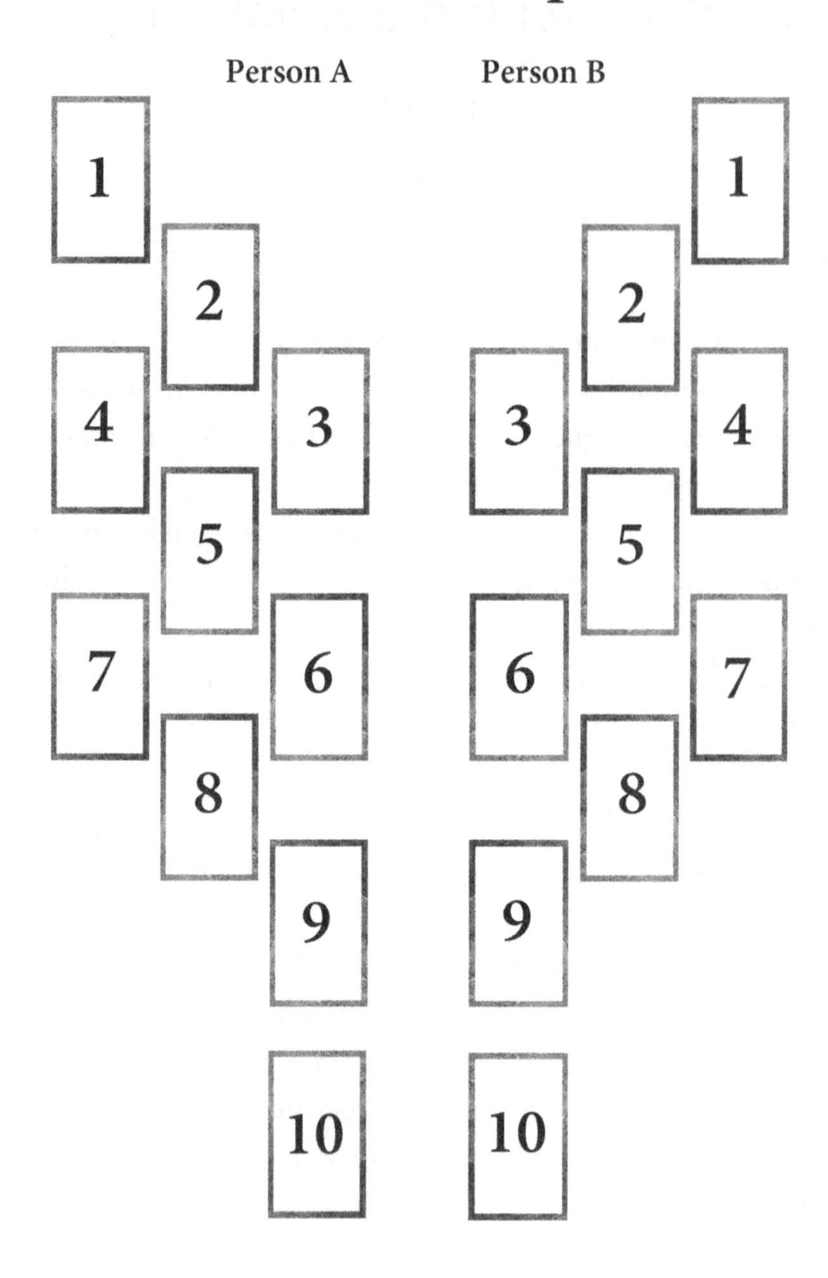

If you think of other questions, please add cards on each side for both partners.

This relationship layout can be used for any type of relationship. Relationships are often your most important teachers and inner mirrors, as well as the most cherished aspects of your life.

My relationships thrive as I look into them as a mirror of my inner workings.

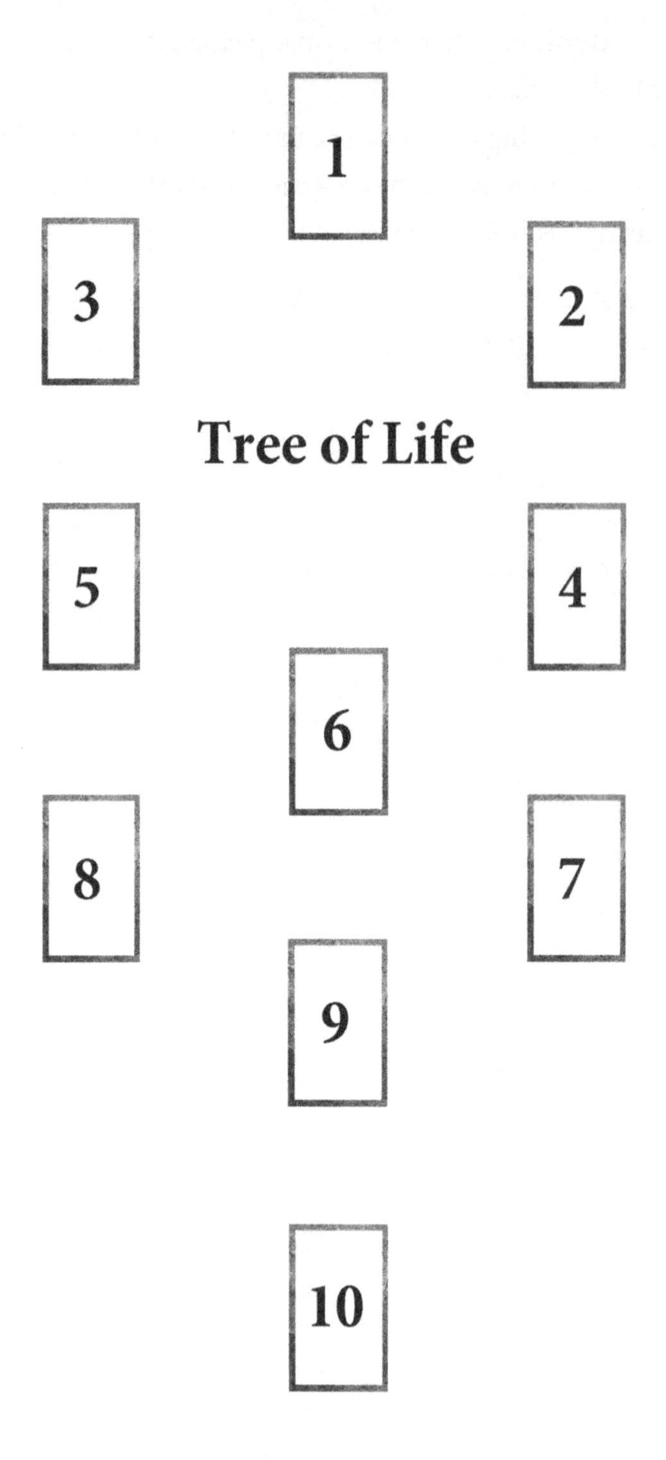
1
3
2
Tree of Life
5
4
6
8
7
9
10

96.

Invoking the Tree of Life Reading

What was once a tiny seed
of belief for me
has grown into the tree of life,
so if your faith is a little tested
in this or any season,
I invite you to lean on mine.

Elder Jeffrey R. Holland

Remember that when you shuffle the cards, you are asking for Divine guidance. When you feel that you have infused the Light of soul into the cards, stop and take the cards from the top and spread the cards in the position of the Tree of Life.

This Tree of Life reading often makes more sense when you start with where you are rather than where you want to go, so I suggest you start reading from the bottom up.

1. Crown: What does the Light of my soul want me to hear so that I can dissolve my barriers to awakening?

2. Wisdom: What inspirational actions can I take to direct my Higher Will to generate possibilities?

3. Understanding: What can I reflect upon or receive so that I can comprehend more clearly where I am on my life's journey?

4. Mercy: What can I do to bring grace and blessings that will help me manifest my intentions?

5. Severity: What do I need to let go of in my life, so that I can clarify my intentions?

6. Beauty: How can I express my Higher Self and my core vision?

7. Victory: How can stay more in the present to make my life more joyful and better?

8. Splendor: What is in my mind?

9. Foundation: What am I feeling, sensing, and dreaming?

10. Kingdom: What is my body reflecting or telling me now?

The Tree of Life is rich in symbolism and gives a multi-leveled way to perceive where you are, what needs adjusting, and what you can do about it.

I see myself through so many different channels.

97.

Understanding the Overview Reading

The Tarot deck is a symbolic mapping of
human consciousness that is timeless and universal.
A reading is a temporal portrait of an individual as it shows
where a person is on the map for a specific time and space.

Angles Arrien

This reading was inspired from a reading that my friend, Richard Ryal gave to me in the 1970's. It is a comprehensive reading that may appeal to you.

1. Present: Where am I now and what do I want to know?

2. Past: What was going on in the recent past?

3. Aspiration: What do I want to happen?

4. Responsibility: What is crucial that I need to do during this cycle?

5. Challenge: What are my obstacles and how can I move through them?

6. Tool: What gift or aid do I have to meet my challenges?

7. Attitude: What is my inner state of mind? What am I focused upon?

8. Environment: What am I drawing toward me in my surroundings?

9. Lessons: What am I learning or implementing?

10. Outcome: What am I drawing toward me with my present frame of mind?

Overview

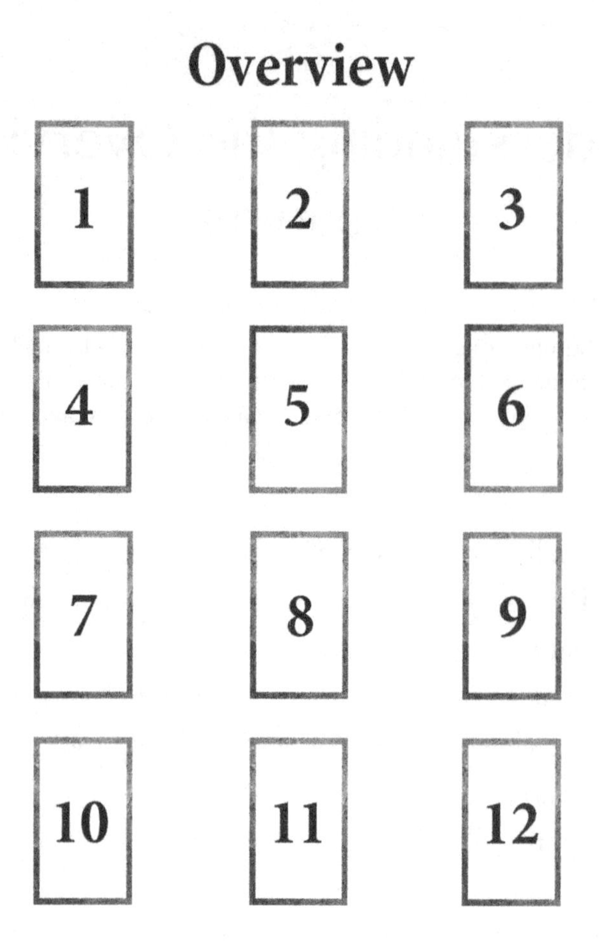

11. Advice: What can I do to that will open doors and bring me opportunities?

12. Soul: What is my spiritual nature asking of me now?

We are on a journey with certain life lessons, and this planet is our schoolhouse. The Tarot is a magnifying glass to look inside yourself so that you can navigate through life. The more I learn the more I see connections between everything and everyone and the more I go within to find my answers.

I find effective ways to reflect my life with the Tarot.

98.

Living as a Goddess Warrior Hero

If we do not bring
a higher purpose to our life
then we only live the ordinary life.

Dalai Lama

The journey of awakening can come through many paths. For me it is through models to emulate. The time-honored mythic archetypes of the Goddess Warrior magnetically creating the Hero's Journey can give you the keys to and the map of the journey. Based on the best of the collective unconscious, they prescribe a way to change and awaken. Basically, embodying this model is integrating Love and Presence.

You can awaken from sleepwalking in your trances and move beyond your conditioned fears. Despite the political polarities, media corruptions, and rampant darkness at this time, you have the tools to dawn a new era in human consciousness. Beneath your conditioning lies the light of your Source and more and more of us are remembering a deeper Self beyond day–to–day so-called realities. Despite your ego's habits and societies' limiting status quo, wise thinkers keep saying, "The time is now!"

As you integrate the Goddess, the Warrior, and the Hero, you are more empowered and inspired to live in a conscious, happy, and supported way. You are better equipped to listen to the cosmic calls, be directed on the path, and find depth and aliveness to your personal exploration.

If you are reading this conclusion, you have answered the call to greater purpose and identity. Since you have started this journey of transformation, you are learning to depart from the past. These Tarot images will help you go within and find guidance. When you realize that positive change and happiness are truly obtainable goals, you can overcome your obstacles and how your ego fixations and emotional wounds refuse the spiritual call. When you acknowledge your responsibility, you also recognize your creative power.

Being a Goddess means you believe that the Divine shines within. You adopt the Goddess when you *love, allow,* are *compassionate*, and open your hearts to others and your inner journey. *Accepting* and *surrendering to what is* happening in the present is how you embody these qualities. The Goddess is a *trusting*, resourceful force of *openness.*

Personifying the Warrior is bringing in *accountability*, *responsibility*, and *motivation*. You become a Warrior when you direct and *focus your will* to bring *awareness* and *combat your illusions* and do it with *conscious choice* and *concentration*.

Living in the moment as a Goddess Warrior allows you to generate positive change and utilize the power of Magnetic Creation. By blending the power of the *Law of Attraction* (Goddess) and *setting intentions* (Warrior), you can manifest your desires. With a willingness to feel your heart's desires as if they are already here, and then flowing positive energy toward attracting them, you can bring them forth in right and perfect ways.

All of these universal patterns incorporate and interrelate with each other. Their combination reflects the timeless Truth that effectively guides you to your spiritual destiny. Here are some of the images created from blending the qualities of the Goddess Warrior that you can embody: Joyful Adventurer; Compassionate Vigilance; Accepting Watchfulness; Receptive Awakener; Caring Commitment; Empathetic Leader; Allowing Motivator; and Peaceful Intentionality.

Learn to make life a wonder and purpose-filled venture. Recognize that what is happening externally is a reflection of your inner dynamics, and discover that help is both abundant and everywhere.

I exist as a Goddess Warrior whose every thought, emotion, and action reflects my heroic journey to assist in bringing healing, compassion, harmony, and peace to the world through Magnetic Creation.

Concluding:
Continuing with the Journey

Take every possible opportunity
to preach your message
but don't open your mouth.
Set an example.

Confucius

Congratulations on completing this Tarot book. My hope is that you are motivated to continue the journey to Awakening, and explore the other offerings in the series, **A Toolkit for Awakening.**

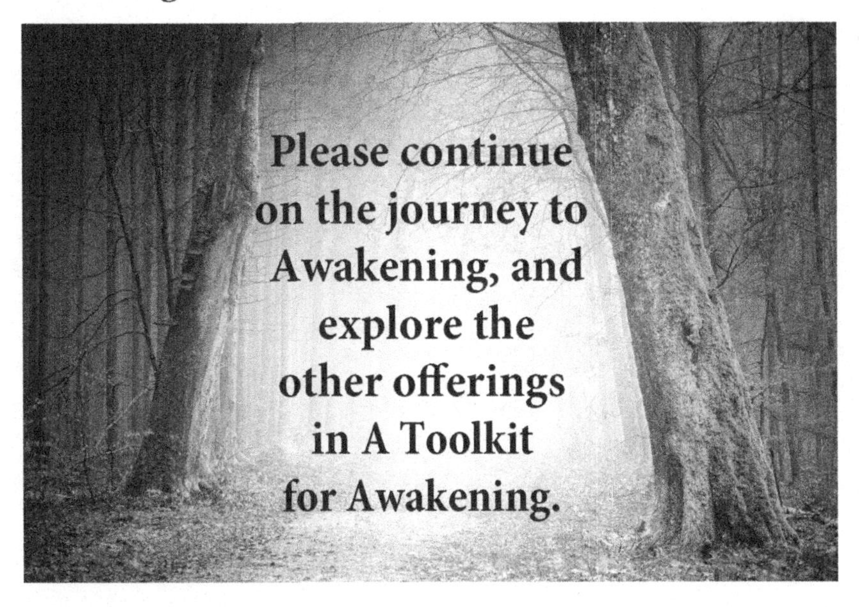

These books and this summary are a recap of Campbell's mythic formula, the Hero's Journey, which is a foundation and stepping-stone to Awakening. Its three parts are presented in bold type and the terms of the seventeen stages are shown in quotes. The title of the corresponding books in **A Toolkit for Awakening** series is shown in semibold italic. The practical directives summarize the stages. This overview of the process bids you to read on.

My first book, ***Awakening Female Power, The Way of the Goddess Warrior***, was published in 1990. I revised and redid it in the style of the series, and changed its name to ***Awaken Female Power.*** This book was highly praised by best selling authors Jean Houston, Terry Cole-Whittaker, Susan Campbell, Angeles Arrien, Ralph Metzner and many more.

Part I of The Hero's Journey is the **Departure/Separation** Stage. It has five stages, which are the motivational and practical steps that help you break through your old forms of being and heal from your conditioning.

Awaken A New Myth, Goddess Warrior on the Hero's Journey explores "Call to Adventure" and "Supernatural Aids." You are to ask for more meaning and purpose; understand how life is transcendent; follow your bliss; learn about the evolutionary stages in the spiritual journey; as well as be open to help from anywhere.

Awaken From Ego, Evolve through the Enneagram looks at "Refusing the Call." It calls on you to consciously choose to awaken from your fixations, beliefs, judgments, and defenses.

Awaken From the Pain Body, Heal Emotionally illustrates the "Belly of the Whale." You are to identify and transcend your developmental wounding.

Awaken Magnetic Creation, Manifest Your Dreams deals with "Crossing the Threshold." You are to intentionally generate change through the Law of Attraction.

Awaken the Inner Archetypes, Explore the Gods and Goddesses Within covers the quest for identity through the emphasis of planets by examining the astrological chart, which is a part of the "Call to Adventure."

This book, ***Awaken To Tarot, Be Your Own Guide, Using Astrology, Numbers and the Tree of Life***, with my new digitally created collage deck, ***Awaken Tarot Cards***, give you intuitive tools to reflect your life and your "Supernatural Aids." You have explored multi-dimentional symbols as your inner mirrors and embraced the magic and richness of archetypical images to give a system to get insights and tap into your inner guidance.

In Part II of the Hero's Journey, you are asked to embody the six Initiations as your spiritual code, for these directives are ways to awaken and transform.

Awaken From Mind, Elevate Consciousness** and **Communications covers "The Road of Trials." You are to be proactive and focus on what you want to become.

Awaken Love, Beyond the Temptations discusses "Meeting the Goddess" and "Woman as Temptress." You are to love and allow and avoid the temptation to control, struggle, and create drama.

Awaken the Spiritual Warrior, Empower the Masculine includes “Atonement with the Father.” You are to be present, forgiving and take responsibility for your time, attention and intention.

Awaken the Sacred, Experience the Ultimate Blessings covers “Apotheosis” and “The Ultimate Boon.” You are to make life sacred and be the change you want to see in the world.

Part III is the Return, for a true Hero serves the greater good. *Awaken the Hero, The Joys of Giving Back* is in development. Here are the steps to serving society with your gifts:

“Refusal to Return”: You are to restore to your community what you have learned and gained.

“Magical Flight”: You are to believe in the flow of the process by moving beyond the obstacles to celebrate what Is.

“Rescue from Without”: You are to trust the world will assist you.

"Crossing the Return Threshold": You are to integrate and teach your changed values.

"Master of Both Worlds": You are to be spiritual beings with practical feet.

"Freedom to Be": Liberation is the true gain.

My hope is that publishing and promoting the other books in the series will provide me first-hand information of giving back what has been learned. I wish to create an anthology and am asking for stories for this last section. If you would like to share your progress, your group's, as well as any stories of how you are giving back to society, please e-mail me at klapuma@soul-source.org.

My hope is that you are inspired to use the Tarot and that the series, **A Toolkit to Awaken**, motivates you to encourage your friends to come together and support each other. Together we can bring positive, personal, and planetary changes as we transition from the old, and midwife new, higher, positive creations. Become a mythmaker. We are the ones we have been waiting for. Let's make a difference!

Glossary of Terms and Archetypes

Adjustment/Justice (Libra, Venus) is the eighth step on the path in the Tarot Journey and signifies balancing and bringing equilibrium.

Adventure is the spiritual journey, the urge for a greater life.

Aeon/Judgment (Pluto) is the twentieth path on the Tarot and illustrates how we are in a process that through time we will refine our familial patterns and ourselves.

Affirmations are positively declaring and confirming desires with emotional confidence.

Air is the mental element that is abstract and communicative.

Androgynous is having the characteristics or nature of both the masculine and feminine aspects.

Anima is psychologically the woman within both men and women.

Animus is psychologically the man within both sexes.

Alchemists were thought to be able to physically convert lead into gold, but they were actually esoteric practitioners designed to transform their gross mental material into the golden radiance of wisdom.

Aphrodite/Venus is the Greek and Roman goddess of sensual love, pleasure, and creativity who was irresistible. She mated with both gods and mortals.

Apollo was the Greek and Roman Sun god whose famous saying, "Man Know Thyself" illustrates our conscious journey. He was the patron of prophecy, music, healing and young boys.

Apotheosis is elevating us to Divine status.

Archetypes are cosmic models, pre-existing cosmic forms from which we derive our fundamental nature. As the original structures that make up our essence, they animate our world.

Ares/Mars is the Greek and Roman god of war who was Aphrodite's most famous lover.

Aries, the first astrological sign ruled by Mars, is energetic, independent, and resourceful. It is Personal, Fire and Cardinal.

Aquarius is a Universal, Fixed, Air astrological sign ruled by Uranus. It signifies a progressive, socially conscious synthesizer of truth, whose symbol is the Water Bearer and called the Age of Synthesis.

Arcana is a major teaching in the Tarot. There are both major cards or Trump cards and minor cards.

Artemis/Diana is the Greek and Roman Moon goddess, who was the virgin huntress and patron of childbearing and fertility.

Aspects are mathematical relationships between astrological planets that create a blending, tension, or flow.

Astrology is an ancient metaphysical language that shows the relationship to the heavens and is an excellent nomenclature of the personality.

Astrological Blueprint is the birth chart or the picture of the heavens at the moment in time at one's birth.

Astrological Planets are like the actors in our life and represent the motivational forces within us.

Astrological Houses are the area in the chart that tells where things manifest—1st house of self and personality; 2nd house of money and security; 3rd house of lower mind, day-to-day communication, siblings and neighbors; 4th home and family; 5th creative offspring and romance; 6th work and health; 7th partnerships; 8th transformation, research, and other's money; 9th higher mind and publishing; 10th career and purpose; 11th friends, groups and social context; 12th intuitive, subconscious, hidden talents and our escapism.

Astrological Signs are the twelve zodiac scripts or ways of being.

Atonement is the act of forgiving and making amends.

(To) **Awaken** is to become conscious of the moment fully without unconscious scripts and with the awareness of the Divine Source of all that is.

Beast is metaphor for our baser and instinctual nature and our programming for survival, the avoidance of pain, and the pursuit of pleasure.

Beauty (*Tiphareth* in Hebrew) is the central sphere on the Tree of Life that represents the radiant inner core or the High Self.

Boon is a gift or favor.

Brahma is the Hindu God of Creation.

The **Call** is the inner urge for more meaning, purpose, and spiritual opening.

Cancer is a Personal, Cardinal, Water astrological sign ruled by the Moon that signifies a love of home, family, and security.

Capricorn is a Universal, Cardinal, Earth astrological sign ruled by Saturn, that patiently and persistently moves toward a goal or ambition.

Cardinal is an astrological modality or orientation for Aries, Cancer, Libra, and Capricorn that dynamically moves out of itself toward a goal.

Cerberus is the three-headed dog in mythology that guarded the underworld.

Chariot (Cancer, Moon) is the seventh path in the Tarot and indicates the principle of contemplative movement.

Chakras (Sanskrit) are psychic centers along the body that appear to be disks that open and close. Traditionally the most popular are the seven, from the bottom up—Root, Sacral, Solar Plexus, Heart, Throat, Third Eye, and Crown.

Childhood Imprints are our conditional patterns we created as our survival mechanism.

Christ is the Divine within.

Collective Unconscious is the Jungian term describing the hidden and ever-changing web of consciousness that binds us all together.

Conditionings are the childhood imprints that we take on misperceiving they are necessary for our survival.

Consciousness is our state of being aware of our own existence, sensations, thoughts, surroundings, and feelings; and collectively being awake.

Core Energetics is a somatic system of psychological therapy.

Cosmic Wake-Up Call is a universal stirring within to grow and evolve.

Cronos/Saturn was the Greek and Roman dual-faced Father god, who was both fertile and stingy, benevolent and punitive.

Crown (*Kether* in Hebrew) is the top sphere on the Tree of Life, which denotes the Divine, the breath of God, the Creator.

Death (Scorpio, Pluto) is the thirteenth path of the Tarot and shows how we are to let go and release all that we have outgrown.

Dialogues are two planetary communications that happen by being in a sign, a house or in aspect with each other.

Divine is the sacred Source within all of us.

Divine Plan is the universal script underlying each human being.

Devil/Pan (Capricorn, Saturn) is the fifteenth path on the Tarot Journey and shows the principle of mirth, sexuality, and practically developing our will to do.

Earth element is the practical, grounded approach that perceives through the senses.

Ego is the "keeper of the plan," the small self that has personal desires, is self-conscious, and wants to look good, be right, and have all the personal comforts and possessions.

Emperor (Aries, Mars) is the fourth path in the Tarot and signifies the pioneering Father who wants rewards in the world.

Empress (Venus) is the third path in the Tarot and symbolizes love, creativity, and wisdom.

Enneagram is a metaphysical system that shows the nine ego fixations and the interplay of naming, reversing and converting the ego.

Essence is a name for the Divine Source.

Father is the archetype of patriarchal authority.

Fire is the inspirational, enthusiastic element that desires freedom and self-expression.

Fixations are the automatic patterns of the ego.

Fixed is a modality or an orientation of Taurus, Leo, Scorpio, and Aquarius that is stable and moves inward toward its center.

Fool is the beginning and ending card on the Tarot Journey, which represent embarking without fear, and is connected to Uranus.

Foundation (*Yesod* in Hebrew) represents the sphere of the Moon on the Tree of Life and signifies the subconscious, dreams and images.

Gemini is a curious, Personal, Mutable, Air astrological sign that is ruled by Mercury and into collecting data and learning vicariously.

Gestalt therapy is a a client-centered approach to psychotherapy that helps clients focus on the present and understand what is really happening in their lives right now, rather than what they may perceive to be happening based on past experience.

Glamour is our collective illusory forces that seduces us into a romantic attachment to outer objects, such as music, fashions, and movies.

Goddess is the archetype of love, compassion, openness, allowing, harmony, and receptivity. The Divine Feminine has many faces and represents nature and Unity.

Hades/Pluto was the Greek and Roman god of the underworld who wore a helmet when he was on earth that made him invisible. He abducted Persephone to be his wife.

Hanged Man (Neptune) is the twelfth path in the Tarot and implies surrender and dissolving blocks and patterns that hang us up.

Hephaistos/Vulcan, the Greek and Roman goldsmith and god of creativity, was Aphrodite's husband, to whom she was perpetually unfaithful.

Hera/Juno is the Greek and Roman goddess who was sister and wife of Zeus. She signifies the commitment maker, but was angry and vengeful of her husband's countless affairs.

Hermes/Mercury, the Greek Roman god of the mind, was the Messenger of the gods and an enigmatic, magical, and versatile god of merchants travelers, and thieves.

Hermit (Virgo, Mercury) is the ninth path in the Tarot Journey and represents the principles of retreating, introspection, contemplation, and completion.

Hero is the archetypical evolved integrated being that has separated from conditionings, learned the initiations and is giving back to the community.

Hero's Journey is a mythological formula created from Joseph Campbell's intensive research of hundreds of stories of the one story underlying all mythology.

Hierophant (Taurus and Venus) is the fifth path in the Tarot and denotes the inner, sacred teacher that practically applies for a greater life.

High Priestess (Moon) is the second path on the Tarot Journey and represents the principles of intuition and balance.

Holy Theurgy is the process of identifying as a god/goddess

"I Am" is another name for Source.

I Ching is an ancient Chinese system, made of hexagrams of yin and yang lines, which is often called, "The Book of Changes."

Identification is where we are focused, what we believe we are, and have become. For example, saying, "I am sad" is identifying with emotions.

Integration is synonymous with Wholeness, the bringing together of the many aspects within.

Initiations are the directives we need to undergo to fulfill the cosmic curriculum. The cosmic curriculum is: Be proactive; Love and allow;

Avoid manipulate or struggle; Be responsible for time, attention and intention; Make life sacred; and Be the change that you want.

Intuition is an inner voice that speaks through whispers, hunches, inclinations, and flashes of thoughts.

Jupiter is the planet that embodies our drive to expand, grow, learn, and be of significance in the world.

Kabbalah is a Jewish and Christian esoteric multidimensional study on the symbol of the Tree of Life. The major cards of the Tarot fit perfectly with astrological planets and signs to enrich the archetypes.

Kingdom (*Malkuth* in Hebrew) is the sphere that represents physical reality on the Tree of Life.

Larger Story is a life that includes the spiritual Source.

Law of Attraction is a universal decree that says like attracts like. Our thoughts create our feelings, our feelings create our vibrations and our vibrations create our life experiences.

Leo, a Social, Fire, and Fixed astrological sign, is Sun ruled and is creative, heart-centered, dramatic and expressive.

Libra is a Social, Cardinal, Air astrological sign, ruled by Venus, and is socially oriented toward balancing, relationships, and others.

Lovers (Gemini, Mercury) is the sixth path in the Tarot and indicates that duality exists and that we see ourselves through the dynamics of relationships.

Lust/Strength (Leo, Sun) is the eleventh path in the Tarot and indicates taking control of one's creative power.

Magician (Mercury) is the first Major Arcana on the Tarot Journey after the Fool and signifies the path and ability to communicate artfully and with timing.

Magnetic Creation is to release resistance, define and align with the essence of our desires, feel the having, and allow and accept it.

Maps of Consciousness are metaphysical systems that operate symbolically, visually and nonlinearly that open our intuitive channels.

Mars is the planet that symbolizes our desire to assert our will toward action and a goal, as well as our energy and individuality.

Maya is a Sanskrit term, which means "Divine Sport," or the illusory ability to create and imagine as well as our conditioned beliefs.

Metaphysical relates to beyond the physical and deals with explaining the fundamental nature of the world and being.

Mercury is the planet of the mind, how we think and what we think about.

Mercy (*Chesed* in Hebrew) on the Tree of Life signifies the benevolent Jupiter and the intention to emulate the Divine.

Midheaven is an astrological term for the career point or the 10th house in the chart, which signifies one's purpose.

Moon is the luminary that signifies our emotional needs and past and our urge to nurture and be nurtured.

The **Moon** card in the Tarot is the eighteenth step and reveals how we are to break our illusions we have through our relationships by communicating and making changes.

Mutable is a modality or an astrological orientation that changes and fluctuates and is good at selling and distribution.

Mythology is a collection of cultural stories or myths that explain humanity's vital history, nature and customs, which are conceived like our world dreams.

Neptune is the transpersonal planet that signifies our spiritual, creative, and mystical urge to transcend the mundane.

Numerology is a metaphysical system of numbers.

Oneness is the name for the Unity and Core of Spirit that is at the center of all of us and all that is.

Opposition is an astrological aspect where planets are positioned directly opposite each other on the wheel, signifying differences, but that objectively generally blend complimentary elements, like air and fire.

Oracle is a medium through which advice or prophecy is sought, like the Tarot cards or the I Ching.

Ouranos/Uranus was the Greek and Roman sky god who mated with Gaia, the earth, and created the Titans or the first Olympic family.

Paradigm is a set of patterns that serve as a model, ideal or mold that contains one's basic assumptions, ways of thinking, and method of living.

Patterns are the emotional conditionings that are imbedded in the unconscious that makes us act automatically.

Persephone was the innocent springtime maiden in mythology who Hades abducted because he wanted her as his wife.

Personality is our individual differences that make-up our behavior and can be read through the Astrological chart, which is the picture of the heavens at our birth.

Personal Myth is our own individual stories that makes up our personality.

Pisces is a Universal, Mutable, Water astrological sign, ruled by Neptune, whose symbol is the two fishes moving in two different directions, which signifies redemption and dissolution.

Pluto is the transpersonal planet of death/rebirth, transformation, and regeneration.

Poseidon/Neptune was the Greek and Roman god of the sea who created earthquakes.

Presence is when we are completely absorbed in the moment.

Right Livelihood is one's right purpose or career.

Rituals are any gesture or ceremony that are designed to induce a feeling of reverence or a sacred space.

Sacred Psychology is a name for the spiritual search for identity and the search for unity.

Sagittarius is a Universal, Mutable, Fire, astrological sign ruled by Jupiter, that aspires toward meaning and learning that is socially inspirational and useful.

Samskara is a Sanskrit term for our karmic impressions or ruts that were created from certain actions and become the cycle of our karma.

Sanskrit is the Hindu ancient language.

Saturn is the planet that signifies the two-faced Father and our drive toward accomplishing through persistence and discipline over time.

Scorpio is a social, Water, and Fixed astrological sign ruled by Pluto that has intense, deep pulls toward the mysteries and the depths.

Scribe is a writer.

Severity (*Geburah* in Hebrew) represents the Warrior and astrologically Mars and the power of intention and discipline on the Tree of Life.

Shadow is the psychological term for the hidden part of us that holds both our negative parts and our gifts.

Spiritual Journey is the path of evolving and growing and is one of many names, like the Quest, the Great Adventure and Soulmaking.

Sun is the luminary that represents our conscious identity, our urge to be and create and is what pulls us into the future.

The **Sun** card in the Tarot is the nineteenth step and represents abundant co-creation.

Supernatural Aids are magical helpers.

Soul is our individual Divine consciousness that holds all our knowledge and never dies.

Soulmaking is another name for the Sacred Psychology, the Spiritual quest, the Great Adventure

Source is another name for the Divine Essence that we are at our Core.

Splendor (*Hod* in Hebrew) is the sphere of Mercury on the Tree of Life and represents communications and systems.

Star (Aquarius, Uranus) is the seventeenth path on the Tarot and signifies self-esteem and recognition of our ability to change our emotions into manifesting power.

Symbols are archetypes, signposts that have layers of meanings and function as a universal language.

Synchronicity is a Jungian term that denotes a "meaningful coincidence," which is not directly related but is symbolically connected.

Tarot is a visual Arcana collection of 78 mystical symbols, a multidimensional, pictorial, and esoteric study. Incorporated inside the Jewish system of the Kabbalah and the Tree of Life, it's an unbound book that became a deck of cards and is a path of God-realization.

Taurus, an Earth, Personal, Fixed astrological sign. It is ruled by Venus and signifies the desire and appreciation for the beauty and material manifestations.

Temptress is an archetype of manipulation—controlling, indulging, struggling, and complaining.

Threshold is a crossing or passage.

Trances are the fixations and illusions we mistake as real.

Transit is what I refer to as the "call of a god." It's what is in the heavens now as it relates to our natal planets. It's like archetypical house guests living and breathing in our psyche and demanding homage.

Trine is an astrological aspect that has harmonious flow but lacks drive that usually joins like elements, such as fire Aries to the fire Leo.

Toltec was an ancient Aztec culture that still exist in the form of teachers like Don Miguel Ruiz.

Tower (Mars) is the sixteenth path of the Tarot and denotes directing energy to clearing away conditioned patterns.

Uranus is a transpersonal planet that represents our urge to be free. to innovate, and to progress.

Vedic Astrology is the ancient Indian study of stars, which uses the Sidereal Zodiac or what is represented by the natural heavens.

Venus is the planet that represents our love nature and the drive to relate, have pleasure, create, and harmonize.

Victory (*Netzach* in Hebrew) is the sphere of Venus on the Tree of Life and represents the pleasure and joy of the Eternal Now.

Virgin in mythic terms is an independent woman who belongs to herself.

Virgo is a Social, Mutable, Earth astrological sign, ruled by Mercury. It is into details, analyzing, and creating order.

Warrior is the dynamic archetype of will, accountability, presence, leadership, and dedication to a quest.

Water is the element that is sensitive, subjective and wants to flow into union.

"**We are**" is the archetypical arena of Sacred Psychology, where we identify with cosmic models.

Wheel of Fortune (Jupiter) is the tenth path in the Tarot and signifies the principles of abundance, expansion, and continual creative flow.

Wisdom (Chokmah in Hebrew) is the sphere of inspiration and revelation as well as the dynamic Father principle on the Tree of Life, which is represented by the whole Zodiac.

Understanding (*Binah* in Hebrew) is a sphere on the Tree of Life that represents the primordial feminine and the fertile aspect of Saturn.

Universal Consciousness is the collective state of awareness.

Universe card (Saturn) is the twenty-first path in the Tarot and shows how we are to branch out into the world and manifest by cutting through our limitations and transmuting them into qualities that enable them to work for us.

Unity is another name for the Divine Source.

Yang is a dynamic energy, and includes the elements of Fire and Air.

Yin is a receptive energy, and incorporates the Water and Earth elements.

Zeus/Jupiter is the Greek and Roman King of the gods and who was married to his sister Hera, but was consistently unfaithful to her.

Illustrations

To find a photo and where it came from, please look at the following list. We are using a four-digit code to present them. The first two digits are for the chapter and the last two are for the number of the photo in the chapter. Pixabay.com has been most generous for its images.

Cover:don-quixote-1170907; flower-3093072; kitchen-2684972; rainbow-2571256; astrology-2792352: sunset-801960

Goddess Warrior logo
Letter Fotolia 49950459
GW sunset-801960
Scroll-Fotolia_49950459
Please note: notebook-3397136

Part I. thank-you4347304

Introduction
0001. sunset-1696207
0002. sean-pierce-Gqo6cuu_UFw-unsplash

Chapter 1
0101.nature-3151869
0102.trees-2562083
0103.oracles.time-711797

Chapter 2
0201.sunset-691848
0202.sky-2667455

Chapter 3
0301.sun-1506019
0302.globe-3408868
0303 birds-1105286

PartII. book-4302990

Chapter 4 bengal-tiger-601965; earth-1207231; earth-2817914; Fotolia_25996526; graffiti-2468336; standard-1401913

Chapter 5
abstract-2350072; beautiful-1274361; galaxy-2377456; monkey-913427 planet-581239; silhouette-1746389; venus-11022

Chapter 6
abstract-1231854; camel-163703; diamond-642131; fantasy-2699194 spiral-2706905

Chapter 7
composing-2808663; fruits-818789; swan-2494925; the-stars-1450362; Womens-Royal-Queen-Robe-Costume-01840; planet-1348079; shield-158587

Chapter 8
achievement-18134; achievement-18134; aries-1799104; luke-fildes-91069; man-796644; mountaineering-2040824; planet-1348079; shield-158587

Chapter 9
elephant-111695; fantasy-3598765; wax-figure-670318; woman-2176687.

Chapter 10
bouguereau-1912791; girls-2032312; Ouroboros; woman-1369253

Chapter 11
horse-175188; horses-83270; men-1276384; toothed-rock-crab-533944; fence-wood-bony-nature-weathered-old--11562908797tnvtg12llv

Chapter 12
christmas-2553837; circle-576797; dance-3134828; dance-3134828; graphicstock.night-and-day-landscape-with-a-single-tree_ BX5Z11zlA-scales-147219; picture of Celestine Star

Chapter 13
cave-3589637; clouds-194840; weimaraner-143753.

Chapter 14
crocodile-931217; fantasy-3574012; flash-731488; fortune-is-in-the-follow-up; lightning-2295075; lucky-clover-437259; squirrel-monkey-505191; wooden-wheel-2490210.

Chapter 15
eco-2221567; fantasy-2530602; fire-2596225; ghost-2935132; lion-3403595; monk-1773597; snake-3279939; sunset-2083771; the-fear-1287669

Chapter 16
ankh-1529464; clouds-2709662; dance-422699; grid-1872374; halo-2646333; snake-2082037

Chapter 17
flower-887443; reptile-242636; scorpion-2789321; waters-3197458.

Chapter 18
bald-eagle-562996; fantasy-landscape-1481184; lion-3284746; woman-1072572

Chapter 19
8657428-6603463-image-m-52_1547743549811; angel-675504; artem-sapegin-229391; couple-1712151; couple-2704469; glencoe-2541548; grapes-2520999; man-3124173; mysticism-3277852; pair-2793407. woman-1386626

Chapter 20
action-1838330; big-ben-3990607; color-1684560; dove-2516641; explosive-1660545; eye-2681783; king-cobra-405623; skydiving-708695

Chapter 21
background-2484300; background-3005303; cosmos-1866820; waterfall-1285221; winter-3006823;woman-3084129

Chapter 22
background-3005303; beetles-1498439; earth-1617121; new-zealand-92460; winter-3006823;woman-3084129; graphic-3729009; meditation-2717462; moon-1217725; moon-3656139; water-3021652

Chapter 23
don-quixote-1170907; flower-3093072; kitchen-2684972; rainbow-2571256; astrology-2792352

Chapter 24
graphicstock-a-woman-lifts-her-arms-out-in-praise-under-the-night-sky_HQlOJyzx0; angel-4928; butterfly-1518060; butterfly-3333179; caterpillar-2066505 light-brown-apple-moth-4021931; moth-3961840; pupa-2191733; time-travel-2910934

Illustrations

Chapter 25
bald-eagle-723540; horoscope-639127; imagination-2699130; lion-1840092; universe-782697

Part III. fantasy-4545911

Chapter 26
crown-4499549; mountains-919040; women-3673977; sword-3144759

Chapter 27
dove-2516641; dove-2901815; woman-3214594; beach-1852945

Chapter 28
heart-1199956; heartsickness-428103; landscape-4255590

Chapter 29
flower-305662; justice-1296381; photoshop-4405807; scales-147219

Chapter 30
clock-4276528; fantasy-4429163; girl-3394947;mystery-1599527; pocket-watch-2771647;sky-404060

Chapter 31
fantasy-2789302; fractal-1280083;people-2616695; rainbow-675832

Chapter 32
girl-1733346; light-bulb-2010022; mindmap-2123973;sky-199154; turkey-3048299

Chapter 33
away-820298; clouds-1037825; fantasy-2420047; question-mark-1872665; work-3585353

Chapter 34
cloud-494739; fantasy-4458063; glass-1497232; landscape-2254945 sun-2942386; people-2570416

Chapter 35
broken-heart-2163735_1280; crosby-beach-3462891;fantasy-4062012; ;love-2055960; seaside-1149687; thunderstorm-3184229

Chapter 36
people-3231252; butterfly-142506; heart-2748340; female 4899179

Chapter 37
brunette-487061; eye-3147494; lake-3261481; man-1503546; man-3161891; sabre-1859774 ; sickle-3369742; woman-2638075;woman-2638078

Chapter 38
fantasy-4257947; landscape-2211587; light-2188464; mask-2060466; mountains-3711350

Chapter 39
beach-1852945; sommerfest-2724649; helicopter-2248989; steel-3369791; sword-308087; steel-3369791; sword-308087

Part IV. mermaid-2522456

Chapter 40
bride-1822488; graphicstock-vvv-0216-img_4978-2887; rose-3142529

Chapter 41
john-westrock-_diTWuLEUFY-unsplash; jonathan-borba-R6LkuS4sl_A-unsplash; sea-2561615; taylor-simpson-wkVg6lNfBMs-unsplash-1.\

Chapter 42
autumn-3772373; waterfall-828948; fruit-2395585

Chapter 43
lotus-3192656; fountain-361048; gorgeous-1906193

Chapter 44
broken-glass-181806; germ-820208; web-4227115; women-2630140

Chapter 45
joy-2483926.; justin-kauffman-eVN9YIaH5P0-unsplash; lotus-992221; snake-1519996

Chapter 46
angel-2693196; fantasy-3057001; nature-dead-1180189; woman-2288359

Chapter 47
beauty-3881159; drip-871152; fantasy-858683

Chapter 48
beach-1852945; beach-4098634; rainbow-676504; wales-1789697

Chapter 49
clouds-1834809; family-2611748; iceland-2243277;rainbow-142701; rainbow-1467988; water-3021652; waterfall-828948

Chapter 50
attractive-1866858; beautiful-16736; clam-2610321; dolphin-2691864; heart-2748340; lotus-963633

Chapter 51
bald-eagle-521492; heart-1213481; lotus-963633; male-731888; man-under-waterfall-2150164; snake-2951621

Chapter 52
a-woman-wears-the-ocean-as-a-dress_HmxzpObxA; bird-3058712; evening-dresses-1591027; lotus-614421; lotus-944379; sea-1930317; sea-snail-345678

Chapter 53
angelic-2743045; crab-165187; cup-1614530; peacock-2740513; tai-qi-1583805; unicorn-2875349

Part V. photoshop-4778071

Chapter 54
fireworks-170110; inspiration-1514296; light-933261-1; light-bulb-3797650; sparkler-1149641

Chapter 55
horses-2904536; landscape-431147; light-bulb-3797650.; sea-1683999; sunset-176939

Chapter 56
fantasy-3341539; sunrise-77677; sunset-75621

Chapter 57
fantasy-4105122; genesis-3922213; lyon-1273841; racing-bicycle-161449

Chapter 58
eyes-730745; gothic-4044838; pasture-fence-1995820

Chapter 59
girl-948246; laurel-1237274; people-294310

Chapter 60
chinese-717344; possible-4062861; sunrise-182302

Chapter 61
fractal-1279939; gothic-3637564; rainbow-209294.

Chapter 62
background-636937; chinese-717352; light-bulb-3797650; yoga-2587066

Chapter 63
desert-3396245; wire-2202773.

Chapter 64
girl-2940655; sun-483989; tiger-500118

Chapter 65
crown-1299141; heart-2748340; light-bulb-3619720; lotus-3047870; mammal-2892906; man-1756907

Chapter 66
crown-1299136; goddess-3575781; grey-crowned-crane-3782242; princess-2750946; woman-1830628

Chapter 67
cd-cover-3002651; fairy-tales-877250; jedi-4391481; sun-209495.

Part VI. fantasy-3712643

Chapter 68
9-90584_falling-coins-png-free-download-falling-gold-coin; angel-2745072. beauty-354565; diamond-161739; NicePng_money-falling-png_43809; NicePng_money-falling-png_90584

Chapter 69
harmony-1229886; pocket-watch-3156771; snake-3279939; yin-yang-99824.

Chapter 70
construction-679973; head-3113192; roof-3633034; time-1485384; woman-2610284

Chapter 71
dawn-190055; todd-gardner-MIOcheoVN40-unsplash; girl-2755611

Chapter 72
away-3206899; composing-2391033; fantasy-1275253; gear-1127518; millstone-897112

Chapter 73
6-point-star-similar-to-sherriff-deputy-badge; background-651752; graphicstock-business-succcss-leadership-achievement-and-people-concept-silhouette-of-businessman-with-flag-_SOllvyhPxjg.; greece-1660546. landscape-3908781

Chapter 74
forward-2349168' man-walks-up-a-scary-set-of-steps_r7-Z0RWeR; old-man-2803645' skull-4221695

Chapter 75
celtic-woman-1880944; field-3130604;tree-3347278. woman-3999428

Chapter 76
girl-1349272; sky-1117008; sunrise-1704585

Chapter 77
buddha-231610;IMG_3537; kisspng-physician-medicine-staff-of-hermes; caduceus-medical-symbol-5b5ebe3e9f38d0.4051291815329357426522; sunset-3314275; treasure-chest-619762; woman-4261102

Chapter 78
bighorn-1721514; python-1689081; trees-3464777;wheat-2190554; woman-3960481

Chapter 79
bull-3769010; joseph-albanese-66332; man-67467; man-1463061; man-1503545; new-home-2538630; people-2604149; sculpture-3101349; south-africa-4126561; sunset-2177324

Chapter 80
apricots-1522680; aries-44188; fantasy-4192303; goat-3916016; mountains-1868715; pineapple-1916996; pure-quartz-6738

Chapter 81
bale-191199; caduceus-2730761; goal-3356125; horse-3600323; kisspng-physician-medicineoc-caduceus-medical-symbol-5b5ebe3e9f3 8d0.4051291815329357426522; knight-164144; man-4331209; money-2156131

Part VII. fantasy-4341459

Chapter 82
8201.book-4302990.; hirsh-1417108
8202.cloud-363075.psd; sword-2993521
8203.splashing 165192
8204.flame-13003.
8205.nature-3289812

Chapter 83
8301.system-3599932

Chapter 84
8401.oldtimer-3709587

Chapter 85
Fotolia_56466695

Chapter 86
8601.spiritualism-4552237
8602 kabbalah-names-and-pronounciations

Chapter 87
8701. sunset 4749228
8702 stones-4011843

Chapter 88
astrology-3479644; zodiac symbols

Part VIII. blond-1866951

Chapter 89
8901.leaf-3341897.psd

Chapter 91
9101 astrology-993127

Chapter 98
9801.just-flower-4610629
9802 poetrait 4820901

Chapter 99
9901.nature-3151869.
9902 book covers
9903 book covers
9904 book covers
9905 book covers
9906 girl 4552492

Thank you letter scrapbook-1365764.
Consultation page.watercolor-2419495

Suggested Reading

Arrien, Angeles, *The Tarot Handbook, Practical Application of Ancient Visual Symbols*, Jeremy P. Tarcher/Putnam, New York, 1997.

Arrien, Angeles and James Wanless, *Wheel of Tarot, A New Revolution, Tarot Anthology*, Merrill-West Publishing, Carmel, CA, 1992 (I have a chapter that blends Astrology and Tarot included within it.)

Case, Paul Foster, *The Tarot, A Key to the Wisdom of the Ages*, Macoy Publishing Company, Richmond, VA, 1947.

Case, Paul Foster, *The Tree of Life*, Internet Version, 1950.

Campbell, Joseph, *A Hero with a Thousand Faces*, Princton Press, 1948, Princton, NJ.

Crowley, Aliester, *The Book of Thoth:*, Weiser Books, San Francisco, June, 1974.

Mann, A.T., *The Mandala Astrological Tarot*, Harper and Row, New York, 1987.

Nichols, *Jung and Tarot, An Archetypal Journey,* Samuel Weiser, New York, 1980.

Oupensky, P.D. *The Symbolism of the Tarot*, U.S. Games Systems, Inc., New York, 1976.

Ronnberg, Ami, and Kathleen Martin, *The Book of Symbols, Reflections on Archetypal Images*, Taschen.

Wang, Robert, *Qabalistic Tarot*, US Games Systems, Inc. New York, 1983.

Wang, R.L. *The I Ching Workbook*, Doubleday, New York, 1979.

Ziegler, Gerd, *Tarot, Mirror of the Sou*l, Weiser Books, San Francisco, CA, 1988.

Praise for Karen's Consultations

"A private session with Karen La Puma was super helpful for me. She shared her gifts of astrology, tarot, intuitive counseling and clearing of old childhood patterns, and wove all of those together very skillfully and insightfully. She helped me understand my wounding, and how these related to my current life. She used a gorgeous tarot deck she designed herself which I enjoyed using much more than traditional tarot decks. I have found the combination of her skills that Karen to be unique and highly effective. I would heartily recommend Karen's books and personal sessions to anyone ready to decode the deep secrets of their emotional body, so they can move ahead and flourish in their lives. I feel much more of that in my experience since my session with her."

-Darren Starwynn, O.M.D. Author, Seminar Leader

"Karen has given me beautiful counsel for over 40 years, keeping me focused on "what I want to become not overcome" and staying clear of those fearful thoughts. Her books have the potential to do the same for many, many people... Maybe you!"

-Devi Jacobs, CEO of Outback, Adventurous Clothing

"Learned more in one hour of her wonderful insight than all my hours of therapy."

Celeste Barnard, Client

"Karen is masterful in how to understand and access enormous amounts of metaphysical information and relate it to your life.

Ivory Sidell, Hairstylist

"Karen saw me better than any psychiatrist I ever experienced, so kind, compassionate and helpful, you can really feel the love."

Joyce Rush, Homemaker

Thank you for reading my book.

I love hearing from you.
This journey is a collective call.
I ask you again to participate, co-create, and share it.

Please tell your friends about this book.

I'd greatly appreciate a review on Goodreads and amazon.com/awakentotarot.

Send comments to klapuma@soul-source.org

Go to my website at soul-source.org and sign up for my blogs and notifications.

Become a part of my social networks.

I'd be grateful if you'd like my author page at facebook.com/AuthorKarenLaPuma/

Join me on twitter.com/1GoddessWarrior
instagram.com/karen_la_puma
Linkedin.com or Goodreads.com

Connect with me and like-minded others so we help each other become the new myth.

Much gratitude for any feedback and support.

Many blessings,

Karen

Made in the USA
Las Vegas, NV
19 January 2024